VAUDEVILLE
U. S. A.

VAUDEVILLE
U. S. A.

By

John E. DiMeglio

Bowling Green University Popular Press
Bowling Green, Ohio 43403

Acknowledgements

For use of the quotations in this book we are grateful to the following originals:

From Fred Allen's *Much Ado About Me*, reprinted by permission of William Morris Agency, Inc., © 1956 by Portland Hoffa Allen (pseudonym for Mary Portland Sullivan).

From Joe E. Brown's *Laughter Is A Wonderful Thing*, reprinted by permission of A. S. Barnes & Co., Inc., including publications of Thomas Yoseloff, © 1956.

From Eddie Cantor's *The Way I See It* by Cantor & Rosenteur, © 1959 by Eddie Cantor. Reprinted with the permission of the publisher, Prentice-Hall, Inc., Englewood Cliffs, N.J.

From Charles Chaplin's *My Autobiography*, reprinted by permission of The Bodley Head, Ltd. © 1964.

From Corey Ford's *The Time of Laughter*, reprinted by permission of Little, Brown & Co. © 1967.

From Larry Wilde's *The Great Comedians Talk About Comedy*, reprinted by permission of The Citadel Press, Inc., © 1968.

From Max Gordon's *Max Gordon Presents*, reprinted by permission of Bernard Geis, Associates. © 1963.

From Norman Bel Geddes' *Miracle in the Evening: An Autobiography* (edited by William Kelley), reprinted by permission of Doubleday & Co., Inc. © 1960.

From John Lahr's *Notes on A Cowardly Lion*, reprinted by permission of Alfred A. Knopf, Inc. © 1969.

From June Havoc's *Old Vaudevillians, Where Are You Now?* Reprinted by permission of *Horizon* magazine. © 1959 by June Havoc.

From Groucho Marx's *Groucho and Me*, reprinted by permission of Bernard Geis Associates, © 1959.

From Mae West's *Goodness Had Nothing To Do With It*, © 1959 by Mae West, reprinted with permission of the publisher, Prentice-Hall, Inc., Englewood Cliffs, N. J.

For use of the Houdini letter to Robert G. Shaw, and the two letters to Dr. Waitt,. permission granted by the Houghton Library, Harvard University.

For use of the Sophie Tucker material, permission granted by the Sophie Tucker Collection of the Theatre Collection, Library & Museum of the Performing Arts.

For quotations from Ferne Albee Burton, (Mrs.) Mary Dentinger, Al Fanton, Ted Lewis, Nancy Welford Morris, Ken Murray, (Mrs.) Jack Norworth, and Benny Rubin, taken in interviews taken 1968-70. Used by permission of the subjects of the interviews.

 The Bowling Green University Popular Press is the publishing division of the Center for the Study of Popular Culture, Ray B. Browne, Director.

ISBN: 0-87972-053-0 CB
0-87972-054-9 PB

Library of Congress No. 73-78161

TABLE OF CONTENTS

Introduction 1
Preface 3
Acknowledgments 7

Chapters

1. "Spare a tear if you wish. I say the hell with it." 11
2. "Don't send your laundry out until after the first show." . . . 19
3. From Burke's Juggling Dogs to Singer's Midgets 29
4. "Don't say 'Slob' or 'Son of Gun' or 'Holy Gee.' " 39
5. "The Warmest and Screwiest People in the World" 55
6. Miner's, Minors, and the "Hook" 63
7. The Show Must Go On [And] So Often, On The Road 71
8. "It wouldn't be so bad, Eddie, if I didn't still hear the applause ringing in my ears." 109
9. "When you leave New York, you're just camping out." 119
10. East Coast, West Coast, Even Al Capone 141
11. Gus Sun, Death Trail, Borscht, and Kalamazoo Garbage Collectors 171
12. Olio 195

Chapter Notes 205
Biography 229
Bibliography 231
Index 247

INTRODUCTION

◆ ◆ ◆ ◆ ◆

THIS STUDY SHOWS THE CHALLENGES A VAUDEVILLE ARTIST FACED WHILE playing the various circuits of the United States and Canada and how he related to those nations. The study also examines the reasons why vaudeville has not received its just dues in historical treatments, especially when compared to other entertainment fields. Too often, vaudeville is credited as having been little more than a training ground for the other arts. Vaudeville was the most popular form of entertainment in a period of American history when many significant changes were taking place through the nation. The rapid changes and titanic decisions which gripped the country and its masses placed pressures upon the American public that demanded their utmost resiliency, sensibility, enthusiasm, and cooperation. In such crucial times the release that entertainment provided deserves attention.

Materials used in research included memoirs and biographies of vaudevillians, works on the theater, theatrical newspapers, articles in popular magazines and scholarly journals, unpublished writings, private correspondence, speeches, and personal interviews. Most of the interviews were tape-recorded. The study consists of a preface, twelve chapters, and a bibliography at the end.

Attention is given to historical background and the status of vaudeville in the first chapter. The next three chapters discuss, in turn, the men who made the rules and made sure they were carried out, the variety of acts which were found in vaudeville, and the audiences that attended the shows. The censorship that was created to insure continued family entertainment, and which persisted through later popular media, is also examined in chapter four.

The vaudevillian himself is the subject of chapter five. Chapter six examines the amateur nights, where many vaudevillians got their start. The general problems and challenges faced by vaudevillians serve as the focus of chapter seven.

Chapter eight treats the black vaudevillian, as he was in "white" vaudeville and in his own black vaudeville circuits. The following three chapters view the vaudevillian's America in distinct geographic settings. In chapter nine, the overwhelming importance of New York City is seen and the great metropolis's environments are examined. Chapter ten gives attention to the other major cities of America, some enjoying good reputations, others quite the opposite. Smalltime vaudeville and small town America are the subjects of chapter eleven.

A summary chapter states that vaudeville, because its major objective was money, refused to experiment with any act that had proven successful. Yet, until success was achieved, vaudeville allowed performers to experiment freely. Vaudeville, vaudevillians, and their audiences were America in microcosm. A typical vaudeville audience covered the spectrum of American society. The very nature of vaudeville, where the opportunity was available to rise as far as one's talent and luck could take him, was representative of the American spirit. The expansiveness of vaudeville, with so many acts doing their separate, highly individual parts, yet all somehow integrating into the whole, served as a symbol of Americanism. The individual vaudevillian stood as a prime example of what could be achieved in a land of free enterprise. The vaudevillian, the most traveled person in America, served as a constant symbol of individual liberty and pioneer endeavor.

PREFACE

◆ ◆ ◆ ◆ ◆

AS I WAS SETTING UP MY TAPE RECORDER BEFORE INTERVIEWING TED Lewis, he commented that he could no longer believe in history and asked if I had read any of the books that dealt with the history of vaudeville. When I indicated I had, he asserted that whatever I had read was not the truth and he guaranteed me that he would certainly tell the truth in his interview. Lewis's criticism was aimed at those stories which were over-embellished at the expense of truth, and at writers, the interpreters of vaudeville, who abused the facts in drawing awkward conclusions. Lewis's statements reminded me of a Groucho Marx observation: "Some day, I'm afraid, the eggheads will take [Red Skelton] up and start reading social significance into his antics. Let's hope they don't, because this has ruined many a good performer."[1]

The anti-intellectual views of Lewis and Marx are typical of former vaudevillians. Jack Benny maintained that a college education would hurt a comedian because the comedian would know too much and his vocabulary would be too good. Benny also felt that a college education would make a comedian feel superior to his audience, whereas a comedian who lacked a college education would be meticulous about his material and delivery.[2] Joe Laurie, Jr., who authored a massive, nostalgic study of vaudeville, also displayed an antagonism toward intellectuals by claiming that professors who had written about vaudeville could make people believe almost anything because of their "way with words."[3]

Perhaps this anti-intellectual attitude explains why nearly all of the former vaudevillians I contacted did not even answer my letters, in which I described my project and requested their help.[4] Probably, if any of them ever reads the finished product of my findings, their anti-intellectual attitude would prejudice their conclusions. If that be so, I would remind them of a statement by one of their colleagues, George Jessel, who once wrote, "Having lived in vaudeville so many years of my career, it may be I miss seeing some of the forest because of the trees. . . ."[5] Hopefully, my objective view will meet with the approval of even the most anti-intellectual vaudevillian.

Vaudeville was, for a short but extremely significant time, the most popular of all fields of entertainment. In a *Life* editorial written in 1953 (when baseball was unquestionably America's favorite national pastime) it was reported that "Vaudeville was once about as big in American life as baseball." Indeed it was! By entertaining the great masses of Americans from coast to coast, vaudeville provided a common experience to a rapidly changing nation. Joey Adams judged that the vaudeville chains "strung America together just as surely as did the railroad tracks," while Joe Laurie, Jr., expressed that the same jokes and songs, in big town and small, contributed to a more united nation.[6]

A look at Bert Lahr's route for one season will show how many communities saw his act. When you consider that this route, or adaptations of it, was followed by all working vaudevillians, clearly it can be seen that vaudeville actors must have exercised a unifying influence, if only by providing a standard base of humor or song lyrics. Beginning in late August, Lahr's itinerary for the 1926-27 season showed the following: St. Louis, Chicago, Minneapolis, Winnipeg, Vancouver, Seattle, Portland, San Francisco, Los Angeles, San Jose, Oakland, back to San Francisco (in a theater different from his first one), then to Los Angeles again (in a different theater), Denver, Kansas City, St. Louis again (in a different theater), Chicago once more (in a different theater), Des Moines, Davenport, Chicago (once again, though in the same house as his second appearance), Cleveland, Toledo, Detroit, Indianapolis,

Cincinnati, Dayton, Louisville, Columbus, Canton, Akron, Youngstown, Erie, Syracuse, Rochester, Ottawa, Montreal, Providence, Boston, New York City, Philadelphia, Baltimore, Washington, New York City (in a different theater), Brooklyn, Newark, Mt. Vernon (New York), Paterson, and ending in early July in New York City, (in a third theater).[7]

If, as Franklin P. Adams suggests, "what persons remember, subconsciously and without effort, may be considered a strong influence"—and I agree that it is—then vaudeville must have exerted a mighty influence in its time. Adams noted that he knew hardly any adult who had patronized vaudeville who could not "remember accurately at least one entire vaudeville act and the words and music of a good many songs that were popular" on the vaudeville stage. When subtle stage mechanics are added, vaudeville's social influence takes on a very significant meaning. If a stage father is the butt of humor, made to appear fumbling and stupid, saved always by the stage mother's ingeniousness, the effect on an audience which passively accepts the scene cannot be underrated, especially if one keeps in mind that "large numbers of children habitually attended the vaudeville shows." So, with each ethnic joke or act, with each portrayal of city or rural life, and so on, the vaudeville stage exercised its influence on American life. More importantly, the mood of the vaudeville stage was a happy and optimistic one, conveying the idea of the spirit of America to its citizenry. The laughs were loud, the songs were lively, the scene was a colorful one. Harry Lauder, one of the major vaudeville performers, was described as a person who came straight from the people, an optimist who painted life as a jolly business.[8] That was what vaudeville did, and at a time when Americans were caught up in the greatest hustle and bustle they had ever faced. Vaudeville, the chief entertainment of all at the turn of the twentieth century, available to all classes because of its broad range of admission prices, may well have been a major factor in keeping a nation stable, of helping a nation to release itself from the compounding pressures of a relatively new and thoroughly overwhelming industrial complex.

Vaudeville was also described as "a treasure house of individuality." Certainly it was. Each performer had his specialty, one which took many years to master, a specialty which was then juxtaposed with others in the assembly line of acts that constituted the typical vaudeville bill.[9] His specialization, his individuality, yet his being but one part of a greater whole, was symbolic of the type of assembly line America that was ever expanding in society.

Vaudeville was the entertainment of the masses and reflected the attitudes of the masses. If no group was dismayed, an ethnic joke was in order. If a group objected, the particular ethnic joke was removed. If any action on stage ever threatened to diminish attendance, it was removed. John Royal, a former manager of a part of the most powerful vaudeville circuit ever developed, made it clear that his boss, Benjamin F. Keith, subscribed to the motto, "Get the coin."[10] Vaudeville thus tended to be anti-intellectual itself. Its job was, as Joe Laurie, Jr., emphatically stated, "to amuse or distract. The idea is that in this vale of tears, the ordinary mortal or non-vaudevillian will pay out good money to forget his cares."[11] The patron's mind was not to be joggled by social questions or matters of import and challenge. It was presumed he had faced his pressures for the day by the time he came to the theater. Now he was to relax, to be spoonfed his laughs and delights. Vaudeville provided something innocent for everyone's taste. It was, in reality, the vast intellectual wasteland of its day. However, just as television's very popular, yet culturally uninspired shows, cannot be ignored in the social history of the United States, neither can vaudeville. It played a major, if brief, role in the nation's development.

ACKNOWLEDGMENTS

◆ ◆ ◆ ◆ ◆

THE WRITING OF THIS BOOK IS THE RESULT OF MANY PEOPLE'S EFFORTS. First, the vaudevillians and people associated with show business must be credited. Groucho Marx was the first I wrote to, and the first to reply. Through the help of Will Jones, entertainment editor of the Minneapolis *Tribune*, I got in touch with Ferne Albee Burton, a former vaudevillian who provided me with my first tape-recorded interview. She in turn let me use her name as a contact in getting an interview with Ben Blue.

Samuel Stark, curator of the theater division of the California State Historical Society, was an excellent source of information and a most valuable reference. Through him I was able to interview Mae West, Amy Norworth, Nancy Welford Morris, and George Poultney, former head of Actors' Equity in San Francisco. Stark also introduced me to Abel Green, editor-publisher of *Variety*, the show business trade journal, who published an article of mine which sought new contacts. Regrettably, only one person, Al Fanton, responded to the *Variety* piece, sending a valuable tape-recording of his childhood memories in vaudeville. Stark, perhaps the best of indexers of works in theatrical history, also compiled the index for this book.

I will never forget the tape-recorded interviews I enjoyed with three giants of the vaudeville and entertainment world, namely, Ted Lewis, Ken Murray, and Benny Rubin. All were extremely hospitable and cooperative. Lou Holtz, still another great entertainer, sent a very interesting tape-recording. Two other former vaudeville headliners, Nick Lucas and Estelle Major Smith, wrote fascinating letters. An article in the Mankato (Minnesota) *Free Press*, written by Lowell Schreyer, discussed my vaudeville interest and led me to interviews with Mary Dentinger and Mitzi Goldwyn. So, I thank the vaudevillians who helped me, many of whom continue to correspond with me, and I regret that I did not have contact with many more.

The thanks do not end there. Through my academic career many teachers and professors have played important roles. I believe they will be understanding when I narrow what could be a huge list to a mention of but two, David C. Smith and John W. Hakola. To these men I am indebted for their enthusiastic interest, their patience, their hospitality, and perhaps most importantly, their example.

I owe gratitude, as well, to three other friends whose "open house" treatment extended to my family and me made it possible to do research and conduct interviews on both coasts. Eugene Slaski, of Bethlehem, Pennsylvania, and Joel W. Eastman, of Portland, Maine, will see the results of my efforts. A marvelous teacher and wonderful man, Myron Stettler, will not. He met an untimely death in an automobile accident in the summer of 1970 near his home in Buena Park, California.

As a novice author, the editing and rewrite suggestions of Carolyn Balducci and Ray Browne deserve special plaudits. They gave me extremely valuable help. It should be stressed, however, that any clumsiness in writing that remains in the book is entirely my own responsibility.

Researchers will tell you that librarians are immensely helpful. Believe me, they are. Particular praise should be given individuals who are associated with the following libraries: the University of Maine, Harvard University, Yale University, the Library for the Performing Arts at Lincoln Center in New York City, the Library of Congress, the University of Minnesota, Fullerton (California) State College, Mankato (Minnesota) State College, Tulane University, and the public libraries of Mankato, Minnesota, Bangor,

Maine, Dallas, Texas, Anaheim and Buena Park, California. A special thanks must go, too, to a wonderful pair of people, the proprietors of the amazing Book Barn in Tatamy, Pennsylvania.

The final indebtedness involves my family. Alice, my wife, and Jean, Mike, Joe, Steve, Mark, and Andrew, our children, have shown an interest and an abundance of understanding. They have made the task of researching, compiling, arranging, and writing an easier one. My mother's constant curiosity and thirst for learning, which continues to this very hour, has no doubt had its effects on me. My aunt Amelia contributed some materials she had saved from her days as a child vaudevillian.

This work, however, is written in the memory of two men. The first is my grandfather, who coincidentally was often billed as "Prof. John DiMeglio." He was a magician in vaudeville and my childhood memories of him are of a jolly, outgoing, big-mustachioed, warm-hearted human being. He was teaching me one trick a week each Sunday visit our family would make to his Allentown, Pennsylvania, candy store. The week that he was going to show me how to pull a tablecloth from a table without breaking anything atop it was the week he became suddenly ill and died.

The second man is my father. Richard A. DiMeglio lived an exemplary life. As a child he performed in vaudeville, then worked in textile mills, and was schooled as both an electrician and barber. He chose the latter profession and for more than forty years, "Dick's Barber Shop" was a mainstay on the South Side of Bethlehem, Pennsylvania. There are no words ample enough to express the meaning he has to me. He was a quiet, resourceful, intelligent, hard-working, dedicated, humble, loving man. May this study of vaudeville serve as a memoriam for him. This is for you, Pop.

"SPARE A TEAR IF YOU WISH. I SAY THE HELL WITH IT."

♦ ♦ ♦ ♦ ♦

AS THE TWENTIETH CENTURY BEGAN, VAUDEVILLE WAS THE UNRIVALLED king of entertainment. It was in the midst of a sensational period of growth that would be followed by an even more sudden decline. Syndication of scattered vaudeville theaters and actors had already begun in 1900. A "star" system was evolving, which would eventually cause disgruntlement among those destined never to succeed. The key to understanding the rise and fall of vaudeville, though, is Willie Hammerstein's proclamation that "the best seats in a theater, for a producer, were seats with asses in them."

Some two thousand theaters, scattered throughout the United States and Canada, played nothing but vaudeville. Mae West observed that it would have taken her six years just to play each theater. The general booking manager for the Loew circuit, Joseph M. Schenck said, at about the same time, that vaudeville of that day was more successful than any branch of amusement had ever been in the history of the stage. According to Schenck, ten people attended a vaudeville show to every one who patronized other forms of entertainment. If three of every five seats in its vaudeville theaters were occupied by ticket-buying patrons, a major circuit enjoyed a profitable year. As vaudeville entered the new century it was already netting half of all theater attendance. A

1920 pamphlet of theatrical information advised its readers that the highest paid profession in the world was vaudeville. It was identified as "the neatest, cleanest, most independence-giving, businesslike branch" of entertainment. Yet, by 1933, this show business giant would be nearly toppled. With the depression, talking pictures, and radio taking their toll, vaudeville was played in only a handful of theaters. Its day was over.

Just what *was* vaudeville, this phenomenon that caught America's fancy during its transition from rural to urban status? Moreover, why does vaudeville, especially when it enjoyed its best days, fail to receive the significant notice that the legitimate theater, movies, radio, and television tend to garner? It is difficult to fathom how a branch of show business that so clearly dominated entertainment for at least twenty years could be dismissed as a virtual nonentity. Certainly television exerts a tremendous influence. The movies, even in their infant nickelodeon days, played a significant role in the development of American society, and like radio, itself important in that development, the movies contributed to the death of vaudeville. Yet vaudeville, the king before movies and radio, receives little serious attention. Vaudeville and the vaudevillians who gave to America its chief entertainment during the early twentieth century are worthy of merit beyond anecdotes and nostalgic memories.

Curiously, contributing to vaudeville's relegation to oblivion is the paternalism of so many supporters of the legitimate theater. In their view, vaudeville was designed to please the tastes of the common herd, giving the public only what it wanted. A playwright remarked of the vaudeville manager that he was "a sure-thing player." Typical of the manager's attitude were the pronouncements of Marcus Loew and Alexander Pantages, two of the more prominent scions of vaudeville. Loew said, "Give people what they want, give them their money's worth, and they'll stand in line at your door just as they stand at mine." Pantages echoed this theme: "Sell the people what they want—that is what brings success in the show business." Apparently, only one vaudeville manager attempted to skirt the popular taste. Martin Beck hired concert musicians and ballet dancers and, even when they flopped, would insist that the vaudeville audience had to be educated.[1] But vaudeville was an industry that could not afford to rock its own boat.

The legitimate theater, on the other hand, was regarded as being experimental, clearly aiming at higher planes, not as geared to the box office as vaudeville. There was also a prevailing opinion in the dramatic arts that the American people themselves were simply "not educated up to the finest productions of artistic genius."

Acton Davies, one of the major drama critics of that time, for example, stated that vaudeville was "a place where a great many bad actors go before they die." Gilbert Seldes felt that the legitimate stage actor could venture into vaudeville only if he intended "digging his own grave, because there is a stigma attached to the two-a-day." An anonymous foreign observer stated that "superior people" were not supposed to patronize vaudeville. Though H. I. Brock allowed that vaudeville "commanded a great public," he identified vaudeville as "low-born, dealing in the common coin of entertainment," adding that it was "a craft that ships a motley crew."

A keen observer of the entertainment scene, Alexander Bakshy, quoted an anonymous critic of vaudeville as saying, "Vaudeville is essentially one of the lower forms of theatrical art which inevitably takes the back seat when faced with the competition of such superior forms as drama and musical comedy." Bakshy's answer was blunt: "What preposterous trash passes here for an aesthetic theory! The popular notion of art is that it is something very serious and very solemn, while entertainment means trivial and light-hearted distraction." Another writer stated candidly, "Man's pleasures are fleeting and his capacity for pleasure equally brief. Vaudeville administers to his need." Still another opinion expressed soon after the turn of the century was that vaudeville was no longer the outcast of the dramatic arts, but had become a respectable medium. Yet, vaudeville has been denigrated and it has been relatively ignored by historians, probably on the basis of its lack of respectability as much as any other factor. Furthermore, even if vaudeville offered only trivial and light-hearted distraction, that contribution alone to its mass audience, would merit distinction. As M. Willson Disher said:

> History must take heed of entertainments before our understanding of the past can be complete. In order to gain insight into the

> mind of another age we should not ignore even the most trivial of amusements. Least of all should we despise those that are termed vaudeville. . . .[2]

Some felt that syndicates were in charge of the theaters and had as their only aim the gaining of profit and that it was regrettable that these theater corporations publicly proclaimed "that the theater [was] a place of amusement, of entertainment, and not of education or elevation. . . ."[3]

Undoubtedly, attitudes like this which ignore the essential fact that vaudeville was patronized by millions of Americans have contributed to the underestimation of vaudeville in accounts of America's social and intellectual development.

In vaudeville's case, its near zero status in historical analyses is even more acutely in error because vaudeville's audiences crossed class lines. Still, vaudeville remains so thinly appreciated by the professional writers of the nation's history that with the death-rattle of the last ancient vaudevillian it may fade altogether. Vaudeville lived briefly and furiously, but not so short a time that it deserves invisibility.

Ben Hecht, in talking of Harpo Marx, said, "He had come out of the early vaudeville circuits which were the slums of entertainment." Groucho Marx supported Hecht's view when he summarized those days in vaudeville in the words, "The so-called glamour of the stage didn't reach as far as the theatres and towns we played." He added:

> Theatrically, we were at the bottom of the social ladder. Five performances a day in a ten-cent vaudeville theatre was about as low as you could get. The only things below us were the carnival shows, one-ring circuses and the crooked medicine hustlers. . . .[4]

In the late thirties George Jean Nathan commented that vaudeville was far from dead and discussed the many acts that were playing in movie houses and nightclubs. He also classified the popular Broadway hit, *Hellzapoppin,* as a gigantic vaudeville show. In making his commentary, though, the type of prejudice that has cheated vaudeville of a more important place in American history shone through: "There is, I thoroughly believe," said Nathan, "as much dyed-in-the-wool vaudeville . . . on tap around New York today as there was in vaudeville's heyday. Which, however, is certainly nothing to go home and brag about." Otis Ferguson held a similar view. He believed that on the whole "vaudeville was pretty lousy. The majority of its acts were dull, stereotyped and crude; its bookers lacked imagination; it employed the minds of the worst writers in this country." Even Alexander Bakshy, in the late twenties, lamented the decay of vaudeville artistry. He felt that only one or two acts on each bigtime bill were "really satisfying numbers. The rest are the veriest junk which only the utter degradation of vaudeville standards has permitted to be performed." As to those who regretted the fading of vaudeville, Ferguson minced no words: "Spare a tear if you wish; I say the hell with it."[5]

Even after the Marx Brothers had achieved great success, the remarks of Groucho Marx could be interpreted as lessening vaudeville's importance in the show business realm. Groucho claimed to be discontented, in need of new worlds to conquer. He ached for the prestige that Broadway stardom carried, a prestige that Groucho claimed could never be given a vaudevillian.

Though vaudeville's money was good, Broadway meant greater stability and less of a grind than the vaudeville stage. Every vaudevillian dreamed of a Flo Ziegfeld offer. Even Edward F. Albee,[6] perhaps the single most powerful administrator vaudeville ever had, tended to put down vaudeville. When asked, "Isn't Vaudeville ever inclined to be jealous when her people are stolen from her by the legit?" Albee replied, "We can spare them. We find pleasure in their elevation to stardom." These statements, while accurate, reflect but one aspect in a very complex development.

In Howard Taubman's work on American theater history, the following view appeared:

> Vaudeville was a highly developed entertainment as well as a remarkable training ground for the theatre. Comedians, singers, jugglers, lariat twirlers, all sorts of performers who achieved distinction as actors in comedy, farce, musicals and even tragedy learned how to catch the attention of an audience, how to pace themselves, how to adapt themselves to crisis in this exigent school of the stage. . . . [Their stars] formed a pool of talent from which the new mediums, radio and television, drank thirstily.[7]

Fred Allen in a letter to Bernard Sobel, said he would place vaudeville in the training ground category, since it offered comedians a chance to experience varied audience reactions. Vaudeville, he continued, "steeled the comedian and enabled him to judge audiences and to adapt himself to any group and adjust himself to meet assorted conditions." There were things performers learned in vaudeville that they could not learn anywhere else; there were varied audiences, economy of method, and timing. As a training ground for musical comedy, gala revues, movies, and the legitimate theater, vaudeville was unsurpassed.

Jack Benny, too, called vaudeville a great school. He made the point that vaudeville allowed a new actor to break in his routine where little notice would be given if he failed. If the new act flopped in Kokomo, Indiana, he said, only the people in Kokomo would know about it. With each succeeding "Kokomo," improvement and experience would result.

Edgar Bergen claimed that a revival of vaudeville would be the greatest benefit movies, radio, and television could enjoy, emphasizing the training aspect. Jack Lemmon, referring to George Burns' remark that there no longer was a place where a "kid can be lousy," agreed wholeheartedly, placing further emphasis on vaudeville as a school that led to better things.

Joe E. Brown's opinion of the vaudeville sketch fits here, too. Comedy or drama had to be conveyed to the audience "with a punch" in the brief time of fourteen to thirty minutes. Brown remarked:

> Where but in a fast-growing young country could dramatics have been able to do that? It took the American mind, the American psychology, the hurried American type to do it.
>
> I think if we could be said to have a distinctively American type of drama, then it is because it grew up through the vaudeville sketch. . . . Vaudeville was the great training ground for the nation's future dramatic material—for both playwrights and actors.[8]

Perhaps because of this conception that vaudeville was merely a training ground, the medium itself has suffered in historical perspective.

Vaudeville had emerged from a rough and tumble background. The early variety halls that it once played, and even many that it continued to play, were far from "high-class." Much of vaudeville was done poorly, much of its comedy was stale, and it was easy for legitimate actors and drama critics to regard vaudeville as low culture and fit only for gross people. A typical view was one which condemned vaudeville patrons as

> . . . too intellectually lazy even to try to understand anything that did not lie immediately upon the surface. Their minds had been so long drugged by such a wealth of cheap and obvious entertainment . . . that they had lost the faculty of thinking.[9]

Sadly, it appears that the low esteem expressed by vaudeville's contemporaries has misled historians into shortchanging both vaudeville and the vaudevillian.

"DON'T SEND YOUR LAUNDRY OUT UNTIL AFTER THE FIRST SHOW."

♦ ♦ ♦ ♦ ♦

VAUDEVILLE, AS A TERM, WAS FIRST USED IN THE UNITED STATES IN 1840, when a Boston "Vaudeville Saloon" advertised itself as an establishment where a variety program could be seen.[1] The word itself is traced back to the valley of the Vire River in Normandy, where Val de Vire was often pronounced Vau de Vire. The area was one noted for its ballads and *vau-de-Vire* became a synonym for "lively songs." A popular drinking song in that part of France was Olivier Basselin's *chansons du Vau* or *du Val de Vire.* Though Tony Pastor, the most important vaudeville producer prior to the turn of the century, preferred the term "variety," once Benjamin F. Keith decided to identify it as vaudeville, vaudeville it was. Keith and Edward F. Albee built the most important vaudeville combine of all.

Vaudeville in its heyday[2] was completely controlled by the huge circuits that developed in North America. These circuits divided into what was usually identified as either "bigtime" or "smalltime." Every vaudevillian aimed for the "bigtime," where the best theaters, the best salaries, the best exposure, and best conditions existed. In the main the "bigtime" meant only two shows a day, an afternoon, then an evening performance. "Smalltime" could mean anything from three to a dozen shows a day.

Yet the situation around 1910 found so many two-a-day circuits that a story made the rounds about an actor who asked, when he was booked to play a circuit he had never heard of, "What is it? Smalltime, medium smalltime, big smalltime, little big time, medium big time or big time?"[3]

Whatever the answer, it was clear that all circuits were in a power struggle with the other circuits. *Variety* stated in 1912, "The big houses that give the biggest shows will get the money."[4] The battle for control of the bigtime raged for years, many contestants slipping in and out of the center ring. Along with the eventual winners, Keith and Albee, there were men like Martin Beck, Alexander Pantages, Sylvester Poli, Percy Williams, F. F. Proctor, Abe Erlanger, William Morris, Oscar and Willie Hammerstein, and the Shubert Brothers, Lee and J. J. When the rivalries flourished, so too did vaudeville. The public benefitted, as did performers, for only the best acts at top salaries were booked into the theaters, very often at very attractive box-office rates. However, the victory of Keith-Albee did not eliminate vaudeville rivalry. The battle lines shifted instead to the smalltime, a smalltime that eventually threatened the survivors of the bigtime war.

When bigtime vaudeville came under the umbrella of Keith-Albee, the bigtime product suffered a noticeable decline. Many of the best performers went into other branches of entertainment, unable to tolerate continued association with the villainous pair. The principle result of the loss of bigtime competition was the growth of smalltime, buoyed by an influx of former bigtime artists. A triangular contest ensued. The Keith-Albee powerhouse aligned itself directly against smalltime, while among the various smalltime syndicates there was a constant struggle for survival. As Keith-Albee cut salaries, smalltime owners raised theirs and offered excellent engagement routes. Many headliners sacrificed prestige for ready cash and better treatment. When Keith-Albee raised its prices for its bigtime shows and stars to as much as two dollars, the largest of the smalltime chains, the Marcus Loew circuit, put its top price at only fifty cents. The Loew circuit and many other smalltime circuits also showed movies with their vaudeville acts, a practice shunned by the proud Keith-Albee management until vaudeville was already dying.

As long as vaudeville lived, however, bigtime was bigtime and smalltime remained smalltime. Prestige, based mainly on tradition and a higher-class clientele, proved more attractive to most vaudevillians than did a high salary. This is not to say that the bigtime offered poor money. Headliners in bigtime vaudeville received the very highest salaries in show business until the advent of radio and movies.

Of course while few vaudevillians got a headliner's pay, in the best years about the lowest any bigtime act received was $150 a week. Lillian Russell, who was paid $35 weekly prior to 1900, was drawing $3,000 a week after the turn of the century. Eva Tanguay drew $3,500 a week. Once he had attained stardom, Al Jolson was assured $2,500 a week whenever he wished to appear. Ken Murray's salary of $2,000 each week during the late 1920's, put him in the same class as the great slugger of the New York Yankees, Babe Ruth. Keeping in mind that other headliners were drawing greater salaries, one readily recognizes the value of a major vaudeville commodity. Ethel Waters, veteran of some of the most rugged vaudeville in the country, was absolutely awestruck when, during the early 1930's, her weekly rate reached $3,500, with an occasional $4,000 thrown in. Around the same time the Four Marx Brothers became vaudeville's most expensive act, at $10,000 a week. In that day of the highest vaudeville dollar, the thirties, an eight-act bigtime vaudeville show generally cost from $6,000 to $10,000. One show at the Palace Theatre in New York in 1932, however, cost the management $16,000. The eight acts ranged from those of Patsy Kelly and Morgan and Stone at $750 apiece to Ethel Merman at $3,500 and the team of Jack Haley and Benny Rubin at $5,000. In the thirties, too, Eddie Cantor put on a Palace show which cost more than $20,000.

Yet, despite the excellent income enjoyed by many stars, the ultimate power always lay in the hands of management. The local manager of each theater was its censor. What he dictated was done, or else. The managers closely observed their opening day matinees and deleted whatever appeared to them to be immoral or unrefined. Each deletion was communicated to the central booking office in New York, where they were filed with painstaking care. A common sight backstage in vaudeville theaters was a sign which read, "Don't send your laundry out until after the first show."

Not only were managers dictators, according to Benny Rubin,

but "they hated your guts." As Rubin emphasized, managers were paid less, sometimes considerably less, than were vaudevillians. When this was the case, "He's gotta hate you."[5]

Not only cancellation hurt the actor. In a letter to a friend, Houdini's bitterness and frustration could be felt when his route was affected. "This Chicago date is an unexpected one, and Mr. Albee has simply loaned us to the Western people for two weeks."[6] The theater managers also were required to file reports of an act's talent with the main booking office. Fred Astaire loathed that arrangement because he felt the managers were too often inconsiderate. In his opinion they never tried to analyze the various conditions that could have been responsible for an act's failure. As he noted, the booking office wanted good news and anything else would hinder an act's progress.

Fines were another method of repression used by vaudeville's administrative authority. The Marx Brothers were playing a small theater in Springfield, Missouri, and the man hired to sing the illustrated songs became ill. Harpo Marx volunteered to fill the breech and the manager let him go on. According to Groucho Marx, Harpo "couldn't sing at all," and the poor audience reaction infuriated the manager. He fined Harpo five dollars. Observed Groucho, "They fined you for everything."[7]

Managers were also responsible for the timing of a show. To go overtime created problems, especially at the end of the day, for overtime pay for musicians and other help was prohibitive. Between shows, or at stipulated intermissions, the house had concession stands going for itself. That meant added profit. Contracts expressly set down an act's time allotment. If an act were set for eighteen minutes and the first run went twenty-one minutes, the manager reminded the vaudevillian of his time limit and said, "Please cut three minutes." Precision timing was very important in vaudeville.

Then there was the infamous practice of blacklisting. The United States Amusement Company was incorporated in New Jersey in 1907, an effort to buck the stranglehold of Keith-Albee. Powerful show business figures combined in the effort, Marc Klaw and Abe Erlanger to procure the acts, Lee and J. J. Shubert to supply the theaters, and William Morris to be in command of the overall booking procedure. The new chain enjoyed tremendous publicity, secured top names at top salaries, and presented its first performances in September. The new competition paid high salaries and forced the Keith-Albee empire to do the same. Some felt the competitive spirit also raised vaudeville's level of entertainment. Raising salaries to stay close to the United States Amusement Company's offers was not the chief strategy of the Keith-Albee offices, however. Edward Albee instituted a blacklist. Any acts deserting the incumbent power for the new challenger would never again play a Keith-Albee stage. Though higher salaries were the big lure of the new group, most vaudevillians remained within the older chain. Those bold enough to go over were hurt, and hurt badly, when the new company folded.

The inspiration for founding what soon became the show business "Bible," *Variety,* was Sime Silverman's hatred of the mistreatment of vaudevillians by their employers. His colleague, Abel Green, expressed about Sime, "He abhorred dishonesty. He set a cardinal rule for his staffers' professional and private lives: *If you tell the truth even the people who don't like it must respect you.*"[8] *Variety*'s persistent opposition to the power mongers finally led to an Albee directive in 1913, that no act which advertised in *Variety* could ever hope to be on the Keith circuit. Even those observed reading *Variety* would be banned. All employees of the Keith chain, not just vaudevillians, existed under this threat. A copy of *Variety* sticking out of an employee's jacket pocket would be an invitation for instant dismissal. Music publishers were informed that their music would not be used in any Keith house if they advertised in *Variety.* It was later observed that Albee's blacklist made "the one of the Joe McCarthy era pale by comparison."[9] *Variety* was powerful in its own right, however, and Albee's all-sweeping edict proved unwieldy.

New excuses for fresh Keith-Albee blacklists appeared on the horizon anyway. If it was not William Morris, it was the Shuberts or Marcus Loew. *Variety* carried a statement issued just after the New Year, 1919, by the B. F. Keith Vaudeville Booking Exchange:

> Rube Marquard will not play any of the Keith time in New York as stated in *Variety* Dec. 20.
>
> Negotiations were on in the Keith offices for time, but when it was learned Marquard had played Loew's Metropolitan, Brooklyn, the negotiations were called off.

> The class of acts that play the Keith high priced houses in New York will be closely watched hereafter, and any act playing a popular priced house—no matter in what neighborhood, where a Keith high price house operates, will lose his or her time on the Keith Circuit.[10]

Harry Jolson felt the sting of the Albee blacklist. When the William Morris circuit folded, he was among hundreds of top performers affected. "I thought I could return to Keith, but such was not the case. . . . Keith's was the only bigtime vaudeville circuit in existence. Those, like myself, who were on the Keith blacklist found themselves without employment." Jolson did go on to point out, however, that when the Keith offices were in difficulty, when headliners would be too ill to appear, they booked him as a substitute. Harry Jolson was used to working no less than forty weeks a year. In the year following the collapse of the Morris circuit, he worked only thirteen weeks. It was years before the Keith bosses relented and removed him from their blacklist.[11]

Albee and one of his chief cohorts, John J. Murdock, put many acts on their blacklist by planting what were known as stool-pigeon acts. It was a motley practice. These acts wrote to Albee and Murdock about backstage gossip and whatever remarks they overheard. Even the Marx Brothers, destined to be the Keith circuit's highest paid act in 1932, did not escape an Albee blacklist. The Marx Brothers emerged luckier than most, for they soon were hired by the Shuberts. Even though their experiences with the Shuberts were far from perfect—"Our new bosses were famous in the theatre, but not for their liberal treatment of performers"--and despite their tour's eventual flop,[12] the Marx Brothers did have work and gained one of the most valuable of all show business commodities, experience.

On another occasion, Harpo Marx alone tried his luck at going against the Albee rules. Frank Fay, an outstanding bigtime monologist, was conducting a series of what he termed "Sunday Concerts," an act which was in open defiance of Albee. Fay asked Harpo, then playing the Palace with his brothers, to do a single. In this way, Harpo and Fay thought they could circumvent the Albee edict, since the officially booked act was the Marx Brothers and not Harpo as a single. Harpo agreed to play Fay's show under the billing, "Arthur Marx," and rendered a piano and pantomine turn.

The next day Harpo was summoned to the office of E. F. Albee, the man he considered "more powerful than the President of the United States." After the conference, Harpo states, "I kept my nose clean."[13]

In the opinion of brother Groucho, "Albee was the owner of a large cotton plantation and the actors were his slaves." He cited Albee's habit of making appointments for an early hour, and not seeing the actor until much later. Ethel Waters described Albee as "usually sterner than a whole Southern Baptist convention."[14]

No matter what their faults, not all vaudeville magnates were judged villainous. Marcus Loew, the king of smalltime, was praised for being sensitive to the problems of others, including vaudevillians working for him. In Loew's opinion a contented employee would perform more enthusiastically than would a disgruntled player. Loew had no discernible prejudices, except against laziness and poor performance. Loew was respected for his human qualities; he was esteemed as well for his eye for talented performers. Both these attributes brought many topflight vaudevillians into Loew's fold at comparatively moderate salaries. It was said of him that he may have been the smalltime king but personally he was strictly Bigtime!

Martin Beck, too, was thought well of by some who worked for him. Beck was the supreme vaudeville impresario in the western towns. His chain of Orpheum theaters stretched to the Pacific. Having started his career as a waiter in a tavern, he was nicknamed by vaudevillians "Two-Beers Beck." He was noted for his policy of "you pay for what you get." He always insisted that his actors stay at the best hotels and to insure they would, he paid his people a higher salary rate. He was convinced this practice was good for his business since performers would be happier and the public would be impressed to see that Orpheum vaudevillians stayed only at first-class hotels. Beck felt the public would judge his players, then, to be only the best. Joe Laurie, Jr., felt Beck was the one man above all others who put class into vaudeville.

Beck did have his critics. Chief among them was probably Buster Keaton's father. According to the famed Buster, most vaudeville performers disliked Beck, although his view could easily have been distorted by his father's resentments. The elder Keaton "called Beck every name in the book," after an incident while The

Three Keatons had the opening spot at the Palace. The bitterness boiled over when Beck began to mock Keaton in the middle of his routine. Moments later Beck was running for his life, out of the Palace and down the street, with the muscular Keaton in hot pursuit. Beck's being alternately admired and disliked was undoubtedly the result of his multi-faceted personality, described by Bernard Sobel as "alternating steadiness and capriciousness, cold critical judgment, erudition and spurts of kindness."[15]

Among New York managers, Percy Williams was deemed the most decent. He controlled theaters in the boroughs of Manhattan, Brooklyn, and the Bronx, and was called "the father of big salaries in vaudeville." His will contained a line, "I made my money from the actors; I herewith return it to them." His thirty acre country estate, Pine Acres, in East Islip, Long Island, thus became a home for "aged and indigent performers." Joseph M. Schenck, general manager of the Loew circuit, was viewed by Mae West to be "a man of great personal charm, soft spoken, and possessed of a manner that made him attractive and easy to like." Another thought of highly was J. Austin Fynes, who had been an editor of the New York *Clipper,* a trade journal, and a drama critic for the New York *Sun.* Keith made him his manager and Fynes' work was so outstanding that Joe Laurie, Jr., credited Fynes with making vaudeville "the nation's amusement."

Then there was Albee's chief right hand, John J. Murdock, called by Max Gordon, "one of the truly great men behind the scenes of vaudeville." Gordon stressed that Murdock enjoyed giving young people a chance and Robert Grau made a point that Murdock was very easy to approach, "a man of quiet and modest demeanor." Marian Spitzer's comments about both Murdock and Albee are perhaps the most incisive: "From all accounts, Mr. Murdock was quite as much of a tyrant as Mr. Albee. Yet everyone who reminisces about Murdock does it with a laugh and a philosophical attitude, while scarcely anyone mentions E. F. Albee without intense bitterness."[16] Spitzer's remarks are based on years of observation, for she was a key employee in the Keith-Albee offices.

Murdock himself praised another top manager, F. F. Proctor, "a quiet gentleman, nothing blowhard about him." Murdock was especially pleased with the fact that Proctor never swore and insisted that his employees follow suit. Proctor also hated drinking men and was accused of having a colorless personality. Proctor, born in Dexter, Maine, was described by another as "a modest, retiring, reticent Yankee, *naturally* reticent." He was supposed to have had "a disposition worth a million dollars." It is interesting to note, in light of this remark, that Proctor willed one million dollars to the Actors' Fund. Proctor was a thorough manager, as tough with vaudevillians as any. At Monday morning rehearsals he would more often than not be seated in a box, quick to censor anything he felt inappropriate for his stage. When interviewed for a newspaper spot called "Mental Photo," Proctor gave his favorite virtue as loyalty, his favorite quality in a man as moral courage, in a woman as modesty, his idea of unhappiness as failure, and as his favorite motto, he chose "Keep Plugging."[17]

Alexander Pantages was viewed by his head usher as a fine man to work for, one who commanded loyalty because he was "absolutely square and a true friend." His word was his bond. Pantages sat in a box and studied the audience reaction to the acts and made a point of mingling with the crowd after the show. One writer pronounced him the best showman in the theater because of his study of crowds and his use of psychology.

Whether liked or hated by the vaudevillians, however, the theater managers knew that the name of the game was box office. In 1909 it was not unusual for Percy Williams to see some of his theaters grossing $15,000 a week. In the same year a single vaudeville theater in Detroit netted a profit for the season of more than $150,000. In 1910 Charles F. Kohl, of the Kohl and Castle circuit in the Middle West, left an estate of $7,000,000. The news generated no excitement because it was not unusual for such a vast sum to be associated with a smalltime vaudeville owner.

FROM BURKE'S JUGGLING DOGS TO SINGER'S MIDGETS

◆ ◆ ◆ ◆ ◆

THE MAJOR CHALLENGE IN THE HIGHLY COMPETITIVE VAUDEVILLE BUSI- ness of managing was making the bill attractive to the public. This meant acquiring not only the best talent money could buy but also putting together a show act by act in the best possible sequence. It was a formidable task. Some houses, like those of William Morris' chain, ran from twenty to twenty-two acts. Others, especially when movies wedged in, played as few as two acts. The standard offering, however, was what the Keith-Albee theaters followed, an eight to ten act bill. Whatever the number of acts, the ideal theater was perhaps best described by Max Gordon:

> A theatre needs to have an atmosphere of friendliness, it must be a place where nothing interferes with the rapport between the audience and the stage. It needs the warmth of intimacy.[1]

This was the aim of vaudevillians, to share a warmth and intimacy with their public. Yet they and their producers always lived in fear of that public. It has been observed that the popular artist, and the vaudevillian was the most popular of his day, actually competes with his audience "under whose control he must work—a notoriously capricious audience of unknown size and composition." Oscar Hammerstein II referred to the public as

"The Big Black Giant."[2]

To appear in front of this awesome public, the vaudevillian had to be booked. The booking system involved four groups: the performer, his agent, the circuit booking man, and the manager of the theater where he would appear. The process has been described as the performer being the merchandise, the agent the seller, the booking man the middleman, and the manager the retailer. The audience, of course, was the ultimate consumer.

The booking man could select from thousands of acts. A typical listing of vaudeville acts in the early 1900's included such intriguing names as Burke's Juggling Dogs, the Imperial Japs, the Piccolo Midgets, the Zat Zams, Musliner's Pigs, Drako's Sheep and Goats, Mr. & Mrs. Earle Gottlob, and even a Bimm, Bomm, B-r-r-r. There were also eye-catching acts like Top and Bottom, Salt and Pepper, Ham and Eggs, You and Me, Kiss and Tell, Yes and No, Stop and Go, Major and Minor, and Back to Hicksville.

The novelty acts clearly demonstrated to what lengths vaudeville would go to entertain. When the Royal Polo Teams, using bicycles instead of horses and the bicycle wheels instead of mallets, gave an exhibition at the Plaza Music Hall in New York City, a review simply stated that the performance was "away from the ordinary run of vaudeville acts." Harpo Marx and George Burns felt that the most original and unusual act they ever saw on tour was Collins and Hart, featuring a cat that blew a whistle. Then there were the world favorite Singer's Midgets. Leo Singer toured certain areas of Germany, locating midgets who belonged to poor families and reaching contractual agreements with their parents in order to put them on tour. Singer used an extra large Packard to drive his troupe of twenty-five to thirty midgets to and from the theater. There were countless animal acts, of course. Fatal accidents to the animals quite frequently created turmoil for these vaudevillians. Kazana, an Egyptian snake charmer, was booked to play the Rivoli Theater in Toledo. When one of her snakes died because of extreme cold, she placed the basket with the three snakes that were still alive next to a radiator. They smothered due to the extreme heat. Kazana kept the engagement, however, doing a Hula dance. *Variety* also cited a dog act in smalltime which ended suddenly when the dog died as a result of flea bites. "The trainer of the dog with the surviving fleas has started a flea circus and latest reports say he is doing better now than he did with the dog act," reported the trade paper. *Variety* also reported the apparent mysterious poisoning of two of Braatz's dogs, when they were allowed to roam outside the Orpheum Theatre in Brooklyn.

Brooklyn's Orpheum was also the site of what was perhaps one of the most exciting single circumstances connected with an animal act in vaudeville's annals. Violet Dale was in the midst of her turn when a trained gorilla from another act escaped backstage. She related, "He was perfectly crazy about women and started for the wings when I was on, doing my act." Before the gorilla made it to the stage, however, he was commandeered by his handlers. Miss Dale who was unaware of what had caused the commotion she heard, finished her act. Another dramatic moment occurred in a theater the Marx Brothers were working. Two lions broke loose, one going center stage and roaring at the audience. The theater emptied in panic while the lions, who harmed no one, were coaxed back into their cages.

Al Fanton vividly recreated in a tape recording what must be classified as one of the most novel acts in show business history when he detailed the act of Hadji Ali. According to Fanton, Ali was one of the most popular vaudeville acts on tour. The act was built around Ali's ability to regurgitate. Included in the act, for example, was the swallowing, then spitting up, of watermelon seeds. The finish of his act, however, was the highlight. Ali had a tiny metal house on stage, made up to look like a castle. He would drink a gallon of water, then a pint of kerosene. While the orchestra played and the drummer hammered loudly, Ali "would, all of a sudden, spit out this kerosene, which would put the little house, the metal house, in flames. The thing would go all over, flames all over." Hadji Ali would then somehow "bring up this gallon of water and spit it all out. The fire would go out and . . . that was the finish of the act. And believe it or not, people would applaud this, really applaud. . . ."[3]

Certainly one of the most fascinating acts in vaudeville history was Motogirl, who was reviewed as the "novelty" of the 1902-1903 season. She was described as "a real live girl, who has by much practice learned to control every muscle of her body so thoroughly that she can stand the closest examination without betraying the fact that she is not a dummy." The examinations afforded the audience were close when one considers that she was literally passed among the theater patrons, "and those who choose may pinch her, and no matter how hard the pinch may be, she never squirms."[4]

Although vaudeville did witness success by the strangest acts, a very interesting one flopped. Sadakichi Hartmann, announced as a Japanese-German inventor, chose for his turn a "perfume concert." Hartmann used fans to blow perfumed smoke toward the audience. Each odor represented a different country. He appeared at the New York Theatre, "explained in irregular English" what he would do, managed to get through England (roses) and Germany (violets) before the hecklers drove him from the stage.

Impersonators have long been an attractive show business feature. One, Willie Zimmerman, impersonated William Howard Taft and William Jennings Bryan, as they would appear if they were orchestra conductors. Then there were female impersonators, premier among them being Julian Eltinge. Of Eltinge, L. Wolfe Gilbert, dean of Tin Pan Alley, said: "As a 'she' he was glorious to look at. Yet he was known to have beaten up many a tough longshoreman and hoodlum. I know he was truly a 'he-man.' Don't ask me how–I know!"[5]

Acrobatic acts were high on a booker's list. Among them one could find "Hayes and Post, Acrobatic Dancers, Tumblers, Comedians, and High Kickers," the Britons and Rita, or an act like Joe Fanton's Athletes. Joe Fanton performed with a rigging composed of pipes that reached twenty feet high, atop which was a supporting bar about ten feet wide. Two rings hung from this bar and guy wires and stage hooks held everything in place. As with many acrobatic acts that depended on apparatus, it was no easy task erecting the equipment. In Fanton's case, in order to get the needed support, he himself would often use a hammer and star drill for hours to anchor the rigging safely to the stage floor. Too many stage floors were only three-quarters of an inch of wood put directly on cement and Fanton would come into a new town, fatigued by dismantling his equipment and the overnight journey, only to face the back-breaking job of putting up his rigging. Once that was done the matinee performance began and Fanton was performing. Sometimes this combination of fatigue and lack of preparation by the stage hands resulted in calamity.

At the end of his acrobatic act, Fanton would stand on the low end of a teeter-board 20 feet directly under the overhead bar. A 200 pound sandbag would be dropped on the opposite end of the teeter-board, Fanton would be catapulted into the air, turn a half somersault and catch his feet in the two loops. It was a spectacular finish. Unfortunately, however, there were times when the stage hands would raise the sandbag too high and Joe Fanton would be thrown completely over.

People in the news were also good for the box office. Willie Hoppe, at the age of eighteen a world's champion billiards player, toured vaudeville. A huge mirror was placed behind him so that the audience could appreciate his artistry. Jack Dempsey and Gene Tunney were booked by Gus Sun in 1926 and later appeared on other circuits. Helen Keller and her teacher also played vaudeville. Oscar Hammerstein was particularly noted for offering acts starring people who were suddenly made famous and whose names were appearing daily in the newspapers.

Variety acts were also popular. One of the better ones in vaudeville's late days was the Albee Sisters. Though the name was the same, they were not related to the infamous Edward Albee, yet played the theaters built and furnished during his reign. The four sisters were a typical variety act. They tap danced, sang, did comedy, and played musical instruments. In their case this meant the cello, violin, piano, clarinet and saxophone. For their finale, the "show stopper," the four dressed in evening gowns but sported handlebar mustaches and derby hats. Another fine act was Major and Minor, two excellent classical ballerinas who would exit doing the buck and wing while playing violins.

Magicians were another dependable draw, chief among them being Houdini. Houdini, a master of publicity, was also a master of concealment. His loud pronouncement during his act that he would undergo any challenge or test generally assured members of his audience that he was on the up and up. Even when searches of his person were made, they were perfunctory, since a thorough search would have delayed the act. Houdini thus was able to hide keys in secret pockets and even occasionally in a bag strapped to his leg below the knee.[6]

Often the highlight of a show was a solo female act such as Nora Bayes, Ruth Etting, or, during an occasional leave from the legitimate stage, Ethel Barrymore. One of the most highly regarded was the sensational Eva Tanguay, a dynamic singer, whose energy was evidently boundless. Her turn was a long one and by employing a pedometer one evening, she discovered that during the course of her act she covered three and one-quarter miles.[7]

The monarchs of the vaudeville stage, though, were the funny men. Marian Spitzer wrote that although vaudeville tried to present as varied a class of entertainment as possible, the main objective was to make people laugh; laughter was the foundation of vaudeville. Ethel Waters called Chic Sale "the funniest vaudeville performer" she had ever seen. Will Rogers, judged by many the wittiest of all vaudevillians, knew the importance of laughter to his success and always made sure that Fred Tejan, a personal friend and one of the heartiest, loudest laughers he knew, was seated right down in front. Perhaps the key to Rogers' success was the fact that an ordinary act rarely went beyond twelve minutes. His lasted forty-five.

Eddie Cantor, one of the greatest, felt that Will Rogers was a performer who, like Al Jolson, came along once in a generation. Cantor felt Bert Williams, another top vaudeville funny man, was the kind who came along just once in a lifetime. Another headline comic, Lou Holtz, said of Bert Williams, "He's the greatest comedian I've ever seen." Edward B. Marks claimed, too, that no white comedian ever surpassed Williams. "Chaplin himself can hold an audience no better," stated Marks.[8] Williams was extremely popular, at one time part of the great Black team of Williams and Walker, and eventually a major star in the Ziegfeld Follies. And there were even those who were of the opinion that Ernest Hogan, another Black headliner, was superior to Williams.[9]

The acts went on and on and the booker had to balance them. Would a Houdini go well on the same bill as a Will Rogers? Would Lou Holtz be the right funny man for a show also starring Sophie Tucker? Could the two headliners be paid their top salaries and still have quality supporting acts fit into the profit-making budget? Then, once the booking agent signed the acts, the theater manager had to arrange them in just the right order. Martin Beck, one of the best, aimed for the best talent, but always so that his bill would have variety, change of pace, and something for everyone. A correspondence school author advised his pupils that there was no better psychologist than the vaudeville manager, who showed not only the best acts but in such a combination as to create a unified whole.

The opening act on a bill, a position referred to as the door-mat of vaudeville, was invariably a "dumb act," one which required no talking, due to the fact as an astute foreigner noted, "Americans are very unpunctual."[10] Unlike Europe, where dumb acts were highly respected and often a headline act, in the United States, they usually were assigned the worst spots on the bill. This irked not only the top dumb acts but also some critics who felt there were such acts that deserved headline status. The opening act had to be one that could succeed despite the constant interruptions of late-comers. Thus dancers, jugglers, acrobats, bicycle riders, and sometimes, animal acts were assigned the opening spot.

The second act could be almost anything at all, as long as it provided more entertainment than the first act. Said George A. Gottlieb, booker for New York's Palace Theatre, "This position on the bill is to 'settle' the audience and to prepare it for the show." Gottlieb himself was of the opinion that a man-and-woman singing act was probably the best type of act for the second spot. Fred Astaire referred to this position as "the lousy number-two spot on the bill."[11]

For the number three position, Gottlieb said the main purpose was to wake up the audience. For Gottlieb that meant a comedy dramatic sketch. For others, though, it could be a magician, a sister act, dancers, a comedy team, even a swimming act. Then came a "corker" of an act, a big name, something elaborate. This number four spot would serve as "the first big punch of the show."

Number five had to be a big act, another big name, a star as important as any other on the bill. For Gottlieb at the Palace the number five spot meant it was right before the intermission. The act had to be excellent in order to have the audience buzzing, generating enthusiasm for the show. Any headline act would fit here.

The number six position was a difficult one to fill. Just before intermission the show had reached its peak. Now the first act after intermission had to somehow sustain the audience's appreciation and yet it could not be an act that would be stronger than the one that was to follow, for that would be the next-to-closing on an eight act bill. Next-to-closing was the most important act of all. The last act was universally referred to as the "chaser," one designed to clear the house quickly, yet be the type that would delight those patrons who would remain seated. It was the last act and it had to be good, in order to keep the audience happy and talking about how excellent the show had been. Martin Beck even went one step further and installed large orchestras in each of his theaters, not only to provide an overture to put the incoming audience in a good mood for the show but also to, as he commanded, "Play the last person out!" He wanted no one exiting from a suddenly silent, cold theater.

Not all managers, of course, thought as Martin Beck did. Very often most of the theater was emptying while the chasers were doing their best to entertain and even the theater ushers would rush through the rows, "clacking the seats back, and picking up the programmes and lost articles under them." No chaser was satisfied with this fate. Joe E. Brown, who started his career as an acrobat, ruefully recalled the days when, just as their act began, he could see half the audience already tramping up the aisles. It hurt especially because Brown knew his act was headline quality. Many spent entire careers playing before rapidly emptying theaters. Eventually, one of the best chasers ever used contributed to the ruination of vaudeville. Very effective chasers in the early days of vaudeville were motion pictures.

It is interesting to compare the results of a question asked of two of the very finest vaudevillians who ever headlined a show, Benny Rubin and Ken Murray. Who would they want with them, and in what order, if they could once again be on a bill at the Palace? Both developed eight act shows and that was where the duplication ended, illustrating even further the abundant variety that vaudeville could offer the public.

While Murray would open his show with Rastelli, a great juggler, Rubin had the Rath Brothers,[12] who did acrobatic hand-balancing. Murray's second spot featured Williams and Walker, Rubin's choice being the Roth Sisters, a singing duo. Both selected dramatic sketches for their third position, Murray unable to decide between Douglas Fairbanks, Sr., and Ethel Barrymore, Rubin choosing Robert Warwick. Then, while Rubin put Val and Renie Stanton into the fourth spot, with their funny act, Murray inserted himself for that turn. While Murray followed himself with the Dolly Sisters, and then intermission, Rubin had Ruth Etting, of "Ten Cents a Dance" fame, for his fifth position. Number six for Murray was Van and Schenck, for Rubin the Gus Edwards' revue. Rubin chose himself for next-to-closing. Murray, instead of naming a top vaudeville artist, settled instead on either Jack Dempsey or Babe Ruth for that key position on the bill. Then, while Rubin was finishing with an act featuring living statues, Murray concluded that an excellent chaser would be Fink's Mules. Murray also wanted Will Rogers near the end of the bill, but was unable to decide exactly where he would include him.[13] Put Murray's bill against Rubin's bill in comparable neighboring theaters, have a family come down the street able to afford to see one show, and that was what vaudeville was all about—money! The acts could be artistically perfect, could get all the praise possible from their vaudeville colleagues and from the numerous reviewers, but if they failed to pack the people in, they were smalltime.

"DON'T SAY 'SLOB' OR 'SON OF GUN' OR 'HOLY GEE.' "

◆ ◆ ◆ ◆ ◆

THE VAUDEVILLE AUDIENCE, LIKE VAUDEVILLE ITSELF, WAS COMPOSED OF a broad cross-section of American society. Perhaps there was nothing more typically American than American vaudeville audiences.[1]

> There it sits, waiting for the show to begin, good-natured, eager to be amused . . . its genuine appreciation is unmistakable. I am not referring to "tryouts" or "amateur nights," where the baiting of the performer is as much a part of the show as the slaughter of horses at a bull fight. . . . But I have frequently heard people speak slightingly of a performance and then applaud at its close from pure goodwill to the performer.[2]

Max Gordon noted the same characteristics. He praised them for their generous applause and laughter and commented:

> They were critical, and they had a right to be, as paying customers. But they were more often than not friendly, too. They applauded frequently, though not overzealously, even when they had not been thrilled or amused especially, but because they may have sympathized with the fellow "up there" who was trying to make a living. . . . The vaudeville audience did not look for moral or spiritual uplift. It distrusted what it considered hifalutin and highbrow. . . . What the vaudeville audience wanted most was good straight entertainment; it was not interested

> in following a story through an entire evening. . . . They wanted variety, and vaudeville gave it to them—variety of which there was no apparent end.[3]

Franklin P. Adams, however, remembered that audiences walked out on an act if it ran too long. Vaudeville appealed "to a public . . . instantly responsive to representations of life. Nothing is lost upon the vaudeville audience. . . ."[4]

Nora Bayes, one of the greatest vaudeville artists, maintained that the vaudeville audience was the most sensitive of all audiences. Nellie Revell, a noted vaudeville critic said of the vaudeville audience, "The more they get, the more they want." Her observation compares with a generally accepted view that vaudeville was a mirror of its times.[5] As the technological age advanced, so too did the demands of the American public for efficiency, speed, and opportunity for action.

Mae West, who claimed she studied audiences, noted that a vaudeville audience was less sophisticated than one on Broadway and more varied. According to her, each town had its own standard for entertainment and the performer had to adapt himself to every city's peculiar "country cousin standards" in order to be successful. In addition, the performer had to be alert for changes from one night to the next. On those scores, Miss West pointed to the importance of the theater manager, whom she found in most cases to be a dependable source of information concerning his locality's idiosyncracies. She observed:

> I usually found that one night a week you would get a top society crowd, and another night you'd get mostly working class people. Other nights there would be family groups—especially on Friday nights when the kids didn't have to go to school the next day. Saturday nights everybody was out for a good time, so audiences were both mixed and terrific.
>
> There was still another type of audience when the house had been sold out to social, charitable or fraternal organizations. These audiences were often rather stiff and reserved. Dressed up, on their best behavior, conscious of themselves and of the other members of their cult—they were careful as to what they applauded or laughed at. This was the hardest kind of audience to play to.[6]

Problems posed by the audience's variety was a challenge that the vaudevillian was supposed to be best equipped to handle. Ben

Blue felt his greatest show business experience was in vaudeville, primarily because of the challenge of playing to so many different types of audiences.[7] Edward Reed wrote:

> The true vaudevillian was a "character." It was the essence of his art to create a stage personality so definite, rounded, unique, and so entirely his own, that he would be recognized and hailed whenever he appeared on a stage—in New York or in Kalamazoo. He was an artist whose material always had a certain universal quality and who was trained to have this material so entirely under his control technically that he was able to mold it to suit the sophistication or simplicity of any audience he faced.[8]

Eddie Cantor recalled that his act, Cantor and Lee, "wowed Chicago—a smash! The next week, two hours away in Milwaukee—with exactly the same act, every word—we died the death of a dog." Heard repeatedly by the performer on the way up was the fact that New York audiences were excellent, whereas what scored there could flop in smaller towns.[9]

Musical acts generally felt that the smaller towns, especially before radio, "didn't know a good thing from a bad thing [and] if you didn't play their country music or something that they were familiar with, they didn't know how to receive it." On the basis that "you had to hit 'em quick," a vaudevillian had to make good in the first minute or he was dead. In certain parts of New York City, he knew he would profit if he worked some Jewish words into his material. In another part, Italian vocabulary paid dividends.[10]

W. C. Fields was a master at what he termed "locals." Fields asserted that every big city had one sure-fire laugh, when the comic hung "some piece of idiocy upon the people of a nearby city or town." Fields kept notes on the areas he played and concluded that "the igloos of the theatrical world" were, in order, Washington, Kansas City, and St. Louis.[11] The success of an act, though the performer might have been a veritable computer of popular idiosyncracies, always remained in the audience's hands.

The audience that sat on its hands was the worst, although vaudevillians abhorred a rowdy gathering just as much. On many occasions a college crowd would literally try to tear a theater apart. At times fire hoses were used to squelch such riots. One theater manager electrified the orchestra pit railing to keep students from leaping onstage. Worse than causing physical damage to a theater, though, were the practical jokes played during a performance. In one theater, for example, students brought alarm clocks, all timed to ring at the same time.

There were those, however, who held that there were no bad audiences. Ted Lewis insisted that every audience he ever entertained was wonderful. Eddie Cantor maintained that "there is no such thing as a bad audience," his point being that an audience had paid for the privilege to be entertained.[12]

One writer felt that "as long as people seek laughter, good tunes, mystification and surprise," vaudeville would endure. "It is a boost to the spirit, a temporary escape from fear, anxiety and pain," said he. Comedians have long maintained that they are satisfied if they bring a smile to the face of one unhappy soul. Eddie Cantor felt, "In every theater audience of fifteen hundred, there must be forty or fifty or more who are not there to be entertained, they're there to forget. The comedian is their Nembutal, their Miltown, whatever medicine they need."[13] Groucho Marx said of comedians:

> But because we are laughed at, I don't think people really understand how essential we are to their sanity. If it weren't for the brief respite we give the world with our foolishness, the world would see mass suicide in numbers that compare favorably with the death rate of lemmings.[14]

Comedy fit the scene in America during vaudeville's golden years and "laughs" were considered the essence of the medium. Musical comedy also flourished at that time, and the early movies highlighted farce. Vaudeville, by providing farce and musical comedy, plus countless other attractions, gained the greatest audience, however. When one considers that vaudeville was the radio, movies, and television of its day, one must also remember that the audience was a group of people seated together before live entertainment—a distinction unclaimed by these other forms of entertainment.[15]

Bert Lahr referred to the first decade of the twentieth century as one where comedy indeed was king. He maintained that the humor of that time "cut deep into the paradoxical fabric of the New World. It was at once a criticism and an acceptance of America's ideals."[16] Vaudeville comedians therefore provided an outlet for their audiences when they supplied laughs on subjects which were sensitive and seemingly unsolvable. Lahr himself referred to "the inefficiency of government and the paradoxes facing an unsophisticated immigrant populace."[17]

The ability of the American public to laugh at itself has been observed by many. Constance Rourke, in her popular work on the nation's humor, stated, "American audiences enjoyed their own deflation; they liked the boldness of attack, the undisguised ridicule." Sir Harry Lauder, the great Scottish comedian who reaped many rewards from American audiences, said of them, "They've a verra keen sense o' the ridiculous, and they're as fond of a joke that's turned against themselves as of one they play upon another pairson. That's a fine trait, and it makes it easy to amuse them in the theater."[18]

Yet, it was not always easy. Even the most talented acts suffered bad days. To Bert Lahr environment played an important part. "Sometimes climatic conditions could hurt comedy; if the people in the audience weren't comfortable." Another top comedian, Bobby Clark, stressed the importance of environment, too. When he got a laugh in the wrong place, he always wanted to know why. Very often the answer settled on dealt with the weather. For example, Clark believed that if it was raining when the audience came into the theater, nothing was amiss. But when it began to rain during the show, a tension developed, uneasiness spread, and the patrons wondered where they had left their lawnmowers or whether the windows at home or in the car were closed.[19] It was no easy task to stay on top as a comedian.

Still, vaudeville was filled with headlining comedians. Corey Ford called the twenties and thirties the "Golden Age of American Humor" and Eddie Cantor insisted that the "Golden Days of Comedy" were those enjoyed week upon week at the Palace, when "unforgettable giants would warm our hearts and tickle our funny bones."[20] To Ford, laughter during the twenties "had a sound all its own."

> The sound filled the packed theaters on Broadway where the great comedians were playing—W. C. Fields and Ed Wynn and the Marx Brothers and Joe Cook—and the musicians in the pit would chortle with the audiences, and the ushers would join in the hilarity, and in the deserted lobby the producer would smile as he counted the profits, because laughter was what poured golden

dollars into the box office.[21]

Constance Rourke stated further that through humor "the unconscious objective of a disunited people has seemed to be that of creating fresh bonds, a new unity, the semblance of a society and the rounded completion of an American type."[22] If that is so, then vaudeville comedians, the most plentiful of their kind in show business during such a crucial period of American history, played an enormous part in the nation's development. As important was the fact that most of the jokes that made their way to the vaudeville boards were written, or stolen from, a small group of writers who were based in New York.[23]

This identity problem of America, a melting pot or not, good or bad, has long been part of the scene. At the same time as a nation's people seek a common bond of heritage, this vast country of disparate ethnic backgrounds clings devotedly to its origins. This duality desired by so many Americans therefore transferred itself to the vaudeville stage.

The popular audience has always been thought to expect entertainment, instruction, or both, rather than aesthetic experience. The appearances on the vaudeville stage of fine actors such as Sarah Bernhardt, Ethel Barrymore, or Wilton Lackaye, were more a novelty than anything else and in order to fill the house the rest of the bill had to be topflight vaudeville entertainment.

The preferences of minorities were disregarded unless the group represented a large enough audience. As long as audiences registered no protest, "coon" acts, ethnic jokes, bawdiness, and other coarse material appeared freely on the vaudeville stage. However, when various groups exerted pressure, restrictive action was taken by theater managers. The first twenty years of the century found ethnic societies trying to rid the vaudeville stage of the acts which caricatured their groups. There were such groups as the Chicago Anti-Stage Jew Ridicule Committee, the Associated Rabbis of America, the Anti-Defamation League of B'nai Brith, the Ancient Order of Hibernians, and the United Irish Societies of New York, all intent on putting pressure on the theater managers. There was no timidness in their approach. The Russell Brothers, known for their "Irish Servant Girls" act, actually feared for their lives because of the intimidating actions of the Irish societies. Many times they were unable to complete their act and were sometimes even unable to begin it. They were driven from the bigtime and in less than six years were out of vaudeville altogether. Criticism was also leveled against the portrayal of Italian girls on vaudeville stages. An article in 1910 accused vaudeville managers of again exploiting a new immigrant group through insulting caricature.[24] To this day many older comics decry the fact that racial and ethnic humor can no longer be done, unless by members of the minority groups involved.

By striving to attract a wide audience all forms of popular art must try to meet the median taste. "Popular art affirms the experience of the majority . . . and it sensitively and accurately mirrors the attitudes and concerns of the society for which they are produced."[25] The broad cross-section of the expanding vaudeville audience represented forced vaudeville to expand its entertainment as well as its geographic horizons. This effort by vaudeville, though, to provide something for everyone and to be ever on guard not to offend anyone could well have diluted it too much. Yet, at the same time, vaudeville was, as expressed by a recent scholar, "the first institution to face this dilemma of modern mass entertainment."[26]

This mass audience, posing innumerable challenges, forced the vaudevillian into many corners. One of the first major decisions made by the theater managers dealt with censorship, a decision unpopular among the performers. The demand for censorship involved not only coarse language, double *entendre* gags, and stage costumes, but also something so innocent as grammatical usage. *Variety* decried that, "Correct English has ever been a failing on the vaudeville stage."[27] Too many comedians, however, were succeeding with their usage of this "evil" and *Variety*'s plea went unsatisfied.

The peculiar circumstances of wartime, though, occasioned a heavy degree of blue penciling. When World War One erupted in 1914, the English variety halls applied instant censorship to all German acts by cancelling them. These German acts, plus hundreds of other European acts, crossed the Atlantic and glutted the vaudeville scene in America. For the German acts it was a necessity. For the others, including many American ones that had been playing England, their arrival was a result of drastic salary cuts, some as high as 50 percent. This sudden influx aggravated the domestic scene and salaries then plummeted in America. The trouble for vaudevillians did not end there. While the United States remained neutral, no censorship was employed.[28]

Once the nation declared war, however, things changed. Thousands of performers were drafted. Edward Marks, the composer, remembers that on the stage men not obviously decrepit were in a delicate position. War sketches were briefly tolerated in 1917 but almost instantly taken out by theater managers. "Cut out war songs and gags" ordered signs posted backstage. There were some acts that only war-time audiences would have stomached; probably the saddest was one called "The Shrapnel Dodgers." The act consisted of Canadian Army veterans. One lacked an arm, another an eye, and the last was without a leg.[29]

Variety summarized another form of censorship:

> The United Booking Offices this week instructed all resident managers of theaters booked by it to report to the New York headquarters immediately any artist or act appearing in their theatres with a "peace song," meaning a lyrical number with peace as its theme.
>
> In the same letter the U.B.O. informed the managers to permit and encourage the use of ad lib remarks or dialog furthering the Third Liberty Loan, recruiting or any movement urged by the Government.[30]

The same article went on to report that federal officials in Chicago had seized copies of a song entitled, "It'll Be a Hot Time for the Old Boys When the Young Men Go to War." German and Dutch acts were banned and Benny Rubin claimed that the only animosity he witnessed or felt in vaudeville was for Germans who might have been in the war. He recalled German acts arriving for morning rehearsals and loudly asking the doorman, "Do you got any mail for the Patricks?" Or, again trying to cover up their German identity, they would walk around the theater, yodelling, announcing to everyone, "Ve are Sviss."[31]

Though there certainly was no freedom of speech for performers in war-time, vaudevillians who proved to be "patriotic" could do just about anything. Most of the actors, especially those who went overseas or to various stateside military camps, were undoubtedly sincere. There were others, however, who tried to capitalize on the situation. Vaudevillians went overseas to join America's Over There League of volunteers,[32] and many of them exploited these experiences on their return. Maurice and Walton, for example, advertised themselves as being back "from France on a short furlough." Chasseurs' Foxtrot was billed "as danced by them at the front for French and English soldiers." During intermission at the Palace, "Corporal Arthur Fields and Private Flatow, that jokester at the piano," sang in uniform as their part of a bond drive. The song was "I Don't Want to Get Well," which was about a hospitalized soldier and a pretty nurse. Nora Bayes wore a red, white, and blue outfit in her act at the Palace and announced that she was going to invest in Liberty bonds instead of a new wardrobe.[33]

Walter Winchell, who had not exactly been a great success in his early vaudeville days, enjoyed his first real acclaim when he carried an American flag onstage and sang of "those wonderful American Stars and Stripes." One writer observed, "It would have been treasonable not to applaud." Others besides Winchell resorted to patriotic ploys. Will Mahoney, who tap danced atop a xylophone, finished his turn by tapping out the "Star Spangled Banner," during which time a large American flag would appear. Other acts used the flag as a backdrop or as a veil.[34] The American flag was not the only one displayed. Used in reverse, unpopular flags drew jeering responses from vaudeville audiences. Theaters also sponsored war song contests. Music publishers were permitted a limit of two songs, the audience serving as judges. If nothing else, the contests boosted vaudeville attendance, for publishers packed the houses with their claques.[35]

Vaudeville's war effort played a major role beyond that of entertaining servicemen, of course. Vaudeville raised money. A subcommittee headed by Albee raised over $27,000,000 of Liberty Bonds, and vaudeville itself, including the Albee effort, sold $400,000,000 worth. For a soldiers' and sailors' smoke fund alone, theaters in 1917 collected $86,000.[36] Many history books celebrate the efforts of movie stars during the First World War, yet *Variety* summarized:

> Vaudeville was the centre of matters theatrical in connection with the war. The many drives, whether by the Government or for charitable purposes, depended in the theatres, to the largest extent,

> upon vaudeville. During any depression in spirits or business vaudeville displayed an amazing strength.[37]

Nils Granlund, director of propaganda and publicity for all areas of show business in New York City, was in charge of nearly all the bond rallies and Red Cross drives. He, too, praised the cooperation of entertainers.[38]

Notable in his contributions to the Allied cause was Sir Harry Lauder. The Red Cross was singled out by Lauder to receive his salary for three performances a week.[39] Lauder, because he was so outspoken against the Germans, was warned numerous times that his life was in danger. However, he made his critical speeches in town after town and no harm ever befell him. Vaudeville demonstrated its powerful service as an agent of the government. Even after the war, vaudeville still was affected by government policies. In 1922, the team of Fields and Harrington was doing an act, "The Sailor and Yeoman." The turn was cancelled in Buffalo when the national government complained that it was discouraging recruiting.[40]

Vaudeville's chief censorship, though, was overwhelmingly attributable to its family trade. In an article which decried the use of loose language by so many comedians, it was reported that one comedian, "in the presence of an audience made up largely of women and children, turned to one of his associates, and said: 'What the hell is the matter wid you?' and he got such a laugh that he will probably continue to use the expression unless he is stopped." The newspaper reporter, writing in 1903, concluded that such humor was acceptable in burlesque, "but in a theatre patronized by women and children they should not be tolerated."[41] By this time, burlesque was returning to an emphasis on anatomy and blue material, after having reformed in the late nineteenth century. Burlesque theaters did excellent business, though not nearly the type of volume that vaudeville enjoyed, since there were many more vaudeville theaters in action. The public associated burlesque with dirty and vaudeville with clean.

Albee throughout his career was dedicated to the proposition that vaudeville must be suitable for everyone in the family. He once proclaimed, "The old variety houses used to be filthy places, but we changed all that. We believed in soap and water, and in a strict censorship of the stage."[42] Keith was just as stringent, saying, "I made it a rule at the beginning . . . that I must know exactly what every performer on my stage would say or do. If there was one coarse, vulgar, or suggestive line or piece of stage business in the act, I cut it out." Keith believed that there were misconceptions regarding the characters of audiences. He maintained that even in theaters in the "poorest quarters," people desired clean entertainment.[43]

Another important owner, F. F. Proctor, stated that his bills were "especially adapted to the tastes of ladies and children." Proctor was reminded of this in a critique of one of his acts at his 23rd Street Theatre. The act contained "bald, coarse 'jokes' about Christmas and Bethlehem," according to the reviewer, who noted that "the refined, decent men, women and children that attend Mr. Proctor's theatre . . . sat in solemn silence and wondered why such dialogue should be permitted in a house which has such strict rules concerning the language permitted on its stage." The writer then put down what is a key to understanding part of vaudeville's impact on the nation. "The regular vaudevillians," said he, "have been gradually educated up to the Keith and Proctor standards of propriety. . . ." Censorship went so far that orders were given to exclude pictures of fires, train wrecks, and similar disasters in order not to affect pregnant women.[44]

A vaudevillian, Edwin Royle, quoted an anonymous lady's remarks about vaudeville houses: "They are the only theatres in New York where I should feel absolutely safe in taking a young girl without making preliminary inquiries. Though they may offend the taste, they never offend one's sense of decency." Royle quipped that, when playing Philadelphia he almost lost things from his dressing room because it was "cleaned so constantly." Alluding to vaudeville, he remarked, "Paternal, austere perhaps, but clean, gloriously clean." Annie Russell, quoted in the official program of Oakland's Orpheum Theatre, maintained that vaudeville was "not so injurious in its influence as many of the legitimate theatres where standards of taste and morality are not of a very high order."[45]

Renee Bonett was one performer who discovered quickly what could and could not be done on a vaudeville stage. Appearing at the 23rd Street Theatre in New York, she was cancelled after her very first performance. Though the content of her act—imitations and songs—was typical vaudeville fare, her costume was not "extensive and seemed to be to expose the figure as nearly as that was possible." Seven years later, in 1924, the Palace banned bare legs. Mae West remembered her manager warning her that the Church would cause problems if she didn't change her material.[46]

Keith houses posted prominent signs backstage in order to keep vaudevillians ever alert to the management's policies. In every theater appeared:

> Notice to Performers
>
> Don't say "slob" or "son of gun" or "Holy gee" on the stage unless you want to be cancelled peremptorily. Do not address anyone in the audience in any manner. If you have not the ability to entertain Mr. Keith's audiences without risk of offending them, do the best you can. Lack of talent will be less open to censure than would be an insult to a patron. If you are in doubt as to the character of your act, consult the local manager before you go on the stage, for if you are guilty of uttering anything sacrilegious or even suggestive, you will be immediately closed and will never again be allowed in a theater where Mr. Keith is in authority.[47]

As for the vaudevillian asking the local manager for clearance of his material, it was often difficult to find more than a few small town managers who were able to recognize "blue" material. Albee, however, was an expert in such matters and had a sign of his own attached to the backstage bulletin board of the Palace Theatre. "Remember this theater caters to ladies and gentlemen and children. Vulgarity will not be tolerated. Check with the manager if you have any doubt about it." The notice went on to list forbidden words, among them "hell, damn, devil, cockroach, and spit." If a performer refused to change his routine when ordered, he was, as Marian Spitzer stated, "O-U-T. And that was that." Spitzer, a valuable aide of E. F. Albee, felt it odd that some acts were able to tour the country without trouble until they tried to use the same material at the Palace. Albee, always the purist, censored material that even his careful circuit managers had not caught.[48]

Yet, even Albee could be fooled, although it took an expert to do so. He received a complaint from a manager of a Keith-Albee circuit theater in New York City, to the effect that Mae West was using bold material. As Harry Richman, then her accompanist, described, she had a line in her "Frankie and Johnny" number that went, "If you don't like my peaches, don't you shake my tree." Richman said, "She did this line as only Mae West could do it, and the men in the audience would scream and yell and go half crazy." Albee ordered a private performance at the Palace. Richman related that when she came to that line, "she clasped her hands close to one cheek and said it very clearly, almost childishly, and at the same time cast her eyes upward, the most mournful creature in the entire world. I nearly fell off my piano stool." Albee resumed her booking, never comprehending the manager's protest. When back onstage, "Mae West was Mae West . . . and the men in the audience again went crazy."[49]

Benny Rubin compiled a list of unwritten laws that vaudevillians abided by. Among them were: Do not try to stop the show, but rather keep it going; Do not say "pants" in Boston, but say "trousers" instead; Do not say "cockeye" or "humpback." Moreover,

> every comic knew that if you stepped in something, you stepped over it and didn't kick it around till it stank. This sounds like it meant stepping in something after an animal act . . . [but] it also meant [that] if the audience misunderstood a word or line or gave your meaning a double *entendre*, you went on to the next joke.[50]

By 1929 the Keith chain was ready to censor seventy-three specific pieces of content. A comic who included lines like "Mother is home sick in bed with the doctor" or "She was taking a tramp through the woods" was in hot water with the management. Girls could not raise their skirts and announce, "I'm a Show Girl." Commissioner Grover Whalen, Mayor James Walker, Fiorello LaGuardia, Aimee McPherson, and Herbert Hoover and his two chickens in every pot were absolutely *verboten* as stage material. Keith-Albee-Orpheum became known to performers as the "Sunday-school circuit." As noted by show business chroniclers, "The Keith taboo list gave acts some excellent new material to use when playing opposition circuits."[51]

As powerful as the vaudeville management was, however, the cleanup battle was not easy. Fred Allen pointed out that the smalltime comedian fought tooth and nail to keep off-color material in his act, since they provided the smalltimer with his biggest laughs. Evidently not only smalltimers resisted the moral edicts from above. R. G. "Dick" Knowles was appearing at Percy Williams' Brooklyn Orpheum over the objections of a certain clergyman. Williams demanded that Knowles eliminate a particularly offensive joke and the vaudevillian proclaimed he would not. When Williams leveled a fine of $100, Knowles refused to pay and his act was cancelled.[52]

Just after the turn of the century an article gave credit to the vaudeville managers for ridding their theaters of acts that had featured muscle-dancers, living pictures, and bronzed models. Those acts had been, according to the writer, an immoral carryover from the "Little Egypt" calamity at the Chicago World's Fair. He judged them unfit for the stage, especially the vaudeville stage which catered to the American family. At about the same time, an article appeared that claimed vaudeville's manners were "on a par with those of the parlor." It praised the vaudeville theater for being a healthful place of amusement.

Less than a decade later, however, an article was published which condemned vaude for having "done more to corrupt, vitiate and degrade public taste in matters relating to the stage than all the other influences put together."[53] The article advised "fathers and husbands" that the vaudeville theater was no longer "perfectly safe entertainment" and that every bill included at least one indecent turn. It was made clear that not only smalltime houses were guilty. Indeed, "first-class" theaters were as much to blame. Al Jolson was singled out for a vicious attack as a headliner who sang one song that was "frankly filthy." Worse, when the audience cheered Jolson to encores, he cried "delightedly" that he should have opened his act with the dirty song. Warned the writer, "Al Jolson is coming to your town, wherever it is, if he hasn't been there yet—Jolson and all his kind." The author believed that "the greatest peril" existed because vaudeville had previously enjoyed such a good reputation that its presentations were then being automatically accepted as decent fare. "Now it is a wolf—but it still wears the lamb's clothing."[54]

The September 21, 1910, issue of *Dramatic Mirror*, in an editorial appeal to Keith, begged him to banish vulgarity and smut from those vaudeville acts that were appearing in motion picture houses.

Before it is assumed that vaudevillians were universally for smut in a war against newspaper editorials and theater managers, it should be pointed out that in their own best interest, most performers were dedicated to keeping their material suitable for family trade. Indeed, many comedians took pride in being able to say that they had never resorted to blue stories. Joe Laurie, Jr., a fine comedian, emphasized that the best laughs in vaudeville houses were the clean ones. Laurie did claim, however, that blue material "was one of the poisons that helped kill vaudeville!"[55] Leo Carrillo, who was a marvelous dialectician in vaudeville, recounted: "Those were the days when . . . off-color jokes meant the cancellation of your vaudeville engagement."[56] Joe E. Brown recalled a time when he was entertaining troops in New Guinea in World War Two. His long act had run its gamut and he called to the servicemen, "Listen, you guys, that's all I know." There were good-natured protests back and forth and a shout pierced through, "Hey, Joe, tell us some dirty stories."

> The kids looked at me, every one of 'em. I could feel 'em wondering what I was going to do. I stood there a minute, not quite knowing myself how to turn it off. And then I just forgot I was a comedian. I said to them, just the way I'd have said it to my own sons:
>
> "Listen, you kids. I've been on the stage since I was ten years old. I've told all kinds of jokes to all kinds of people. I've been in little flea-bitten vaudeville theatres and in big first-class houses. I've been in movies, I've made 65 pictures in my life—and there's one thing I've been proud about. In all that time I've never had to stoop to a dirty story to get a laugh."
>
> They were quiet and they looked a little guilty, the way kids do when somebody speaks out loud about something like this.
>
> "I know some dirty stories," I went on. "I've heard plenty of 'em in my time. I could tell them to you fellows if I wanted to. But I made a rule a long time ago that I'd never tell a story that I wouldn't want my mother to hear me telling."
>
> Then the applause came. Not just a trickle of it but the biggest, noisiest gale of hand clapping I've ever heard anywhere.[57]

Bigtime vaudevillians took pride in "clean" material. They were the products of a stern age, performed in theaters governed by moralistic owners, and added their own influence to the family society of America.

"THE WARMEST AND SCREWIEST PEOPLE IN THE WORLD"

◆ ◆ ◆ ◆ ◆

TO UNDERSTAND VAUDEVILLE IT IS NECESSARY TO APPRECIATE THE vaudevillian and his life. Here were people who faced formidable challenges, and often for little recognition and meager pay. Their backgrounds and ambitions molded them.

Considered to be different from other performers, vaudevillians were called "the warmest and screwiest people in the world," "a different kind of breed," "unlike anybody else in the world."[1] When I mentioned to Ted Lewis that my father always remembered from his days in vaudeville that they were ever one big, happy family, he instantly affirmed, "Then your father was absolutely right. And I miss it today. I miss it."[2] Most vaudevillians feel the same way. The cohesiveness of the group was similar to that of a religious group. Moreover, faith certainly played a part in every performance. "In the theater . . . you see the boys and girls crossing themselves and kissing mezuzahs . . . and asking The Almighty to make them a hit!"[3]

Vaudevillians formed a tightknit family indeed. June Havoc felt that when anyone achieved status as a "standard act" in vaudeville, this meant they were legally adopted into "the royal family of show business. . . . Vaudeville wasn't just a career or living, it was a way of life. It was home, it was school." There was a saying that if three actors started talking, they ended up forming a club.[4] Performers plainly enjoyed each other's company. A typical Saturday night vaudeville hotel room, vintage 1927, was portrayed by one writer:

> We had played five shows and were relaxing at a get-together in Fanny's room. Cheese, ham, and sardines were spread invitingly on a hotel towel along with crackers and bread. Bottles of beer filled the sink; cool water ran from the tap and gurgled as it escaped down the drain. Fanny went on talking [but] spoke quietly because her baby lay asleep in the bathtub a few feet away. The faucets were carefully tied with towels and the child was padded with pillows against the cold porcelain.[5]

Charles Bickford had one of the most interesting appraisals of vaudevillians:

> And as I look back, vaudeville was to me the real "Show Biz." Here, among the midgets, trained seal acts, wire walkers, Salome dancers, monologists, girl acts and acrobats was to be found a sincere spirit of good fellowship and warmhearted generosity. Gauche perhaps, and often ludicrous in their "always on" efforts to impress, they were none the less people who always had their hands out, not to take but to give, whether money or whatever else might be needed to help a fellow in distress.[6]

In the book, *Show Biz,* it is shown that vaudevillians contributed freely for the sake of charity and that even the fines levied for the breaking of management rules ended up being used for a benefit fund. George M. Cohan was one example. Eddie Cantor, himself one of the greatest benefit performers, said of Cohan, "He was one of the softest touches in show business. For many years he sent weekly checks to unemployed actors, disabled wardrobe women, stagehands, and others who, at one time or another, had been associated with him." At one point in her career, Marie Dressler suffered typhoid fever and was inactive for months. Many vaudevillians, among them Eddie Foy, Blanche Ring, Fay Templeton, and May Irwin, presented a benefit show at the Victoria. Miss Dressler was the beneficiary of $7,842. After a severe earthquake in Japan, vaudevillians raised $300,000 to aid the afflicted. Vaudevillians also regularly performed at the Home for Incurables at 183rd Street and Third Avenue, where the hospital bills of many actors were taken care of by the Actors' Fund.[7]

Many an oldtime vaudevillian out of work resorted to the traditional substitute for an electric blanket used to ward off the cold—a copy of Sunday's New York *Times* over his chest and tucked under the overcoat.[8] Harry Jolson recalled when he and younger brother Al worked up an act they believed was surefire. They had rehearsed it until they felt they could do no better. With an original stake of $300 rapidly diminishing, they set out cocksure they would be hired. Not one theater manager even let them begin their act. Soon they were broke, and they learned what it meant to "carry the banner," slang for spending the night on a park bench. They soon discovered that nobody boasted as much as did an unemployed performer. However, Jolson stressed "there was method in their madness." The down-and-out vaudevillian would maintain his facade until he ascertained that those to whom he was speaking were not theater managers searching for an act. Then, "he would try to borrow a dollar, and would even end his plea by sponging a schooner of beer in a saloon that had a free lunch counter." The brothers learned the difference between wanting something and needing something. Yet both continued to go to vaudeville shows. "One of our *necessaries* was going to the theater. In fact it was a *must.* Otherwise we would be like a doctor without medicines or a banker without money." They considered the shows as part of their education.[9]

Fred Astaire remembered being fired several times and even being replaced one time by a dog act. He never quit. Astaire said, "What keeps all performers going is the belief that the next try will surely be a wow." In vaudeville there was always hope. An actor could be out of work for months, but changing partners, trying a new act, or altering his finish, he could suddenly find himself in demand.[10]

A popular story concerning out-of-work vaudevillians was one where a married vaudeville team emerged from a delicatessen with ten cents' worth of food, about all they could afford in their unemployed state. Headed back to their lowly abode, they saw a Rolls Royce drive by, occupied by ladies decked out in furs and men in white tie and tails. The wife, eyes all aglow, said to her husband, "Oh, Bert, weren't they marvelous?" The husband agreed, "but," he added, "they can't act."[11]

Another contribution that the vaudevillians made was done

later on a lesser scale, by performers in other fields. That contribution was that the vaudevillian was a scapegoat for his public. The patron could readily identify with the egotism of the actor and in doing so, would fail to see himself. The theater patron, at least momentarily freed of any feelings of guilt could then fit more easily into the American way of life, where humility was esteemed and pride was considered a sin. Only an egotistical person would go on the stage, or so the American public believed. And though it was not "the American way" to be egotistical,[12] the entertainer on the vaudeville stage was accorded the adulation of American audiences. Though American theatergoers respected tradition, they admired the exception, as long as it constituted no threat to their well-being.

Public favor was absolutely necessary to a vaudevillian's success. Eddie Cantor maintained that anyone who has not been onstage could never really comprehend the heights and depths that a performer experienced. An appreciative audience meant everything.

> You don't eat, you can't sleep, your stomach churns, your head throbs, and you're seven kinds of psychomatically sick. This is your life—and you haven't long to live. At least you hope not. And then they haul the curtain up, and suddenly it's all right. All right? It's all you ever want in life![13]

Cantor was a tiny orphan faced with life in a very poor New York City neighborhood and its peculiar challenges. He emphasized he had always been frightened of being alone, "I longed for crowds." He recalled his graduation day from grade school:

> My grandmother has gotten me a pair of knickers, new, and a blouse. . . . Today I'm no orphan. I forget the endless delicatessen, the toilet in the cold back yard, everything. I'm it. I stand on the stage and recite *The Soul of the Violin*. . . . When I finish, there's not a dry eye in the house. The teachers are crying! I'm crying! Talk about stopping a show—I've stopped the graduation.
>
> Can you imagine what that meant to a kid who was cold, hungry and lousy-looking? The sound of applause was heat and food, mother and father, pink champagne.[14]

Neither Cantor's views about entertaining, nor his childhood circumstances were unique among vaudevillians.

Milton Berle was born in Harlem, on West 118th Street, between Lenox and Fifth Avenue. George Burns was also born in New York City. One of fourteen children, he left school when he was thirteen to help support his family. Bert Lahr was another born in New York. The first home he knew was on the fourth floor of a five story walk-up on First Avenue and 84th Street. Lahr said of his childhood, "I never got anything of consequence as a child or else it would be very vivid in my memory. . . . I was a lonely kid. I lived in an ordinary house in a coldwater flat." Lahr was contributing to his family's welfare before he was nine years old. Both members of the famous team of Weber and Fields emerged from the Lower East Side slums of New York. As young boys they went out on tour throughout the nation. Joe Fanton, from the Lower East Side, ran away from home and its poverty to join a carnival.[15]

That Lower East Side of New York was often "the first America" for a great conglomerate of immigrants, Jews, Italians, Irish, Chinese, and Poles, just to mention a few of the ethnic groups that lived in their own neighborhoods. The area has been described as "a stopping-off place, where you lived until you could afford to go to Harlem, the Upper East Side, the Upper West Side, the Bronx, Brooklyn, or out of town." From the Lower East Side came many entertainers, befitting a further description: "It was a creative crucible which gave birth to great ideas and great men."[16]

Ethel Waters, raised in a poor section of Philadelphia, wrote, "It never occurred to me to grumble about the discomforts connected with playing those little theatres. One of the few advantages of being born poor and hungry is that you expect very little and learn to take everything in your stride." Benny Rubin was born in the slums and was a tough, young hoodlum, a fact which he claimed worked to his advantage occasionally during his show business career.[17] Harpo Marx, raised in a New York ghetto, commented:

> When I was a kid there really was no Future. Struggling through one twenty-four-hour span was rough enough without brooding about the next one. You could laugh about the Past, because you'd been lucky enough to survive it. But mainly there was only a Present to worry about.[18]

W. C. Fields was one of five children in a very poor family and was frequently beaten by his father. Fields ran away from home when he was eleven. W. C. Fields' sense of irony has been viewed by some as an expression of the hostility he felt for his father. George M. Cohan was born in the attic of a frame house in Providence, Rhode Island, that rented for only six dollars a month. His biographer claimed "Cohan was seldom a happy man."[19]

Sophie Tucker showed her devotion to her vaudeville colleagues by saying:

> We all sprang from the same source, the same origin. We were all swept to the shores of this country on the same tidal wave of immigration, in the same flight from prejudice and persecution. Our life stories are pretty much the same.[20]

She could have been speaking for Eddie Parks, who ran away with the Buffalo Bill Show in 1909, and who remembered, "Most of the time I slept under steps." Or she could have been thinking of Al Mardo–before he was sixteen, he had a lady forge his mother's signature so that he could join the Six American Dancers. Or George Jessel–having first purchased a fake birth certificate, he not only gave fourteen performances a week in "Gus Edwards' Song Revue," when he was twelve, but also sold music during the intermission and made the rounds of clubs at night to plug songs, often until three in the morning. Or Belle Baker who was only twelve when she started singing songs in a cheap ghetto movie theater. The Marx Brothers would have qualified, too. When his mother gave him fifty cents a week for piano lessons, young Chico Marx scouted around the East Side of New York and located a teacher who charged only thirty-five cents.[21]

The over-all view of vaudevillians is that having emerged from the lowest classes though destined to entertain a basically middle-class America, they were considered social undesirables. A staunch middle-class citizen would probably oppose his child's wishes to become an entertainer. Jack Benny's parents, for example, felt disgraced that their son became a vaudevillian.[22]

In an interview, Larry Wilde queried Jimmy Durante, "Most comedians came from poor families and had unhappy childhoods. Do you think these emotional and psychological scars were the reasons they became comedians?" Durante replied:

> No. Now, I was born in back of the barber shop on the East Side of New York . . . washroom is out in the yard . . . my dad owned a barber shop. But we wasn't what you call poverty-stricken. My dad made a nice living [and] we never wanted for bread or a meal. I went to work when I was a kid, selling papers—I worked after school. But that don't mean we were poverty-stricken, that we didn't eat.[23]

This is reminiscent of my father's childhood. He came to the United States at the age of eight and went right on to the stage in an Italian song-and-dance act with his older sister, Amelia. They worked with my grandfather, a magician billed as Prof. John DiMeglio. My father was the oldest boy, second of eighteen children, of whom nine survived to adulthood. To help the finances of the huge family, he also worked in a silk mill, became an apprentice electrician, and ended up being a barber. Though he lived in Brooklyn tenements and in rugged ethnic neighborhoods on the South Side of Bethlehem, Pennsylvania, he never felt as if he had come from a poor background. The family ate well, he remembered, they laughed and played, and though they were often crammed into just a few stifling rooms, he accepted this. The America my father enjoyed as a youth was one of teeming urban growth. Living in Little Italy-type neighborhoods, the transition from one culture to another was easier for him than for many who were thrown into completely alien circumstances. In addition, he was lucky to have as his first American acquaintances, some of the most unprejudiced, openhearted people in the country, vaudevillians.

That big family relationship among vaudevillians, the acceptance that American audiences gave the young performers, the extensive tours through the vast area from New York to Chicago—all must have bolstered the confidence and made life itself at least tolerable, if not enjoyable for the young vaudevillian.

At that time, it was not uncommon to find hordes of children holding full-time jobs, or simply wandering the streets, looking for menial work, but no one was interested in them unless they committed a crime.[24]

It is possible to see that, though the circumstances were, by current standards, probably dismal when compared to our standard of living today, these young artists could not have sensed this, for they did not take themselves that seriously. Though their determination and fortitude was in great part due to the hardships they endured as children, most vaudevillians who rose from poor backgrounds to stardom and financial success would naturally throw accolades to the country in which they succeeded. And their acts would reflect that very devotion they felt for the United States. Vaudevillians symbolized what could be achieved in a land of opportunity. Furthermore, an audience of recent immigrants and first generation Americans must have identified with this.

Vaudeville was in that sense America in microcosm. Vaudeville headliners represented that kind of success that the American public had come to expect for themselves. When the vaudevillian succeeded, in essence the American system succeeded.

MINER'S, MINORS, AND THE "HOOK"

◆ ◆ ◆ ◆ ◆

THE LURE OF THE STAGE WAS AN OVERPOWERING ONE FOR COUNTLESS ghetto children and for restless youths from the hinterland. The offer of riches and adventure was too much to resist. Groucho Marx wrote that he went into vaudeville because of Al Shean, his uncle. Shean was a vaudeville headliner and Groucho stated, "He was netting $250 a week (sans taxes) and I quickly decided that if this kind of money was laying around in show business, I was going to get a piece of it." Harpo also was impressed by "Uncle Al." "He was our Celebrity, and he played the part to the hilt. Once a month, Uncle Al came to visit, decked out in expensive flannels and broadcloth, matching fedora and spats, and ten-dollar shoes. He sparkled with rings and stickpins and glowed with the scent of cologne."[1]

The sparkling rings and stickpins were a vaudevillian's trademark. A story circulated about the English vaudevillian who returned home and said that American vaudeville acrobats "wore the filthiest underwear and the largest diamonds he had ever seen." Said Fred Allen, "To the smalltimer, a diamond represented security. It impressed the booker, the manager, and the audience, but, more important, the diamond was collateral." Jewels were looked upon by vaudevillians as a solid investment and a "diamond craze" pervaded the entertainment field during vaudeville's best years. Will Rogers, too, pointed out that the vaudevillian was supposed to buy a diamond ring. Al Fanton agreed wholeheartedly that "Diamonds was the vaudevillian's best friend." He related how his mother and father, both vaudeville stars, would constantly have the diamonds "in and out of hock." He recalled their favorite New York establishment, the Prudential Pawn Shop on Broadway. "We'd come to New York, we'd go to the pawn shop, one way or the other, either it was a bad time . . . or a good time. . . . I became very familiar with the pawnbroker. . . ." Any performer could contract for diamonds on credit, absolutely no red tape involved, as long as he was fairly well-known.[2] The flash of these diamonds had to excite youngsters into giving vaudeville a fling.

Add to the diamonds the fact that male vaudevillians had the reputation for being successful with women and it becomes even easier to understand why down-and-out youths trekked to the theaters for tryouts. Many a young man noticed vaudevillians and the way they seemed always to be surrounded by women. Groucho Marx felt this had something to do with the fact that they were New Yorkers and, on that score alone, impressed the "girls in the sticks." He added, though, "Naturally, the town boys hated us, and for years we never left a theatre at night without blackjacks tucked away in our back pockets." Fred Allen spoke of the "gaudy womenfolk" who accompanied the vaudevillian.[3] One vaudevillian, and a great one, who admitted that the opposite sex played a major role in his decision to go on the stage, was Bert Lahr:

> You know, when you're a kid your thoughts are on women. What attracted me more than anything else on stage was that you'd see the comedian holding the women around the waist and walking them across the stage. And I said to myself, "Wouldn't it be wonderful if I could do it." Just to be around the women, that impressed me more than anything.[4]

While vaude life held definite lures for the uninitiated, his entry into that life was often humiliating. A starting point for many new performers in vaudeville was in amateur night shows. Benny Rubin played amateur nights for eighteen months before he was finally spotted and able to get his first professional job. Just about anyone could get onstage at an amateur night. The aspiring newcomer generally had to compete against "professional" amateurs, for as Bert Lahr observed, "There were even people who made a living getting the hook." The usual prizes at the amateur nights were from a dollar up to five dollars, though there were some as high as twenty-five dollars. One always got fifty cents merely for appearing. Rubin claimed that many of the "pros" worked seven nights a week and sometimes even appeared at two theaters during three or four of those nights. Rubin made the point, "Let us say, they made an average of four dollars a week. At that time four dollars could feed a family of three for a week. *It became their business*!" Fred Allen put it mildly when he expressed, "The Amateur Night audiences were difficult. They came to enjoy themselves, and while they appreciated talent, they were primarily in the theater to deride and laugh."[5]

Yet, Allen had fond memories of those amateur nights:

> I enjoyed the company of the other amateurs. Every night there was a new theater and a new group of kids. . . . The young singer, dancer, or acrobat knew that he had no chance to win the twenty-five dollar first prize if there was a "sympathy act" on the bill. A "sympathy act" was an old man, an old woman, a child, or a crippled person who performed and traded on the sympathy of the audience.[6]

A winner, though, did not necessarily win the sympathy of all. Al Mardo remembered when he won an amateur night prize of five dollars. "And there was a hundred kids at the door wanting to beat me up 'cause I won over their friend."[7]

Many of the bigtime feature acts got their start in amateur nights. Fanny Brice was one. Like so many others, she came out of New York's East Side. Her first amateur night appearance was in Brooklyn, at Keeney's Theatre. She was either thirteen or fourteen and she wowed the audience and won the amateur contest. Her brother Lew told how, while Fanny sang onstage, he had to fight off the stagehands to retrieve the coins that the appreciative crowd kept tossing onstage. Fanny collected five dollars for winning the contest and Lew claimed he picked up five dollars scooping up the coins. Frank Keeney, the owner, urged Fanny to appear at his two other theaters and Fanny Brice's career was launched. Her consistent winning of these amateur night contests, plus her brother's scrambling for coins, placed her weekly income at sixty to seventy dollars, a fact which astounded the teenager. Her instant vaudeville success encouraged her to quit school, a decision not uncommon for aspiring young performers. She won every amateur contest there was to win in Brooklyn, crossed over into Manhattan, and remained a winner.[8]

Amateur nights themselves began in burlesque, at Miner's Bowery Theatre in New York. They had taken the idea from the English music hall. H(enry) C(lay) Miner was the originator of the hook, a device which pleased the raucous amateur night audiences and which later expanded to the point that performers were squirted with seltzer bottles. A show paper reminded its readers that Friday nights were the regular amateur nights at Miner's and that the theater never wanted for amateurs:

> [There] it's a common sight to see lads of ten or twelve years of age practicing jig-steps on the street corners, in the hope that when they became expert they may get a chance to appear at Miner's. . . . Once in a while Mr. Miner discovers a diamond in the rough at these amateur performances, and he gives the lucky individual a few words of encouragement. . . .[9]

Miner's was the scene of Eddie Cantor's first appearance. His friends, knowing how Cantor loved to entertain, challenged him to go on. His memory of that night was vivid:

> I'll never forget that night. I was scared to death. I stood in the wings shivering in my pants . . . while the regular burlesque show ended and the amateurs went on, were jeered, hooted, and got the hook. Most of 'em were pretty seasoned amateurs, too. Then the announcer was saying, "Next, Mr. Edward Cantor. He *says* he's an impersonator." Someone pushed me, rushed me out into a blaze of lights and Bronx cheers. Things were flying onto the stage. Rotten fruit. I ducked. They wouldn't let me say a word. Suddenly I had an inspiration. In the burlesque show was a comic named Sam Sidman who had a stock line. He'd grimace, stamp his foot, put up one hand, and whine, "Oh, dat makes me *so mad*!" In my extremity I held up one hand, there was a slight pause in the clamor, and I whined, "Oh, dat makes me *so mad*!" They roared. They let me go on. There were even cheers from the gallery, "Stick to it, kid, you're lousy!" But coins began to pelt the stage. I won first prize and picked up several dollars besides.[10]

Cantor was sixteen at the time.[11]

The first vaudeville theater to utilize amateur nights was

Keeney's in Brooklyn, soon followed by many others.[12] Among them was the Royal Theatre on Brooklyn's Fulton Street. Making her debut in an amateur night there, Mae West recalled the theater being large, with two balconies and boxes, and a twelve-piece orchestra. After her appearance there she, like many others, made amateur night turns a regular matter. As a child she impersonated Eva Tanguay, Bert Williams, and Eddie Foy, and like many other future headliners who came out of the amateur night contests, she was used to winning. She also recalled the prevalent mood of amateur nights:

> When the professionals were finished on the stage, there was a chord of horn music and a roll of the snare drum, and the manager would step out . . . and announce to cheers and cat-calls: "And now we have those talented amateur performers with us tonight. Tell 'em they're welcome by a nice big hand, and show yer generosity by yer offerings tossed at them. . . .[13]

Another amateur night theater was the Circle, located at Broadway and Sixtieth in New York. About fifteen amateur acts generally competed. The stage manager there was George Weiss. He announced the acts and was described as "a terror to the bunch" of amateurs who chose to try their lot at the Circle. If any act were failing, Weiss placed a sign on an easel in full view of everyone. The sign commanded, "Beat It." At the Columbia Theatre in Boston, the biggest amateur night house in New England, the manager used several devices, including the infamous hook. He also employed a large inflated bladder, with which he pummelled acts from the stage. The theater also had a special curtain, split from top to bottom at regular intervals across the stage, enabling the manager to sneak up on the amateur no matter where the hapless actor stood.[14]

The victor in an amateur program often got his reward as a result of ethnic appeal. Bert Lahr gave as an example a theater in New York's Jewish section, where he watched the brother of the famous Willie Howard try his luck.

> At the finish, they'd have all the amateurs line up on the stage. If the prize was five or ten dollars, they'd put the money over the amateur's head. The audience would judge who was the best. Every time it came over a new head, the audience would applaud. When they put the money over Sammy Howard's head, he went

down to the footlights and said, "Ich bin ein Yid." Naturally, he won.[15]

Pearl Bailey broke into show business in an amateur night at the Pearl Theatre in Philadelphia. Her victory won her not only the five dollar prize but an offer of a week's work, as well. In high school at the time, she took the job, which was worth thirty dollars. She went directly from school to the theater, in time for each matinee performance, did her homework between shows, and gained valuable vaudeville experience.[16]

Still another to make his debut at amateur nights was Joey Adams, who broke in at the Madison Theatre at the age of twelve. His slight appearance and tender age did not matter to the hardened crowd. As Adams said, "I charged out on stage like a tiger, [yet] I never even finished my first number. I slunk off like a whipped dog with the boos and catcalls of a hostile audience ringing in my ears."[17] Though crushed, Adams persevered.

At an even younger age, Jimmy Savo began his career at the Olympic Theater, an upstairs vaudeville house on New York's 129th Street. He was only eight, already working as a newspaper boy. With some papers still to sell, Savo approached the stage door man at the Olympic and told him he wanted to sing on the amateur night program. Little Savo was allowed in and when his turn came, out he went to face his first audience. He had newspapers under his arm, holes in the knees of his pants, a big patch on his coat, and he had not had a haircut in six months. As he sang his selection, "Wait Till the Sun Shines, Nellie," his dog, Nelly, joined him onstage. They were a hit. As Savo recounted it, "To put it modestly, we murdered them." They won the prize, a watch, and Savo's career was on its way. Two or three nights a week, he appeared at amateur nights. "My family complained at first about my staying up so late at night," he recalled, "but after I won five dollars several times in succession and a number of gold watches as well, they let up on their objections."[18] Even younger than Savo were two who won amateur night programs in Philadelphia. Molly Picon, at the age of five, won a five dollar gold piece, plus loose change from the audience, and Sammy Davis, Jr., was only three when he was victorious in a dance contest.[19]

In Harlem, the famous Apollo Theatre also had a wild, weekly amateur night. There, a comic named Puerto Rico packed a pistol and "shot" performers off the stage if they were not being received well. At the Majestic Theatre in Brooklyn, amateur dancing contests were staged on Saturday nights. Twelve boys competed against each other, six Black versus six white each week. A twenty dollar gold piece was first prize.[20] Amateur night was a rough way of breaking into show business, but it was a quick way of finding out if the entertainment industry would offer a way out of the tenements. The vaudeville artist was popular, a picture of success. To children who were already fighting the battle of life, an amateur night audience was easily endured in exchange for the opportunity of vaudeville riches.

THE SHOW MUST GO ON [AND] SO OFTEN, ON THE ROAD

◆ ◆ ◆ ◆ ◆

ONCE PAST AMATEUR NIGHTS THE ENTERTAINER DID NOT NECESSARILY GO directly into vaudeville. Dime museums, described as "the lowest rung on the ladder of theatrical entertainment," presented variety shows to supplement their exhibits. They paid very low salaries and demanded extremely hard work. As in vaudeville, no offensive material was permitted onstage. The museums seldom ran fewer than six shows a day and there were times when there were as many as twenty shows a day. If a performer was able to work less than twelve hours a day, he was indeed fortunate.[1] The daily grind of the dime museums was so gruelling that even the rigorous demands of vaudeville were pale by comparison.

Jimmy Durante's background included Diamond Tony's, a honky-tonk in Coney Island, where he got only seventy-five cents a night for playing piano for ten hours, starting at eight. It was a seven nights a week job and a police raid was not unusual. Durante commented, "It was the kind of job if I wanted to get to the gent's room, the boss'd say, 'What you tryin' to do? Take advantage?' " Durante also remembered a cabaret named Maxine's, where, "if you took your hat off you was a sissy."[2] Here, too, like the dime museums, even smalltime vaudeville would seem a vacation to the honky-tonk graduate.

Minstrel shows had schooled many a vaudevillian. Such prominent performers as Bert Swor, Al Jolson, Eddie Foy, Bert Williams, Julian Eltinge, George W. Walker, and Eddie Leonard, to cite a few, were its alumni. Leonard built his vaudeville act around the minstrel framework, as did Jolson and others.[3] The minstrel show, which had preceded vaudeville as America's favorite entertainment, was a faded product, however. By virtue of the variety it offered, the vaudeville stage seemed better suited to the bustling America of its time.

Medicine shows, burlesque, carnivals, dog and pony shows–all formed Ted Lewis' background. Lewis asserted that "in those days you had to work from the bottom up and that's why I think I acquired enough showmanship . . . that I've been able to stay on top so long." Joe Besser, a comic, finished the eighth grade, became a popcorn and candy vendor with a carnival, then worked as a song plugger, before entering vaudeville. A varied background was often helpful to vaudeville success. As Harry Jolson put it, "A comedian was expected to do anything. You were either versatile or out of a job."[4]

Versatility was synonymous with Benny Rubin. From amateur nights he went to tab shows, which were like a long vaudeville act, each show lasting about an hour:

> We did an hour show eight times a day. There was a movie in between. The feature picture was two reels in length, approximately twenty minutes, a comedy was a one reeler, about ten minutes, and the news ran ten minutes. There was a ten minute intermission, to sell popcorn, peanuts and homemade lemonade.
>
> This was the best medium in which to learn, because in order to stay in a small town for a week, you changed shows (called bills) every day.
>
> That meant, you learned how to play different kinds of characters –that included–dialects, brogues and accents. Different types of songs and styles of dancing.[5]

From tab shows, Rubin caught on with a showboat troupe. To him, "this was great." He was paid the same as with the tab show, sixteen dollars a week, but showboaters had distinct advantages. "We'd call it sixteen and cakes. Cakes would mean you got the food for free." In addition there was no hotel expense since the performers lived on the boat. But what Rubin emphasized was that, in order for him to get the jobs he did and to make it eventually into the bigtime, he "had to perform as a fair singer, an expert dancer and a competent actor and comedian."[6]

Vaudeville was the goal of nearly everyone. For most, once the amateur nights, tab shows, showboats, dime museums, and the rest were put into the past, then came still another source of challenge, a series of hurdles up through the various grades of vaudeville. In retrospect, the experience was viewed as all important.

Vaudeville life may not have been as tough as what was faced in dime museums and honky-tonks, or even burlesque, but it was tough enough. Added to the toughness, of course, would be the extra pressure faced by the vaudeville artist. Once the vaudevillian made a name for himself, he certainly did not wish to forfeit his status.

The pressure upon a vaudevillian was noticed by those from the legitimate theater who took temporary flings in vaudeville. Ethel Barrymore pointed to the fact that a vaudeville audience insisted on perfection. She found vaudeville to be demanding, yet very rewarding. "I learned so much watching the other artists. I found out that you have to be awfully good in vaudeville. . . ."[7]

Elbert Hubbard felt that vaudeville demanded "the very life's blood of the performer." According to Hubbard, "There are two big things to do in Vaudeville–interest and amuse the audience and keep yourself in shape to do it again tomorrow."[8]

The vaudevillian was alone on the stage. As emphasized by Ken Murray, actors in a play could share the blame for a failure or blame the playwright, and some could even emerge as individual successes though the play might be cancelled. But not so for the vaudevillian.[9] In vaudeville the actors were entirely on their own, and they got help from no one. Without anyone to rely on but himself, the vaudevillian was a sterling example of independence.

Of course, there was always an ulterior motive. Vaudevillians tried to give a good performance [because] someone important might be out front. One vaudevillian learned that the hard way. Jack Donahue was considered to be an outstanding comedian-dancer by Eddie Cantor. At Cantor's suggestion, Flo Ziegfeld went to Brooklyn to check on Donahue. At that show only a sparse audience was in attendance and Donahue gave only a half-hearted show. Ziegfeld did not hire him until four years later. According to Cantor, "If he'd given a good performance on a certain Friday in Brooklyn, he could have saved himself four years of hoofing in vaudeville. . . ."[10]

Besides the ability to withstand pressure, above all, vaudeville demanded endurance and dedication. Though there must have been many exceptions to the rule, "The show must go on," few acts in vaudeville would be found among them. Lillian Roth once said, "Every entertainer can pull himself together on the stage, even if he collapses a moment later in the wings."[11] They just went on, no matter how they felt, and apparently they forgot about their illnesses anyway.

Harry Jolson perhaps summarized it best:

> To the layman, it may seem that the ancient tradition, that the show must go on, is carried to extremes. The actor will not agree. If it were only his own welfare that is at stake, the matter would be simplified. But he has an entire show to think of; the manager who has sold hundreds of tickets, and the other actors, most of whom are probably but one jump ahead of poverty and a park bench. There are the musicians and the stage hands, as well as office employees and many others whom the public does not see. The show must go on! One assumes a tremendous responsibility when he chooses the field of entertainment as a profession. Many are depending upon him, and he would die rather than fail them.
>
> I have seen people get up from a hospital bed, rush to the theater, put on an act of singing or violent dancing, and return immediately to the hospital, burning with fever and with doctors and nurses screaming maledictions.
>
> I shall never forget one bitterly cold winter when everyone on the bill was sick at one time or another. When we left St. Paul, Cleveland Bonner, the classic dancer, was so ill that he could hardly stand, but he went on with his act and did a good job of it.
>
> The strange part of this tradition, that the show must go on, is that no actor wants it known that he is not in the best of health and spirit.[12]

Once the bill was underway, the show had to keep moving. The worst problem was what was called a "wait." To vaudevillians, it was totally inexcusable if anything ever happened to cause a delay. A letter written by Houdini depicts the vaudevillian's somewhat bizarre feelings on this score:

> We had a terrible accident last night at the Hippodrome . . . and

> there was a helluva time. I wanted to go out in front of curtain to do a stunt, for the stage was in a sad sight splattered with blood, and nothing is so bad as a stage wait.[13]

"Next to the audience, in its importance to the smalltimer, stood the theater orchestra," claimed Fred Allen. Sometimes there were as many as eight pieces in a smalltime vaudeville theater, though the usual count was three–piano, cornet, and drums. The drummer was very important, since he accentuated the falls and crashes of the comedians and played long rolls for the aerialists' sensational slides.[14]

There were times when three pieces would have been a luxury. DeWolf Hopper was playing a small town and asked how many pieces the orchestra had. The manager replied, "Two, a piano and a stool."[15] Many actors felt that the orchestra could make or break their acts.

Even the bigtime had its problems with orchestras. Tony Pastor's theater orchestra was described as being old and unique. The second violinist was deaf in one ear. And when the cornetist began to play, the whole orchestra was out of tune. Pastor himself acknowledged his orchestra's poor quality. He said he knew they were terrible, "but they're my old boys and they can die here." On the other hand, Morris Meyerfeld and Martin Beck, partners who ran the Orpheum circuit, even included a harp and an organ in their orchestras.[16]

For comics, material was extremely important. One of the primary sources for material, especially for the smalltimer, was James Madison's *Budget.* Madison published a yearly paperbound assortment that included jokes, monologues, sketches, and parodies, and sold it for one dollar. Madison earned between $15,000 and $20,000 a year on its publication.[17] Bob Hope, as a frequent Master of Ceremonies, needed a lot of fresh material, and he constantly asked other acts on the various bills he played if they had any jokes he could tell. He also pirated from *College Humor,* changing its jokes to suit his style. "I did anything just trying to get material to do," he admits. George Burns also resorted to taking his jokes from *College Humor* and other magazines, including *Whiz Bang*. Like Hope, he adapted the jokes to suit himself.[18]

Jack Benny claimed that, aside from paying thirty-five to fifty dollars for a routine, he did a lot of his own writing. However, he found himself "walking down the street staring and people would pass me by and say hello and I would not even know who they were. I was always thinking of jokes." John Hazzard referred to "jokesmiths," too, except that he mentioned that they would write an act for anywhere from five to fifteen hundred dollars. He claimed the jokesmiths would write acts "full of wheezes and anecdotes guaranteed to play half an hour. If you get three minutes of actual playing time when you have boiled it down, you have got your money's worth." Hazzard stated that many jokesmiths kept scrapbooks of stories and jokes. One, Henry Blossom, "used to have them beautifully arranged as burglar jokes, stenogs, steeplejacks, mothers-in-law, marital battles, and so on."[19]

In his quest for material the vaudevillian too often stepped on his fellow artist, causing bitterness among the performers. *Variety* observed in 1928 that not only was material being lifted, but many acts credited the source of their piracy. Joe Laurie, Jr., believed that the stealing helped kill vaudeville because eventually it seemed as though everyone was doing the same act.[20] Comedy acts were the easiest targets for piracy and for many years there was nothing that could be done. At any Palace opening matinee many small-timers sat in the audience, on the prowl for fresh material. Small-time bookers condoned lifting material from headliners, since it afforded their theaters topflight material. Often an entire act was stolen. As Benny Rubin related, "Mel Klee did Al Herman, Marty May did Jack Benny . . . Sid Marion did Jack Pearl [and] there were more." Among those who lifted from the Palace headliners were The Borscht Belt comics, those who served as social directors for the hotels in the Catskills.[21]

The Borscht Belt, in its way, became the new vaudeville. Many great entertainers cut their teeth in the "Sour Cream Sierras," much as many stars had received their baptism or chief education in vaudeville. A list of Borscht graduates would fill pages, but included among them are the likes of Gene Baylos, Joey Bishop, Red Buttons, Myron Cohen, Joey Faye, Phil Foster, Jackie Gleason, Danny Kaye, Alan King, Jack E. Leonard, Jerry Lewis, and George Tobias. The Borscht circuit has become a string of prominent playgrounds, known worldwide. Brown's, the Concord, Grossinger's, Kutsher's, and the Tamarack are but a few of the more than five hundred hotels that comprise the Belt. Today, these hotels play the top names in show business and opportunities for new talent are slimmer than in the more reckless days of its infant and puberty stages. This does not mean, of course, that material is safe from show biz thieves. Good material has never been safe.

Though the situation was tolerated, hard feelings definitely arose over stolen material. When Fred Allen learned that Al Jolson used one of his lines, he wrote Jolson a letter. Though Jolson's reply stated that Allen could have his joke back, Jolson kept using it. From Allen's attitude after so many years it is clear the episode still bothered him. Even John and Bert Swor, brothers headlining in separate acts, had a dispute over material. When a line he delivered fell flat, Bert asked the theater manager about it and he was told that the same line had been used the week before by his own brother. Bert angrily informed John that he had better drop the line from his routine. John did.[22]

Ben Blue was once accosted by W. C. Fields, himself notorious for lifting lines, and was accused of stealing a routine. Blue called Fields a liar and other performers finally convinced Fields that he had originally stolen the material from Blue. In an open letter to *Variety,* Bert Lahr once accused Joe E. Brown of having stolen the Lahr character. Though Brown never replied, Sam Sidman, an old-time Dutch comedian, did, angrily. He claimed Lahr had stolen the character from him and not only that, but Sidman had stolen it from Sam Bernard. "I admit it, why don't you?" demanded Sidman of Lahr.[23]

From so much thievery evolved the Vaudeville Managers' Protective Association, which acted as prosecutor, judge, and jury in cases where a vaudevillian was accused of stealing from another. Many vaudevillians registered their acts in the Protected Material Department of the National Vaudeville Artists, Inc., by enclosing their material in a sealed envelope and handing it in at the N.V.A. office. The envelopes were opened whenever one act accused another of stealing.[24]

When an accusation was made, "court" was called into session. Officially the court was known as the Joint Complaint Bureau of the Vaudeville Managers' Protective Association and the National Vaudeville Artists, Inc. Both management and performers sat on the bench. Contractual disputes were settled and other types of performers lodged protests about copying. An acrobat could be angry about someone appropriating his cartwheel technique. A magician could lodge a complaint about certain tricks. During its first eight years of operation, this "Supreme Court" of vaudeville heard some 14,000 cases, of which only four ended up being referred to the regular courts of law.[25]

Though plagiarism was considered detestable, the competition made theft inevitable. True, in vaudeville's best years, comedians repeated the same act year after year. Yet, even during those golden years, there were demands for new material and artists who, if only for their own sakes, frequently changed their patter. Mae West was one who did this, which for her meant costume changes as well, even though she acknowledged that it was an expensive habit. "I no sooner had an act perfected than I became bored with it," she said, adding that it was considered bad luck to change an act. The changes, when they came, were not impulsive. As pointed out by Jack Benny, every detail of a routine had to be set. "If we wanted to change something we had to go out of town and break it in, that's how nervous we'd be."[26]

Vaudeville audiences, until drawn away by the novelty of radio and movies, were not attracted by curiosity. Audiences came to see the acts they knew. Audiences tolerated no deviations. The famous team of Smith and Dale, for example, were together for well over a half century, but always did their "Dr. Kronkheit" sketch.[27] Their infrequent television appearances in the 1960's found backstage personnel reciting their lines with them, due to the material's familiarity. Eddie Cantor put it this way:

> Half the fun was listening to the same song, the same story, the same routine again and again and again, chuckling louder and louder, as those great comedy masters built steadily to the "boffo." The more often you heard the punch line, the louder you laughed.[28]

Change was demanded by the trade papers, though. Just after the turn of the century, the New York *Dramatic Mirror* strongly advised performers to convert to new material instead of clinging to the same old lines. No trade journal was strong enough, however, to affect the dollar-and-cents' figuring of vaudeville's bosses. There was a fear in the upper administrative offices about changing material. The management felt that if a headliner was going well, success at the box office must not be endangered by unnecessary experimentation, so management and the almighty dollar triumphed continually over desire to improve the art.

Though most headliners were quite satisfied to do the same act year after year, one who was not was Bert Lahr. Over a four year period on the bigtime, he felt confined because vaudeville management refused to let him do anything but his standard act. Lahr repeatedly tried to convince managers that they were wrong, that he could be a success with a different act, but he was always denied the opportunity. Ben Blue also eventually left the vaudeville scene because it restricted him too much.[29]

Variety also decried the apparent lack of concern that managers and agents felt for newcomers.[30] Fred Allen told of his discouraging early days in New York after his arrival from Boston. He did appear at Keeney's in Brooklyn but then got nothing, even though his turn had been a good one. He was then taken to Barney Myers, an important theatrical agent in the city. "Day after day I sat in Barney Myers' office hoping, and talking to other acts who seemed to be sitting there because they, too, had no place else to go."[31] The plight of so many newcomers was set forth with clarity in a letter to the editor of *Variety*:

> . . . I started out one morning with gay abandon to have a little heart to heart (?) talk with various managers and agents. . . . Suffice to say that I would have had a far better chance of gaining an audience with the President of the United States than I had with any of the gentlemen who claim they are looking for something new.[32]

One writer said, "There are two hardest things in the world: One is breaking into vaudeville and the other is the same."[33]

Despite the pitfalls and sufferings associated with finding a job, thousands made it into vaudeville. Once vaudevillians, their struggle was to remain vaudevillians and to aim for the top. The biggest boost to success was a good review. Ken Murray insisted that reviews were more important then than today and Amy Norworth recalled how vaudevillians always rushed to read their reviews.[34]

All the newspapers reviewed the shows on opening day. On the road, this practice particularly disturbed Ken Murray. He recounted that the very show the critics reviewed was a show where the performer was not sure of the orchestra, was still feeling fatigued from the overnight trip to get to town, probably had worried about his baggage, and faced other minor problems. Yet one did his show and was reviewed. Good reviews generally meant packed theaters but poor reviews could kill a show and, as Benny Rubin pointed out, a performer's billing and pay depended on how he sold tickets and not on how much talent he had.[35] Too many bad reviews and a performer would get no billing.

With so much depending on a review, especially one that appeared in *Variety* or the New York *Clipper*, it was not uncommon to have under-the-counter transactions. An advertisement in a trade paper usually meant a guarantee of a good review. *Variety* boasted of its efforts against this practice and by virtue of its example, to have discouraged most other journals from doing it. Notwithstanding *Variety*'s pronouncement, Fred Allen catalogued a time when he claimed that a representative of *Variety* approached him on the opening day of a three day stint. Allen's salary for those three days was to be $62.50. The *Variety* agent suggested Allen take a $125 advertisement in the trade paper:

> When I was obdurate, he played his trump card: he told me that Sime, the editor of *Variety*, was going to review the show that night, and that he, the representative, would like to go back to the office and tell Sime that I had taken an ad. I told him what he could tell Sime. I don't know what, if anything, he did tell Sime, but I do know that Sime appeared at the theater that night, reviewed the show, and panned the life out of me and my act.[36]

Sime Silverman who was noted for his caustic reviews, once lost a job on that account. Working for the *Morning Telegraph,* part of his job was to review vaudeville performances. Sime, who loved vaudeville, pulled no punches in his reviews. Acts which Sime panned cancelled their advertising, so the easiest thing for the paper to do was to fire Sime. Because Sime always insisted on telling the facts,[37] he earned the love and admiration of the entertainment world. In his early vaudeville career, Fred Allen experienced much difficulty. It is unclear exactly what Allen wished conveyed to Sime, or in what manner the agent reported to Sime. It is doubtful, however, that a man of Sime Silverman's prestige and dedication would maliciously attack any vaudevillian.

Variety's reviews were respected by theater managers, many of whom depended on it to point the way to the better acts. A good review in Sime's tough sheet often led to a full season's booking. On the other hand a poor review was ruinous. In the editorial offices of *Variety,* a kingsize baseball bat was always within reach. A particular fear was that tough, muscular acrobatic acts would come to avenge a bad review.[38]

Even headliners were not safe from *Variety*'s reviews. When Mae West appeared in masculine attire, the trade sheet was very critical and added that she would "have to clean up her style–she has a way of putting dirty meanings in innocent lyrics." Jack Benny also drew less than top rating when *Variety* summarized his "Jack Benny and Marie" spot, which was next-to-closing, as a standard act. Observed *Variety*: "Benny should lift his voice a bit for the rear of the house. It is possible to be overconfidential. Benny becomes rigidly exclusive at times, eliminating all but the front rows in addressing his flip stuff." In the same review, the entire lineup of acts came under fire. The reviewer complained of the Palace bill, "It has all the fleetness of a tired turtle."[39]

Of course, not all reviews were so critical. A vaudeville and *Variety* favorite, for example, was Eva Tanguay. Here was a woman who, by the testimony of Mae West, practically made vaudeville. "There are two kinds of headliners in vaudeville–the kind that draws and the kind that makes good, with occasionally a combination of the two, like Eva Tanguay, who does both."[40] Excellent reviews were not confined to *Variety*'s pages. One of the most outstanding reviews she or any artist ever received appeared in 1915 in the *Dramatic Mirror*:

> We can't imagine anyone sitting back in his theater chair and placidly observing Eva Tanguay. There's no passive way of watching the Cyclonic One. When the spotlight centers upon the corner of the stage and the trombones blare, as the Tanguay moment comes, you have such a feeling as we suspect a staid resident of London harbors when a Zeppelin hovers in the English evening mists. There's a tingling sensation of electrical expectancy. . . . If ever the United States becomes involved in war, we recommend Miss Tanguay as recruiting sergeant extraordinary.[41]

The better the reviews, of course, the better the billing, and billing played an extremely important role to the vaudevillian. The billing generally appeared in the following format:

VAN AND SCHENCK
The Snow Brothers
Hortense Wayne
BENNY RUBIN
Everett Sylvester
George A. Wichman
Haveman's Animals
RUTH ETTING

At the top was the headline act, at the bottom was the second headliner, and in the center was third billing. Fred Allen emphasized that the smalltimer was extremely concerned about his billing. The headliner, more likely than not had it written in his contract that he would get top billing. Sometimes, in his hometown, a performer would be given top billing.[42] Brotherly love did not exist when it came to billing. The manager of the Fifth Avenue Theatre seemed to be in a bind when three of his acts on a new bill, Lafayette, Papinta, and Della Fox, all claimed top billing. Shrewdly for that bill, he had the names of the acts printed in vertical rather than horizontal lines and thus solved the dilemma.

It would be difficult, however, to find anything more symbolic of the meaning of billing to a vaudevillian than what occurred after the deaths of Ole Olsen and Chic Johnson. Johnson died in 1962 and was buried in Las Vegas. A year later Olsen died and was buried in Wichita, Kansas. Their daughters subsequently decided it would be appropriate if the two madcaps were buried together. Olsen's body was transported to Las Vegas and as it was being lowered into its place, Olsen's daughter insisted that just as in their billing, Olsen should be placed on the left, Johnson on the right. The bronze plaque overhead is inscribed "Olsen & Johnson."[43]

Though crap games, billiards and poker were highly popular diversions on the road, not all vaudevillians squandered their money. Many looked to the future and tried to plan accordingly. Some invested in annuities, stocks, and bonds. Many set a particular goal for themselves, perhaps $25,000 or $50,000 put away for retirement. Though many reached their goals they kept on because they could not quit. Jack Benny often proclaimed that "when they put me in the box, I'll retire."[44]

"Every vaudeville actor dreamed of his personal utopia," according to Fred Allen. Many acts either sent money home or put savings in the bank every week. Writing of the smalltime, Allen stated that the purpose for saving was to someday "quit the business" and open a restaurant, dancing school, gas station, or some other type of permanent venture. "The few that did realize their ambitions found that after the travel and excitement of vaudeville, the dull and sedentary routine imposed on them as they tried to run some picayune enterprise in a small town was boring." Moreover, many vaudevillians simply were not qualified to manage restaurants or specialized businesses. Most had no training or education for "civilian" jobs and the transition to those responsibilities often ended in failure.[45]

The shortcut to fortune, as viewed by many, was in the stock market. News of killings in stocks when they appeared in the trade journals no doubt encouraged others to take chances. Roger Imhof bought property in Chicago and Beverly Hills, which paid off nicely for him but with the crash he lost quite a lot of money. There were those, however, who were quite successful. The comedy duo of Block and Sully became experts in the stock market and traded their headline act for Wall Street profits.[46]

Fairly typical of vaudevillians was Joe Fanton. His son Al believed that his father, like most, never seriously planned for the future. He felt that if they had their forty weeks booked, that was sufficient. The present seemed to count more heavily than a distant future that demanded the trouble of planning. However, vaudevillians did invest considerable sums in "pipe dreams," or real estate investments which were prematurely scratched because they didn't yield quick profits.[47]

Mitzi Goldwyn felt that smalltimers knew the time would come when they would go down and out.[48] Those who had been raised in vaudeville families were especially aware of the need to prepare. Their savings and investment programs, though, required austere living for many.

Next to playing the Palace, the vaudevillian had only one ambition: to own his own home.[49] But so many never realized their dreams.

If anything, the mobility of the vaudevillian exposed him to more get-rich-quick schemes than most people. The uncertainty of his chosen profession, where success had "the life expectancy of a small boy who is about to look into a gas tank with a lighted match,"[50] must also have encouraged the average vaudeville actor into taking chances that the average American would never have risked.

That same uncertainty probably accounted for superstition playing such a major role in vaudeville life. If Fate itself seemed against you, there were two ways to battle it. The first way was to do what all vaudevillians had to do, perform, and hope that the act alone would turn the tide. The second way was to obey the accepted superstitions. "Good luck" wishes were bad luck in the theater. So was whistling in the dressing room or throwing a hat on a bed at home. No one was overjoyed to see peacock feathers anywhere in a theater or a bird on a window sill. No one threw away his old dancing shoes. Comedians considered it a bad omen when J. J. Shubert laughed at their routines in rehearsals. Fred Allen considered Shubert's laughing "the kiss of death." A disappointed vaudevillian, one Stan Jefferson, claimed that, "quite by accident, I happened to notice that my name had thirteen letters in it. I figured the superstition department might be the cause so I decided to make a change." Stan Jefferson thus became Stan Laurel.[51]

There were those who even had their own private superstitions. Bert Wheeler, for example, never wanted to hear the act before him get any laughs. Described by Benny Rubin as "the sweetest little man you ever met in your life," Wheeler ran the water in his dressing room and, not satisfied with that noise, he and his wife sang as loudly as they could in order to drown out the sounds of any laughter in the theater. Jack Pearl would be panic-stricken if anyone touched his ears. If his ears were touched, Pearl had to touch that person's ears in return or else suffer sad consequences. Knowing this, there were performers who deliberately touched his ears and ran, leading Pearl on many a merry chase.[52]

Not all superstitions were tied to bad luck. If a vaudevillian put his undershirt on inside out or, if he touched a hunchback, he believed good luck would result. But probably the spirit of optimism that was so much the vaudevillian's was best illustrated by his staunch belief that every bad break which encountered him only served to bring him that much closer to the good one that waited for him.[53]

In a more practical vein than superstition, the vaudevillian learned quickly how to supplement his income. Song-plugging was one of the best things that ever happened to vaudevillians, as far as extra income was concerned, but it proved to be extremely controversial. From the standpoint of artistry, song-plugging proved detrimental.

The practice of song-plugging originated in the 1890's and steadily grew until the music publishers were in such fierce competition that bigtime stars like Belle Baker, Fanny Brice, and Sophie Tucker were making small fortunes by holding out for the highest bid. Music publishers even had to pay the silent acts to use their melodies. But vaudeville provided the tunesmiths their best exposure and because of that, the "music business became one big auction sale, with the plugs knocked down to the highest bidder." At its height, music publishers paid out over one million dollars a year to vaudevillians. Many acts actually made more by plugging songs than they were paid by their contracts.[54]

The whole idea of vaudevillians giving plugs in their acts for anything was considered reprehensible by the entertainment journals. The *Dramatic Mirror* (November 10, 1900) attacked what they called the "advertising nuisance" that pervaded the vaudeville stage and referred to plugs for such items as molasses taffy, pianos, and typewriters. The newspaper advised, "It would do well . . . for managers to use the axe relentlessly on the sketches of performers who have the advertising habit."[55]

The Gus Edwards Music Publishing Company took out an angry advertisement in the January 20, 1906 issue of *Variety*, which clearly displayed their sentiments:

> READ! READ AGAIN!! READ SOME MORE!!!
> We NEVER Did, We Do NOT and We Will NOT PAY
> Singers to Sing Our Songs

Among the acts the Gus Edwards Company claimed used their numbers were such luminaries as Lillian Russell, Louise Dresser, Nettie Vesta, and the Avon Comedy Four.[56] Soon after *Variety* itself intoned, "Nothing appears so largely on the horizon as a possible menace to vaudeville as the music publishers who are paying artists to sing their songs." The trade sheet complained that the audience enjoyed little musical variation as a result and that, therefore, the performers were "cheating themselves."[57]

With the efforts of John J. O'Connor, the business manager of *Variety,* vaudeville management applied a crackdown, although it did not come until a decade after *Variety*'s early warning. Albee's power monger, John J. Murdock, and O'Connor got together. O'Connor acquainted him with the various and sundry facts associated with the evil of song-plugging. O'Connor pointed to the repetitiveness of vaudeville programs, when a single publisher managed to corner the key acts on a bill. He also advised Murdock that, because the bidding was so hotly contested, only the large music publishing houses could continue to afford paying song-pluggers, dooming the small competitor to extinction.[58]

Murdock accompanied O'Connor to the Alhambra Theater, a Keith house in New York. Acrobats opened the bill to the melody, "I Didn't Raise My Boy to Be a Soldier," then a very popular hit. The same tune was sung by a duet in the second act. Before the show finished, the song was used five more times, as background music for several, for an entrance cue, and even for a dozen choruses by a quartet. Murdock was infuriated. The following day Murdock's office was a scene of action. Maurice Goodman, attorney for Keith and Albee, was ordered to work with O'Connor in forming an association of music publishers that would have as its chief purpose the elimination of song-plugging. Any publisher who chose not to join would have his songs barred from the vaudeville circuits. The group took the name of Music Publishers Protective Association and enlisted thirty-five publishers, an excellent number. They unanimously agreed to terminate the bidding war and to cease providing the vaudevillian any recompense for using their material.[59]

Before it is assumed that the MPPA agreement of 1916 solved the whole problem, reference must be made to a work on Tin Pan Alley that was compiled in 1930. The author, Issac Goldberg, contended that it was optimistic for anyone to believe the practice of song-plugging had been eliminated from vaudeville. He even cited an example of Al Jolson being given a race horse for singing a particular song. According to Goldberg, vaudeville singers were generally receiving from five to a hundred dollars weekly for singing the right tunes. During the thirties, the Albee Sisters—and undoubtedly many other groups and individuals—had free arrangements done for them by music publishing houses, in exchange for singing their songs.[60]

For the vaudevillian any extra money was most welcome. Charles Bickford, when in vaudeville, drew $275 a week. Of that, fifty dollars went to the writer-producer and $13.75 to the agent. Railroad fares approximated sixty dollars, although he computed that on the basis of playing split weeks—one-half week in one town, then the rest of the week in another. He added, "Then there was the tipping. The stage hands had a racket operating which made it imperative for an act to tip. Otherwise, dire things could happen." Bickford tipped an average of ten dollars a week.[61] Thus, his gross of $275 for a week was reduced by those expenses to $141, which represented a loss of nearly 49 percent of his salary. After that came the necessary deductions for food and lodging.

Tipping was an essential. A trade journal noted that performers "suffered severely at the hands of careless expressmen in New York city and elsewhere." Trucks arrived late, even if only in transit from Brooklyn to New York. The paper also reported that the expressmen were "frequently overbearing and insulting to performers who do not tip them liberally, and it is more than likely that these delays are arranged on purpose to compel the actors to 'give up.' " Stagehands passed the word from one theater to another by chalking symbols on the trunks of those vaudevillians who had not tipped them. A non-tipping act could find itself the victim of "lost" trunks, missed cues, sloppy lighting, anything that a member of a stage crew could do to disturb a performance. Benny Rubin tipped the elevator man, the doorman, "if he was nice," and the property man, if he had done something extra that aided the act.[62]

The big expense, though, and often the biggest problem, was transportation. Ethel Waters remembered her early days in vaudeville, when there were times that her act, which included two people, only received thirty-five dollars a week. At those times, as she related, "the big trick was to avoid long railway jumps between engagements." Theaters advanced money for the railroad fares but never paid the traveling expenses.[63] The vaudevillian, though, was not always in command of his engagements. In a letter to a friend, Houdini wrote, "We are in Providence week April 13th, then go to New York and then come to Boston. Bad jumps, but I cant [sic] pick my route." Houdini also had a route which, in consecutive weeks, required him to jump from Chicago to Kansas City, Omaha, and Richmond, Virginia.[64]

In the earlier years of the twentieth century, vaudevillians generally traveled by train. On the trains, headliners had drawing rooms and some, like Nora Bayes, even had private cars. For practically all, though, a drawing room, or even a compartment or single bedroom, was unattainable. Many sat up all night in the day coaches or, as some referred to them, chair cars. Harry Jolson described them as "but a glamorous caboose for a freight train." In these cars, passengers brought food aboard. Will Rogers became a "seasoned vaudeville trouper" when, among other things, he was able to "travel for twenty-four hours in a day coach, duck his head under a water tap, and go into his routine without a rest."[65]

Sleeping berths offered great temptations, even though they were more expensive. Harpo Marx recalled that a Pullman upper berth cost $1.60 more than the regular coach fare. Once aboard the train, his younger brother, Groucho, scouted for vacant upper berths. When he found one he propositioned the conductor, offering him a dollar for the berth. If the porter caught the four Marx boys crowding into the upper berth, Groucho gave him a quarter to keep him quiet. As Harpo summarized, "The most we had to spend would be $1.25–a saving of thirty-five cents [which] was not to be sneezed at. It was worth a movie show and a game of pool for the four of us."[66]

It was not at all uncommon for friends to share upper berths. Benny Rubin remembered being frozen in an upper berth, despite sleeping with a companion. Both used hot water bottles, something Rubin always carried with him after that. Leo Carrillo once shared an upper with Corny Brooks, of "Burton & Brooks." Brooks had only one arm, a fact which Carrillo emphasized saved them from being "squeezed to death" in the narrow quarters.[67]

Vaudevillians generally stayed together on the trains. Some traveled as units, often coast to coast. Sometimes, though always starting the tour in a friendly fashion, familiarity bred contempt. On the other hand, Amy Norworth recalled her tours where the troupe fast got acquainted, went out after the shows for coffee or sometimes were hosted at a local fraternal organization. By the time they reached California, she described the entourage as "one happy family." Even when trains were late and the tired band of players had to wait around the station, the relationships evidently did not break down. "Some of the boys would play cards and they'd have a merry time," she said.[68]

For most, though, train travel was a necessary evil. Mitzi Goldwyn got trainsick. Ken Murray added that there were times when the actors had to change trains in the middle of the night, getting off a train at three in the morning. Then "you'd sit in the station and suffer."[69]

Murray supplied a vivid, depressing account of a vaudevillian on the road, traveling every week. "It was rugged," he related, "And I still think of it in horror." The show would end at about eleven. At midnight, the railroad station's restaurant and most of the restaurants in town were closed. No diner would be available on the train. Therefore, the performer sought out "a little lunch place [where he could] grab some sandwiches and bring 'em on the train." Though the vaudevillian may have eaten at six o'clock, it was six hours later, he had done a show and packed his trunks, and he was hungry. Since there usually were no lounge cars on the milk trains, the sandwiches would be eaten in the men's room. A good deal of the time the trains would be sidetracked and picked up several hours later that morning. Murray's face looked worn when he remembered how he would be awakened when "the bump would come . . . Bang!"[70]

At seven o'clock, after a rough, nearly sleepless journey, the train would arrive at its destination. The weather might be cold, and the actor's hunger acute, but he would consider himself lucky to find any restaurant open. Then he would wend his way over to his hotel and another strange room. Murray lamented, "This went on every week. . . ." And there was no time to rest. The rehearsal was at nine, so the vaudevillian only had a chance to sit down for awhile before dashing over to the theater. That early in the morning, many theaters had not yet turned on the heat and the entertainer had to request it be done.[71] What kept them going? Benny Rubin's answer may be the best: "We wanted to be actors, and we would have gone on a hundred times a day. . . . [We] were full of piss and ginger and we wanted to get on there."[72]

Opportunities to trim their transportation expenses came when midgets or young-looking performers were part of an entourage. Often the railroad conductor was fooled, but there were times when the full fare was exacted. Bert Lahr once teamed with a midget named Jeanie and passed her off as his daughter. On a train to Pittsburgh, one conductor asked Lahr if the little girl in the neighboring compartment was his. The comedian confirmed that she was. Apparently Jeanie was inebriated and telling off-color stories. The Marx brothers wore sailor suits and paid only half-fare, until a conductor let their mother know that one of her sons was shaving in the washroom, while another was enjoying a cigar.[73]

The railroad was indispensable to the various animal acts. Whether it was Fink's mules, a dog act, monkeys, goats, or even elephants, the "iron horse" accommodated them.[74] Had it not been for railroad travel, animal acts could not have played such a major role in vaudeville bills.

Automobiles were used to great advantage in the later days of vaudeville. Gypsy Rose Lee recalled that her mother purchased a second-hand Studebaker for its roominess and also to save money as compared to railroad costs. The Albee Sisters had an Auburn, although only one of the girls could drive. On many occasions that meant driving all night, even though the next day was show day. Not unsurprisingly, autos were not always totally efficient. At the beginning of his career, Lawrence Welk was stuck with an ancient oil-burner. According to his biographer, if Welk traveled over twelve miles, the car's oil gave out. Fortunately for Welk, like so many others did at times, he was soliciting vaudeville appearances on his own, therefore was not committed to a major circuit's route. Even motorcycles were utilized. The Marx brothers used them briefly in their vaudeville days and sometimes carried chorus girls on the handlebars.[75]

Still another mode of transportation was to travel by ship. The Albee Sisters would never forget their jump from San Francisco to Vancouver, a voyage up the Pacific Coast that was standard for vaudevillians. This time, however, the trip proved a miserable one, for all four got sick. The rough waters had not only made them ill, but had delayed the ship's arrival, as well. Instead of arriving early in the morning, the ship pulled in about noon. By then, the Albees had changed into their stage costumes and had their instruments and luggage ready. They were the first to leave the ship, rushing to the theater, where the show had already begun. With no rehearsal, and after three days of sickness and loss of weight, they went onstage, were received very well, and then staggered to their dressing room. Ferne Albee Burton recalled, "Oh, were we just dead when we got off that stage. We all laid on the floor in our dressing room." But they did not sleep. Three more shows were scheduled and they played them all.[76]

Food and lodging presented its peculiar problems, too. Dressing room walls all over the country had stickers designed to help the vaudevillian decide where he should eat and sleep. Actors then scrawled their own opinions on these stickers, such as: "Terrible, flies get in the soup," "Do not stop here unless you have your mother-in-law with you," and "This place gives you all the eggs you want but you don't want more than one." Performers also warned one another when a boardinghouse or hotel was connected with the theater management. Even with the stickers and graffiti the search for accommodations was not easy, especially for food. Benny Rubin stated that Chinese restaurants were good bets, "they didn't serve you anything that was from yesterday. It's made fresh, right now." If Chinese cooking was not available, he then searched for a German restaurant. The worst foods, he claimed, were to be found in the fancy hotels, where "they had to put some cockamamie sauce or something on it."[77]

Eating in "dingy Greek restaurants . . . where pork chops cost only fifteen cents" was one of the memories of Ethel Waters when she was in vaudeville. Restaurants often issued meal tickets to vaudevillians, once their names were on a bill. In that way the actor could enjoy a week's food on credit, then take care of the tab on pay day. The male was expected to pay only for himself when dining with his female co-workers.[78]

The Albee Sisters always tried to find tea rooms since "they specialized in home cooking," but when they were in any metropolitan area for an extended time, they made every effort to rent an apartment instead of a hotel room. In this way they could enjoy home cooking, for their mother accompanied them. Not all were so fortunate. Fred Allen often shared only a single room with other hungry vaudevillians in order to save rent. Their meals at those times consisted of doughnuts and coffee.[79]

Max Gordon "especially loved" boardinghouses and said of "the good ones":

> . . . where for a dollar and a half a day I could get a room, gorge myself on breakfast, lunch and dinner, and in addition, get a sandwich and a bottle of beer after the theatre. Three squares and a bluff they called it, the bluff being the after-dinner snack.[80]

But different boardinghouses had different standards. Some had the habit of serving excellent meals on the first and last days of each troupe's stay. However, as Gordon expressed, "In between, the menu was terrible."[81]

In the case of the Marx brothers, their father scouted ahead. If the cooking of any boardinghouse was poor, the father cooked. When their father was unavailable, they were forced to eat left-overs:

> Boardinghouse leftovers were the same from Seattle to Sandusky: cold macaroni and cheese with all the cheese picked out, stiff, cold dabs of mashed potatoes turning yellow at the edges, a lonely pickle floating amongst seeds in a bowl of pickle juice, moldering masses of stale bread pudding, and coffee three times warmed over with milk in it, turned into a sickening mauve in color and covered with a pucker of scum.[82]

Groucho, remembered the problems presented by bathroom facilities:

> The boardinghouses usually had a bathroom at the far end of a drafty hall, and in the morning as you sneaked down the corrider, you were apt to glimpse four or five heads of varying sexes peeking around half-open doors, waiting for the bathroom door to open. When it finally did, the race down the hall would reveal some fairly startling sections of anatomy.[83]

The weekly rates usually found at boardinghouses were seven dollars for a single, six dollars apiece for double occupancy, and $5.50 apiece for three in a room. For this the vaudevillian received meals, slept on a lumpy mattress on an iron bed, had a bowl and pitcher, a few odd pieces of furniture, and one pair of face towels and bath towels per person. "By the end of the week the towels would be so dirty you would usually bypass them and fan yourself dry," wrote Groucho Marx.[84]

Good food or bad, lumpy mattresses or not, the boardinghouse, with its own peculiar atmosphere, was home to the actor. Usually they were places of good fellowship where vaudevillians would give impromptu shows for each other, trying out new gags or doing bits that could not be done on the censored stage. Joe Laurie, Jr., went so far as to say that the only thing that topped playing the Palace "was the gathering in comradeship after the show to exchange laughs, dreams, and hopes!"[85]

Yet, the life of the vaudevillian, even in the midst of that type of camaraderie, could suddenly be depressing. Sophie Tucker confided:

> I've said there were no lonesome times. But sometimes I used to stare at the four walls of my boardinghouse bedroom and wonder if I had really ever had any other home. Whitewashed walls, or walls papered in nightmarish designs. The bed, the dresser with its mirror that made you wonder why they ever let anyone who looked the way you looked get on a stage, the straight chair, the rocker, the one window with white cotton lace curtains, the washstand with pitcher and bowl, the little rug beside the bed, the one electric light above it and the white china night pot beneath it. From Worcester, Massachusetts, to Kansas City, Missouri, from Dallas to Duluth, the pattern of those rooms remained the same.[86]

Another who felt alone was Joe E. Brown. His memory, as Miss Tucker's, illustrated the type of loneliness many vaudevillians endured. Brown revealed that his youth in vaudeville had given him many homesick days, though he claimed he had become accustomed to the hardships involved and that he rarely felt depressed. One night stood out, however, apart from his customary acceptance of the conditions of his show business life. It was a Christmas Eve in North Adams, Massachusetts. Then fifteen years old, Brown spent the evening in a typically dingy hotel lobby, watching all the merriment outside, as townspeople crowded the streets and rushed home with their gifts. Looking back, Brown sadly observed, "I had no one to wish me one little Merry Christmas."[87]

Ken Murray combatted his loneliness by taking a "great big RCA radio" on the road. He remembered listening to a Miami Beach station:

> That guy was saying, "And here we are, down with the lovely breezes," and then he'd say, and he'd play, "Let Me Call You Sweetheart," [and] he says, "So we're leaving you now," and I'm

thinking, "Oh, no, don't leave me."[88]

The loneliness of all those strange towns and strange rooms made idleness itself a major enemy. It was this loneliness that drove Murray to take up photography,[89] a hobby which made Ken Murray the film historian of Hollywood. Ted Lewis, on the other hand, claimed that vaudevillians "never got lonesome because there was so many performers in the different cities that would all stop at the same place." They would then get together and "always have a good time." Lewis noted that unlike his vaudeville days during his recent tours, frequently he was the only entertainer in town. "You're all by yourself. . . . Yet you're stopping at the best hotel. And things become a little lonesome."[90]

Buster Keaton recalled that his father also enjoyed the excitement of vaudeville travel. For the elder Keaton it "meant constant and pleasant surprise encounters with his pals. . . . Every week was old home week for my Pop."[91]

But life on the road was gruelling, especially on the smalltime circuits nicknamed "The Death Trail" and "The Aching Heart." Even the best hotels could not offset the agonizing fatigue of constant pressure, weekly travel, changing food and climate, and absence from family. When Stan Laurel decided to go into movies, he did so because it meant he would no longer have to work at night, barnstorm, or put up with hotel living.[92]

Charlie Chaplin, too, hated America's "cheap vaudeville circuits" and referred to them as being "bleak and depressing." Chaplin did three and four shows daily, seven days a week, and called English vaudeville "a paradise by comparison." In England he had worked two shows a night with one full day free. The only advantage he saw in the American system was that the lack of leisure time allowed him to "save a little money." Saving money was made a bit rougher by some smalltime managers who would pay the acts just before train time. Using the pretext that they were forced to use the cash box receipts, acts were paid in coins. By the time they were miles away, counting showed they were several dollars short.[93]

Leisure time was enjoyed by those in two-a-day vaudeville, though. Benny Rubin recounted that when he played bigtime two-a-day, he had the entire morning free, did the afternoon show, and was free till the evening show. The schedule enabled him to sleep as late as he wished and to get in several rounds of golf during the week. As a next-to-closing act, he went on after five o'clock, so that he was able to take afternoon naps and appear fresh for his performance. Between shows he ate a fine dinner and often went to see other shows before going onstage himself. Bert Lahr also took up golf while in bigtime vaudeville. Another two-a-day artist, Violet Dale, used her free time to go horseback riding. To Harry Jolson, two-a-day allowed the actor to be a gentleman. Time was virtually his own. He performed the matinee, dressed leisurely afterward, and enjoyed several "hours for pleasure and dinner before the evening show." My father remembered the luxury of sleeping late in the mornings. Their schedule included a light lunch at noon, the afternoon performance, a very light snack at six o'clock, the evening performance, and then "all would go to a place to eat—and it was always like a party—then about 1½ or 2 hours later we would go our own separate place. . . ."[94]

Not all vaudeville was two-a-day, of course. Even the bigtime went to three-a-day when it added a supper show. The actors detested this and their anger became acute when even more shows were demanded. Depending on the theater or the circuit, vaudevillians could be working all day long, bigtime or not. The luxury of free time became unknown.

The extra performances also created additional hazards to the vaudevillian. It was one thing for an acrobat to do his vigorous act twice a day, but quite another to be forced into more. Joe E. Brown had to soak his ankles, which "were taking an awful beating from the three-a-day" program he faced. What of the acrobat who was called upon to do more than three shows? Bert Lahr was constantly doing pratfalls in his slapstick comedy. His left wrist, which he used to break the falls, became much larger than his right. Even animals were affected. The extra shows forced dog acts to carry surplus dogs to substitute for those whose hind legs would have become overly strained by an extra show.[95]

Through all the trials and tribulations, however, the vaudevillian retained his sense of humor. Practical jokes were frequent. Bobby Clark was one of the best in rigging them, to the point that several vaudevillians on the bill with him dressed in their hotel rooms instead of taking the chance that he might hide their costumes at the theater. Other performers asked for dressing rooms as far away from him as possible. During his career, Clark indulged in such tricks as loosening bolts in bicycles and putting water in the horns used in seal acts. Jack Benny always had to be on guard against colleagues who hid his violin. Just before he was due onstage, Julius Tannen was the victim of Joe E. Brown. Though an admirer of acrobatic ability, Tannen could stand on his hands only by bracing himself against a wall and by depending on someone to help him get down. After displaying his acrobatic feat to Brown, Tannen found that Brown had walked away just as Tannen was called to go onstage. The entire theater reverberated with Tannen's yell, "Get me down! Get me down!"[96]

The pursuit of sex was a serious business to many. The Marx brothers always flirted with the girls in the audience, no matter what scene they were playing. Ben Blue matter-of-factly said, "Well . . . you never have to worry about actors in a town. The girls come looking for them." Actors leaving town would also leave notes for those coming in, including girls' names and phone numbers. Many of the men arranged to either have prostitutes sent to their rooms or they went to the red light districts for their pleasure.[97]

On the road the vaudeville performer was away from his family, staying at shabby hotels or boardinghouses and desperately in need of diversion. Groucho Marx emphasized that to "these lonely pariahs" sporting houses were important. While the invitations that these houses issued to vaudevillians did not always include one to go to bed, there were enough that did. The houses also offered free food and liquor, as well as "miscellaneous fun."[98]

The double standard prevailed, however, for the female trouper. Mae West received attention from both men on the bill and those in the hotels. Mitzi Goldwyn received letters written by admirers: "I'm in love with you, Banjoist. Please meet me after the show." She also recalled the time in Pittsburgh when a theater manager offered her top billing in exchange for a date. The Pittsburgher was not unusual. Many theater managers, as well as stagehands and musicians, went out of their way in their quest for actresses and their favors.[99]

In the opinion of Nils Granlund, female entertainers were "subjected to more temptation in a day than most other women encounter in a lifetime." Occasionally, as in the case of Ethel

Waters, severe problems cropped up. When she was on tour with the Hill Sisters, the three girls were hustled by all types, from college boys to pimps. Because of that, the trio looked out for one another, though they dated freely. One night some knockout drops were put in her drink. Luckily, the Hills saw what was happening and rushed her home, averting what she felt was sure to be a "gang-up."[100]

Although Joe Laurie, Jr., referred to the unmarried girls on tour as "poor gals [who] couldn't go with anybody on the bill, because the wives and partners were jealous," Benny Rubin claimed differently. He stated that if the girls in the show wanted sex, they had to find it right on the bill. If this meant breaking up couples, then breakups occurred. "I saw it and saw it and saw it," lamented Rubin. Pat Rooney, Sr., who was teamed with his wife for decades, also recalled the numerous breakups. His observation was that "there were mainly two reasons for this–liquor and another woman or liquor and another man." But Ken Murray believed that very few vaudevillians lived together, which he attributed to "spillover from the Victorian era." There was dating, yes, said Murray, but no flaunting of sexual relationships. But others claim that despite some Victorian limits, extra-marital sexual relations existed and many marriages were destroyed because of it.[101]

From the standpoint of sexual availability, being married was a distinct advantage, of course. But children were a serious problem. Family life in vaudeville was unlike family life anywhere. Opinion is sharply divided as to how beneficial vaudeville life was for the troupers' children. To Mitzi Goldwyn, it was "a horrible, horrible way to raise children, [for] it was in those days a dog's life, really. And I feel sorry for anybody that was raised in it." Ken Murray told of walking into a dressing room and seeing a child of three, leaning her head on the dressing room table, fast asleep standing up. To him, life on the road was "a rough thing" for kids.[102]

Groucho Marx's son, Arthur, recalled the hotel rooms. "It seemed to me we were always traveling–for what purpose I didn't know." Both his parents were in the same act, so Groucho would arrange to have the opening act on the same bill fulfill the duties of babysitters. Steve Allen was the son of vaudeville parents. His father died when Steve was only eighteen months old. Allen wrote of "watching countless movies and endless vaudeville bills, waiting for my mother to come on." Just as often he was left at "home," which meant being "boarded out with a succession of aunts, uncles, grandmothers, strangers, and boarding schools." When on the road with his mother, babysitters were not always available. There were times that he would awaken "in the middle of the night in various hotel rooms, wondering where I was and where my mother was. Sometimes I would get up, get dressed, and go out into the night looking for her."[103]

Another who journeyed alone into the night was Al Fanton. His parents were playing the Palace and Al, who was only about five at the time, was left in the care of a babysitter in their room at the Mansfield Hall Hotel, just off Broadway on 50th Street. As Al related the story:

> . . . I'll never forget it—I eluded this person, this babysitter. I was ready for bed. I had on my pajamas, my bathrobe, and my slippers and I got out of this hotel and started walking Broadway because I wanted to see my parents. . . . And by an amazing coincidence, who should be coming toward me but my mother and father. . . . I could have gone left and gone uptown and wound up at 138th Street. . . .[104]

Fanton spoke of education, too. In his opinion an education then, even a high school diploma, mattered little. His own education was in show business—"the idea was to get an act together." He learned his profession, was able eventually to juggle, dance, do acrobatic stunts, tell jokes, and sing, and that enabled him to be prepared for the career he chose. Ken Murray was the same way. His father was in vaudeville, too, and he learned whatever he could in the trade, including how to accurately snap a whip.[105]

There were laws about education, however, or as Murray expressed it, "there was hell to pay" in connection with children and their schooling, or rather, lack of schooling. Despite Murray's career coming along late in the glory days of vaudeville, he stated that even then, the school-going children did not brag about the fact their "folks were vaudeville." The police constantly quizzed child actors on school matters, according to Gypsy Rose Lee and June Havoc, and their mother finally relented and hired a private tutor, who accompanied them on the road. Sammy Davis, Jr., related how his grandmother, who took care of him when he was not on tour, had been visited by the truant officer. When he and his father came home, the grandmother excitedly implored, "You gotta get him a tutor when you're on the road 'cause the bulls are going to lock me up sure if they catch me!" The tutors turned out to be anyone on the bill willing to work with young Sammy on reading and writing. Ferne Burton observed that the stage mothers usually acted as teachers and that many children took officially assigned homework on tour.[106]

How valuable such tutoring was depended, quite naturally, on the abilities of teacher and pupil. Fred Astaire was tutored in boardinghouses, hotels, theaters, and trains, and remarked, "Incidentally, geography on a moving train is a good idea: the lessons are less painful when you see the geography moving by." Evidently the tutelage he and his sister Adele received paid dividends, for unable to procure bookings, the family moved to New Jersey, where both children entered the public schools. They were put in with their age groups, but within a week were promoted to the succeeding grades. Joe E. Brown, on the other hand, came off a tour, enrolled in school, and experienced considerable difficulty before he was able to complete the term. He acknowledged, "I could never have done it without the help of understanding teachers, God bless them." Buster Keaton, who always regretted the fact he had been to school for only one day in his entire life, was just as proud of the "best catch-as-catch-can education [that] anyone could have wanted" that he received from his fellow performers. He made the point because he "was so successful as a child performer . . . it occurred to no one to ask me if there was something else I'd like to be when I grew up."[107]

Keaton also remembered how angry his father became whenever agents of the Society for the Prevention of Cruelty to Children would pressure the Keaton family about his welfare. Buster himself called them "a pain in the neck." What disturbed the elder Keaton was the fact that thousands of children roamed the streets of New York, abandoned, hungry, and homeless, doing their best to scratch out a living. Then, too, many children who lived at home worked side by side with their parents in the sweatshops of the time. Why, wondered Keaton, did the S.P.C.C. hound him instead of devoting their full time, energy, and money on remedying the much more serious problem of needy children? The father also became angry whenever theater managers would advertise Buster as a midget, in efforts to fool the authorities. Keaton would have none of that.[108]

Most vaudevillians sent their children away to school. For many, this meant a military academy or boarding school or, as it did for Ben Blue's daughter and many other girls, a convent.[109]

Keeping a family together on the road was no easy task, as the following colorful description of Fred Allen attested:

> Vaudeville families endured for generations. The female of the species foaled on trains, in dressing rooms, in tank towns, and in big cities. The show must go on. At the theater the baby slept in the top of the trunk in the dressing room. At the hotel a crib was improvised by removing a large bureau drawer and placing it on the bed or between two chairs. A large blanket filled the drawer nicely; the baby, wrapped in its quilt, rested serene in his drawer bassinet. . . .
>
> The smalltime vaudeville mother had the endurance of a door-knob. She did three or four shows a day as part of the act. She cared for her baby on the road and prepared its food. She did the family washing: there was always a clothesline hanging and dripping away in the dressing room and the boardinghouse, and the sinks were filled with diapers. As the family grew larger, the kids were packed like sardines into upper berths. . . . Many wives cooked the family meals in the dressing room; before electricity became promiscuous, vaudeville wives carried tin plates, cups, knives and forks, and prepared tasty meals over flaming gas jets, and blazing Sterno cans in dressing and hotel rooms.[110]

The theatrical trunk was indispensable to vaudeville families and the best of them all was the Herkert and Meisel, or H&M, as vaudevillians referred to it. Al Fanton, who always believed that the expression, "born in a trunk," actually meant "borne in a trunk," pointed out that the top drawer of the H&M would convert to a tidy bassinet. The next drawer down contained spaces for milk bottles and Sterno. The trunk also contained a metal compartment designed to house an electric iron, special rubber-lined compartments for holding wet sponges, washclothes, and soap, a hat compartment, and spaces for shoes and jewelry. There was even an ironing board that fastened securely to the H&M. Since they were so expensive, the H&M trunk advertised that the vaudevillian who owned one was either a headliner or well on his way toward headline status.[111]

Not all vaudeville mothers used trunks as cribs. Lillian Roth, herself a child star, remembered that Rosie Green, of the comedy song and dance act, Keno and Green, kept her baby in a little basket. But Lillian's chief memories were sad ones. Her mother accompanied her on the road, while her father remained home, so that for six years, starting at the age of nine, she rarely saw her father. Unlike many other children who loved the train rides, Lillian felt they made for loneliness. Train whistles have ever since filled her "with haunting sadness." In one sentence of her autobiography, she thrice used the word, "lonely," to describe train rides, hotels, and cities where they knew no one. Through her vaudeville childhood, she "yearned for a home, a garden, a hammock, a sense of belonging."[112]

Sammy Davis, Jr., on the other hand, cited the fact that he had been in ten states and over fifty cities by the time he was only four years old. His father always rented the cheapest room available to save on expenses. Rarely were they in a city for more than a week or two. Yet, Davis stated that "there was never a feeling of impermanence. Packing suitcases and riding on trains and buses was as natural to me as a stroll in a carriage might be to another child." Davis never felt as if he were without a home. "We carried our roots with us," he said.[113]

Games of hide and seek were the favorite pastime for many vaudeville children, an especially good game for the backstage areas because of the many trunks, pieces of scenery, and stage equipment that could be used for concealment. While traveling, the children enjoyed the run of the trains.[114] Miriam Young, who stated sadly that she was fifteen before she found what it was like to be at home at Christmas time, described the privileges of a vaudeville child:

> If I was spoiled, blame the Spanish wirewalkers, the German jugglers, the sister teams, the animal trainers, the country yokels, and chin-whiskered grandpappies; the women who wore men's clothes and sang baritone, the female impersonators with their veined, muscular arms, padding, corsets and chalkwhite make-up. Blame the strong men, blame the pretty, dainty toe dancers with their heavy thighs and jutting calf muscles; blame the Arabian tumblers, the Chinese magicians. You might even blame the big dramatic stars who, having no play on Broadway that season, were slumming in vaudeville at huge salaries. Don't forget to blame

> the stagehands and musicians, too, and the men up in the flies. They all petted, spoiled, and flattered the one child among them.[115]

She remembered her joy at seeing and memorizing new acts. She lived in the world of the trouper, "no home town, no home. But at home in any town."[116]

Benny Rubin gave Eddie Cantor as a prime example of a performer who rarely saw his family. Rubin claimed the comedian "sometimes saw his kids once a year, once a year-and-a-half, once in two years." Cantor was away from his family a great deal. He wrote home every day, sent most of his salary every week, and also mailed "silver spoons from every town in the USA." Even when Cantor was based in New York for an extended period of time, the demands of his schedule contrasted to that followed by his family.[117] Cantor wrote a touching, yet not atypical, summary:

> Any marriage should be a partnership. Ours has never been a matter of fifty-fifty. Most of the credit for our success goes to my wife. She accepted show business and put up with it. One situation became a standard joke. If I was on the road I'd try to get home for Sunday, my time with the youngsters. I'd take the midnight train after the Saturday-night show and get in Sunday morning. Then I'd sit quietly in the living room, reading the paper until they got up. As if I'd been there right along. One Sunday morning Marjorie went running to say, "Mama, that man's here again."[118]

Not everyone was lucky enough to get a home in a suburban colony or even get a heated room. At one point in his career, Houdini and his wife were down to their last $1.50. They used that to rent a small unheated bedroom for a week. While Houdini hunted for a job, he took advantage of a "professional courtesy" that many vaudeville houses allowed performers—a free seat in the balcony. There, at least, his wife could be warm.[119]

A similar but more somber recollection because it involved a child was that told by Sammy Davis, Jr. When only six years old, their act was stranded somewhere in Michigan. With the temperature below freezing, their landlord had locked them out and kept their possessions. They walked to the railroad station in order to be warm. To avoid arrest for vagrancy, his father and Will Mastin took turns looking busy, while young Sammy, covered by his father's overcoat, slept on a bench. At midnight, though, the station closed. The bus depot was also closed. They walked, "looking for any place that would be warm and open, stopping in doorways every few minutes for a break from the fierce wind." Spotting a hotel, the older Davis failed in his attempts to rent rooms, even when he pleaded for his young son. Luckily, a woman overheard the distraught father, approached him outside, and supplied lodging for the night.[120]

On the road, two did not live as cheaply as one. If a wife traveled with her vaudeville husband, but was not herself a performer, she was termed "excess baggage." For most then, a long tour generally meant a long separation. Some wives joined their husbands for a week or two at a time, mostly in the big cities. Will Rogers used an Orpheum tour as a honeymoon vehicle, introducing his wife to a life that often meant sandwiches after the show, unless they were able to find a restaurant "where Will could get his beloved chili."[121]

When vaudeville families were talked of, however, the ones that loomed largest were those that kept the children with them on the road and eventually worked them into the acts. These families were noted for being very close, yet even they were aware of the strain on love that the pressure of making good, performance after performance, could have. There was an unwritten law with family acts whereby no one said anything until the makeup was off and the street clothes were on. By that time any temperament caused by awkwardness in the act would be calmed down.[122]

Violent temperament sometimes seized even the best of the family acts, however. Buster Keaton was only a pre-schooler when he was already an integral part of his father's no-holds-barred acrobatic turn. During one performance, Buster's father became so infuriated at an ill-mannered clod down front that he literally fired the child like a missile directly at the offender. The young Keaton had been fortunate to survive to that event. He had nearly suffocated in infancy, while sleeping unattended in a costume trunk. At the age of six months he survived a fall down a flight of boardinghouse stairs, a fact which prompted Houdini to dub him "Buster." Several hotel and theater fires, plus a train wreck, were also involved in Keaton's youth. Despite all of that and his sorrow at losing out on a formal education, Keaton said he "enjoyed both the freedom and privileges of childhood [plus] the thrill of being treated as full-grown years before other boys and girls."[123]

There were times, of course, when like any parent, the vaudevillian would have to administer discipline against his cantankerous child. My father told of the time when, just before he was to go onstage and sing a prisoner's ballad, he refused to budge. What happened is best told in my father's words: "My Father warmed my behind real well that I went out and sang it and I was crying—boy did I make a hit."[124]

From numerous standpoints, then, family living in vaudeville was no lark. Yet, the great majority of vaudeville marriages and families evidently were happy and tight-knit. In a medium that appealed chiefly to a family trade, the family act certainly had to be an asset. Depending on the nature of the act, the vaudeville family could well have projected its image to the public as a kind of American ideal: the respectful child, the subordinate wife and the like. There were acts, however, where mischievous children gained the upper hand. In theaters that so often enjoyed a heavy trade in children's admissions, no doubt there was more than a bit of imitation going on in that particular section of the audience.

Indeed, many were concerned about the negative influence that show business could wield on its numerous child-patrons, especially since children attended the lowest priced theaters, where the worst vaudeville was offered. Though the medium itself was viewed as being educational, there were critics who concluded that vaudeville was very injurious to children. For one, children would develope appetites for emotional excitement and have a "restless craving for constant excitement of the eye and ear." As well, they would gain a "premature knowledge of life," lose their reasoning power, and have "unusual opportunities to become delinquent." Their habits of study would be greatly disturbed, they would increasingly demand "artificial amusements," and the end result would be substantial "weakness of character."[125] The warning was emphatic:

> When parents and educators wake up to the fact that the theatre really is an immense educational force, one way or the other, they will begin to see the bad intellectual effects of frequent indulgence in the variety-show habit and will require better forms of entertainment in the theatre.[126]

An investigative committee, headed by the President of Reed

College, Portland, Oregon, examined vaudeville in that city and reached some interesting conclusions concerning vaudeville's effect on children. The committee discovered that over 70 percent of Portland's children, grades one through nine, attended vaudeville, while 24 percent attended at least once a week. This factor was foremost in the committee's investigation, as it sought to insure that Portland's children would not be detrimentally affected by the popular medium. Some of the committee's findings may have influenced the Juvenile Court of Portland which a year later concluded that amateur nights had a demoralizing effect on young girls. They pointed to testimony in eight delinquency cases where girls had stated that their participation in amateur performances had contributed to their plight.[127]

The Reed College committee concluded that vaudeville was more objectionable than motion pictures and was more likely to corrupt the morals of youth. The committee had observed 58 vaudeville bills and maintained that only ten had been "free from positively objectionable features." They added, however, that more than 80 percent of the acts were "harmless." Specific complaints were lodged against a pantomime act, "A Night in the Slums of Paris," which was judged to have a bad influence on youth. The act showed young girls smoking, gambling, drinking, and dancing. The act, which "put low ideals before those in attendance," was described further as "one of reckless abandon."[128]

The report of the Portland group referred to a similar study conducted by the New York Child Welfare Committee, in which the most striking characteristic of vaudeville was stated to be its "simple stupidity." The Portland investigators agreed with the New York findings, which stressed that any person of moderate intelligence who would attend a dozen vaudeville shows would have to be "disgusted at their vapidity." The New York report also noted that vaudeville audiences often appeared bored.[129]

Vaudevillians circulated and supported established opinion, besides transmitting their own personal reactions to life. To influence the minds of people who were seeking relief from mental activity was easy if they were in a mentally lax state unwilling to resist what sifts into their thoughts while they are being entertained. Thus, "a vaudeville philosophy of life" was definitely influencing Americans in their daily affairs, and this influence of vaudeville was not to be taken lightly.

One writer felt this influence to be a poor one and wrote a very interesting summary of what he believed to be the dangers of the vaudeville theater:

> There are certain standard subjects that are used almost every night on the vaudeville stages throughout the country. An audience, composed of many persons mentally fatigued after a day's work, learns a philosophy that embraces such precepts as: Marriage is an unfortunate institution to which the majority of us resign ourselves; women are fashion-crazy, spend money heedlessly and believe that their husbands are fools; politics is all bunk, prohibition should be prohibited; mothers are the finest persons in the world . . . next to grandmothers; fathers are unfortunate persons upon whom fall most of life's woes; marital infidelity is widespread; clandestine affairs of most any sort between at least one married person and another of the opposite sex are comical; and finally "nothing in life really matters. The main thing to do is to get all the money you can and keep your mother-in-law as far off as possible."[130]

The vaudeville audience spread over an entire continent. Its vagaries presented a constant challenge to the touring artist. As he mastered the audiences from coast to coast he acquired that refinement that stood the vaudevillian so well when he performed in other branches of show business. And the successful vaudevillian had to master those audiences. They were his America and, in a great sense, he was their America.

Whether the vaudevillian took to "The Death Trail" or "The Aching Heart" circuits, or to the "Sunday School Circuit," his impressions of America came from the audiences. Benny Rubin felt that beyond the theater and the hotel room, most vaudevillians never got to know the town they played. Rubin himself rode street cars and busses as much as he could in an effort to get to know the town as well as possible in a short time. Ethel Waters, too, cited the fact that she and others would chip in together in order to take an hour's tour of the town they were playing at the time. "If we were flush we'd get up six dollars and buy a long two-hour ride," she said. As little as even the exposure of two hours could show, it was still more than most saw.[131]

For foreign players American geography itself was staggering. It was difficult to get accustomed to the great distances one had to travel. A route often had him jumping five hundred miles to get to the next town. Harry Lauder spent a great deal of his train travel seated on the observation platform and remarked of the landscape, "It's grand scenery—and there's sae much of it."[132]

Stan Laurel was another foreigner to the shores who thought he sensed the spirit of America: "There was still the rawness of the Old West not only on its home ground but all over the country." That statement, made when the "affable" William Howard Taft was President, was made of a nation Laurel recognized as being "young—ready and willing to grow in all ways."[133]

If an entertainer was a success in a given town, his opinion of the town was that it was great. If he flopped, however, it was "a jerk town." There were other factors, as well, that influenced a vaudevillian's judgment. He faced, especially in the small towns, a public which thought him to be no good, untrustworthy, and immoral. Vaudevillians knew that when they walked the streets, they were viewed as "bums [and] drinkers."[134] Groucho Marx phrased it more sharply:

> [An] actor's position in society was somewhere between that of a gypsy fortune teller and a pickpocket. When [he] arrived in a small town, families would lock up their young daughters, put up the shutters and hide the silverware. To give you an idea of the actor's social status, a Southern planter in Shreveport, Louisiana, once told one of my brothers that he would kill him if he ever spoke to his daughter again. Only the fact that the planter was busy attending a lynching that afternoon prevented him from shooting my brother.[135]

Thus, though a major force of vaudeville was the intimacy of the performer with his audience, there appeared to be a great distance separating them once outside the theater. Only "those who had attained stellar rank" were accepted outside the theater. June Havoc related that she had been given a sound bit of advice along this line by a daredevil named Big Gurn. Her guinea pig had nearly been torn to shreds by a pack of rats and Big Gurn stated simply that the pet should have known to stay among his own kind.[136]

Fred Allen insisted that the vaudevillian could be content only with other vaudevillians. Even during "vacation" season, vaudevillians flocked together. They understood each other's terminology, hopes, and fears. Their terminology alone created an alien world. Walter J. Kingsley held that if an outsider were put backstage in a vaudeville house, "he would understand as little of the conversation as if he were suddenly cast away upon a cannibal island." A *fish* was a poor act. A *chooser* was a performer who stole material. *Handcuffed* meant an audience which did not applaud. *Morgue* defined a theater that did not do business. *Deucing* was to appear second on the bill. Those and countless other expressions set the vaudevillian in a separate category. They were part of a profession that long had been scorned by a "decent" public. The very conditions of life on tour forced them together, into the available boardinghouses or hotels, to eat at the conveniently located restaurants, and to take the same trains, often to go to the very same towns. As Al Fanton commented, "We had nothing in common with [the public]."[137]

"IT WOULDN'T BE SO BAD, EDDIE, IF I DIDN'T STILL HEAR THE APPLAUSE RINGING IN MY EARS."

♦ ♦ ♦ ♦ ♦

THE BLACK ENTERTAINER, JUST AS THE BLACK IN EVERY SEGMENT OF American society, had exceptional problems. In vaudeville, Joe Laurie, Jr., said, talent had no color. Laurie pointed out that in 1907, there were hundreds of blacks in the medium, many as headline acts. He observed, "If you had talent, a good story, or were just good company, that was your ticket to get in the magic circle of performers." A work on the blacks in show business attests that there existed less intolerance among entertainers than in any other group of people in America. Sammy Davis, Jr., was a young veteran of vaudeville before he heard the term, "nigger." Not knowing what it meant, he asked, learning it was "a nasty word." At the same time it was explained to him that show people were different, were not prejudiced, that "most of 'em don't care about anything except how good is your act."[1]

In 1912 *Variety* published an article on the black vaudeville team of Fiddler and Shelton. In their five years in the medium, Fiddler and Shelton had played theaters all over the country and were convinced that people of their own race had an excellent chance for success in the entertainment field. Though the team claimed they were "ready to file affidavits that not once in their lives have they had any 'run in' or tilts with theatre managers, stage crews or hotels," the rest of their remarks indicated the type of prejudice that did exist in vaude. Fiddler and Shelton knew they were regarded highly as entertainers, and said that they gained and held that regard by showing respect. They selected their material "with a view of giving no offense" and emphasized that "the colored man should always be prompt at rehearsal" and should keep in mind that he would receive "good treatment from orchestras by showing the leaders and musicians proper respect."[2] Therein was the message. If the black had talent, he also had to know his place.

A standard story about Bert Williams, probably the greatest black vaudevillian in history, relates to the knowing of place. Lionel Barrymore, in vaude for enjoyment and added experience, stood in the wings during the black artist's turn and was asked by a stagehand if he liked Williams' act. When Barrymore affirmed that he thought Williams was "terrific," the stagehand remarked, just as Williams passed, "Yeah, he's a good nigger knows his place." Williams retorted, "Yes. A good nigger. Knows his place. Going there now. Dressing room ONE!"[3] Williams was paid a huge salary because he was regarded as the number one comedian. But on the road, the black comic's skin brought him in contact with offstage America. Often, while his fellow vaudevillians stayed at the best hotels, Williams, the headliner, was obliged to seek out the usually dilapidated, segregated ones. Williams said that in this respect it was no disgrace to be a Negro, but it was very inconvenient.[4] Even while vaudevillians I interviewed told how friendly they were with blacks–"They weren't any different than anyone else"–they always seemed taken aback when asked where the blacks lived while on the road. Naturally, they assumed, the black stayed with blacks. One must hasten to point out that onstage, in many restaurants, in their own homes and apartments, racial differences meant little or nothing. (Only very infrequently, as when the Four Small Brothers, a group of white Southerners, complained because they had to participate in the same act at Loew's State as Louis Armstrong,[5] was there any sign of onstage prejudice.) But when the greater offstage America closed in, there was nothing the vaudevillian could do.

Onstage America stretched from coast to coast for the black vaudevillian. Those who traveled in the South knew what Jim

Crow railroad cars were like. Southern trains stopped at hundreds of places, according to Ethel Waters, "and people would get on carrying pots, pans, their bedding, and even live chickens." She mentioned, too, the resentment shown her by Southern blacks. The fact that she was a smalltime performer meant that she was "considered not much better than cattle by respectable Negroes." With the blacks she encountered in the Jim Crow cars, they "would do everything to pressure me out of my seat, spitting and poking, elbowing and knocking my hat off," when they recognized her as a Northerner. White Southerners, too, showed an antagonistic attitude when they saw she was from the North. Clerks in stores would say, "I see you're one of those fresh Yankee niggers."[6]

Miss Waters also vividly recalled arriving in Macon, Georgia, and learning that the body of a black youth had been tossed into the lobby of the theater where she was scheduled to appear. A "white mob" had lynched him. His offense: he had been accused of talking back to a white man. Yet, that very night, she probably entertained the killers of the boy, for when good black acts played the black theaters, special performances were given for white audiences only. As she pointed out, "So we found ourselves applauded by the ofays in the theatre and insulted by them on the streets."[7]

Miss Waters herself talked back to a white theater owner in Atlanta, Georgia, and feared she would be severely beaten. The man was a "hard-bitten old Georgia cracker" who had a reputation for beating black performers and having them put in jail if they gave him any trouble. With police watching her hotel both front and back, and even the conniving black chauffeur of the theater owner spying, the hotel manager helped her to escape. From there she went to Nashville, Tennessee, where she found the theater owner to be a direct contrast. She described him as the first white man to ever address her as "Miss Waters." His theater, however, had rats which she described as "heavyweights. They were game as bulldogs and big enough to climb ladders." One, she claimed, literally held a Coke bottle in his front paws and drank from it. "Their cockiness gave me the chills," she remembered.[8]

Many theaters, especially on the black circuits, were dilapidated. Miss Waters recalled the Lincoln Theatre in Baltimore, absolutely one of the worst houses on any route. The dressing room was located beneath the stage, with a thin partition separating the men from the women. Plaster fell on any actors unlucky enough to be changing costumes or putting on makeup when any dancers took the stage. To get onstage, the performer exited through the orchestra pit and climbed a ladder. Miss Waters summed it up: "Glamorous is not quite the word for the Lincoln Theatre. . . ."[9] In contrast, Baltimore also had the Royal Theatre, a "colored house," as it was called. Located on Pennsylvania Avenue, this black vaudeville theater held a capacity of about one thousand, had excellent dressing rooms, plush carpeting, and what was described as a "serene, church-like atmosphere."[10]

Offstage America included a Joplin, Missouri, restaurant known as the Green Room. The theater bulletin board recommended the establishment as a good place to eat. Sammy Davis, Jr., related the time when he went there with other members of the show, both white and black. The greeting they received was, "Evening, folks. You niggers'll have to sit on the other side." The countertop was painted two colors. Whites sat where it was painted white. Davis and his fellows sat where it was painted brown.[11]

One did not have to be black, however, to be aware of prejudice. Benny Rubin clarified that there were hate towns, where a Catholic, black, and Jew were automatically in trouble. Rubin particularly mentioned the black, emphasizing that the black entertainer had to be humble. Alluding to the performances of black stars in the 1960's, Rubin asserted that, had such attitudes been used by black performers in vaude in the South, "they'd lynch him on the spot."[12] The black had to know his place.

There were other subtle prejudices besides the black always having to show respect to the whites around him. Whereas a white could perform in serious drama the black could not.[13] He could dance, he could sing minstrel and "coon" songs, and he could be funny, but he could not be taken seriously. New Yorkers, as well as any on the vaude routes, were shown a stage black who was a stereotype. Without a doubt vaude contributed heavily to the maintaining of a Negro stereotype which affected the American public's later assessment of the black.

How could a white American respect the black he thought he knew, the black he laughed at in so many vaudeville shows? When the "Jonah Man" shuffled across the stage and spoke in his stumbling dialect, in his representation of the illiterate Southern black, as he did in countless vaudeville theaters, American culture had to be affected. As Gilbert Osofsky concluded in his excellent study of Harlem, the black portrayed onstage was "totally the reverse of what Americans considered worthy of emulation and recognition. The major and traditional values were all absent from the Negro stereotype."[14]

Though we may shudder at these blunders, Joe Laurie, Jr., did not see it that way. He loved the vaudeville that had acts billed as "Irish by Name but Coons by Birth," "The Watermelon Trust," "The Merry Wop," "The Mick and the Policeman," and the like. Laurie claimed that the acts built around such themes were "taken in good humor by the audience, because that is what everyone called each other in everyday life. There were no pressure groups and no third generation to feel ashamed of immigrant origins."[15] His view, as interesting as it was, totally neglected two points. First, that pride in one's immigrant origins, rather than shame, would propel an individual to resent his nationality or race as being characterized as ignorant. Secondly, whereas the white man could become absorbed in the mainstream of White America, the black man could not. He would suffer as long as the stereotype existed.

Laurie and others in agreement with him cannot be labeled as prejudiced. Laurie, a superb vaudevillian himself, related as well as any other to his black colleagues. He saw little prejudice in his medium, worked his active vaudeville day, saw blacks do Jewish acts onstage, Jews do Italians, Irish do Dutch, and representatives of every group, including Black, do blackface. The friendships developed in the theater and the sincere respect one performer had for another who put on a good turn made it difficult for someone like Laurie, especially when placed in the context of the society of his time, to recognize the tragic consequences of such stereotyping on the American way of life.

Another factor which contributed to the white vaudevillian's lack of full appreciation for the plight of the black performer was the use that whites gave to blackface. Blackface enabled many young performers to look more mature or, because of its exaggerated application, to look funny even before the comic material came forth. Blackface was an ordinary prop used to elicit laughter.[16] Blacking up involved no prejudice on the part of the user.

It was business.

Al Fanton testified:

> As far as I can remember, we had no prejudice whatsoever. It was never taught to me one way or the other. My mother and father . . . never said to me you must never differentiate, you must never dislike, you must never like. It was just something that they left with me and as I recall, there wasn't any prejudice backstage. . . . We were travelers, like in space. There were Arab tumblers, there were Hungarian teeterboard performers, Spanish dancers, there were Negro dancers, there were Jew comics. . . . And you had to get along. There were Catholics and there were Hindus and there were meateaters and there were vegetarians and there were all these kind of characters, and we didn't know any of these [towns] people around, so that we had to be friends with ourselves.[17]

Fanton added that if there was any prejudice, it was against the untalented performer, although he hesitated to use the term "prejudice" in that regard.[18] So, as long as the minority performer was among his colleagues, prejudice was non-existent.

Booker T. Washington said of Bert Williams, "[He] has done more for the race than I have. He has smiled his way into people's hearts." Yet Williams was constantly in touch with reality. Eddie Cantor recognized that Williams was extremely sensitive to the problems of his fellow blacks. Even in happy moments, Cantor noticed a "deep strain of melancholy" in Williams, a strain that would occasionally surface. He cited a New Year's Eve when the two entertainers had agreed to celebrate the holiday event together. As they left the theater together, Cantor told Williams to meet him at his hotel. Williams retorted, "Okay. I'm on my way to the back elevator." Cantor said that it marked the first time he had seen bitterness in his "turn-thine-own-cheek friend." There was a silence, a moment of understanding between the two, Cantor claimed, and then Williams sadly remarked, "It wouldn't be so bad, Eddie, if I didn't still hear the applause ringing in my ears." W. C. Fields once observed that Williams was the funniest man he ever saw, yet was the saddest man he ever knew.[19]

Williams emphasized, "I am *what* I am not *because of*, but *in spite of* who I am." Whether his appearances onstage significantly helped race relations in the nation, it is a problem which drew an interesting analysis from Heywood Broun. Broun observed, "Somehow or other, laughing at Bert Williams came to be tied up in people's minds with liberalism, charity and the Thirteenth Amendment."[20] Therein is a premise that transcends vaudeville and the followup Ziegfeld Follies that Williams starred in. Show business and athletics, the two areas where blacks have enjoyed their most prominent success in the twentieth century, are made for the spectator. Therefore, the audience can, without any thought of race relations, applaud, cheer, whistle, to signal its approval. Once the theaters and stadiums and gymnasiums empty, the spectator is once again the middle class man, with a home and family to protect. It makes no difference that the entertainer who made him laugh and applaud, or the scoring athlete is black. America's history of racial problems takes the story from there. For example, George Walker, Bert Williams' partner, and Ernest Hogan, the famous "unbleached American," were well-known headliners in many New York theaters. When a bloody race riot erupted there in 1900, both were badly beaten, as was every black found on the streets.[21]

Black audiences were far less inhibited than white audiences. It seemed to Ethel Waters that black audiences "gave a peppier performance" than the acts onstage:

> Rugged individualists all, they did whatever they pleased while you were killing yourself on the stage. They ran up and down the aisles, yelling greetings to friends and sometimes having fights. And they brought everything to eat from bananas to yesterday's pork chops.
>
> But they also were the most appreciative audiences in the world if they liked you. They'd scream, stomp, and applaud until the whole building shook. Years later, when I first stepped before a white audience, I thought I was a dead duck because no one tried to tear the house down. They merely clapped their hands. Such restraint is almost a sneer in the coloured vaudeville world I came out of.[22]

However, years later, after she had become accustomed to the white audience, she feared returning to black theaters. The same noise and boisterous reactions she had enjoyed formerly frightened her after her success in bigtime (i.e., white) vaude. Also making her uncomfortable was the familiarity black audiences showed. "Certain men out front would sometimes shout vulgar and insulting remarks at you," she said.[23]

The Monogram Theatre in Chicago was a particularly bad memory for Miss Waters. In her opinion, "any old kind of dressing room" looked good to her in comparison to what the Monogram offered. There the vaudevillians "dressed away downstairs with the stoker." The room featured a low ceiling, which necessitated the player's bending over, and also had a ladder as the only exit from the dressing area to the stage. The ladder impressed Miss Waters as one "that looked like those on the old-time slave ships," an impression that was reinforced by the fetid and sickening air of the Monogram's basement. In addition the theater was situated near the elevated, which forced entertainers to stop in mid-joke or mid-verse whenever a train hurtled by. Miss Waters also played Chicago's Grand Theatre, where conditions were noticeably better. According to her account, she brought the business that had been drawn to nearby white theaters back to the Grand. Black musical revues had been booked at these theaters, featuring top name stars, and the Grand's regular patrons had been going to the balcony areas of the white theaters instead.[24]

For blacks to appear before black audiences was one thing. For some white performers, it was something else. The Empress Theatre in Chicago turned out to be a nightmare for a pair of teen-aged whites who were booked there unsuspectingly. The two "were scared to death" and when the audience began to laugh at their fright, one of them quite noticeably "started to pee his pants," which not only brought the house down, but brought the curtain down, too. They were paid for one show and fired.[25]

The fact that there were all-black and all-white audiences demonstrated that, though performers were democratic, the box office was not. According to Ethel Waters, even in New York City only Keith's Alhambra Theatre at Seventh Avenue and 126th Street permitted blacks to buy tickets in the peanut gallery, or as it was less delicately termed, "nigger heaven." In 1905 the Orpheum company was sued by two black patrons when they were ejected from the Circle Theatre. Five years later, at Fifty-first Street and Seventh Avenue, the New Palace opened its doors, the first showplace to cater to blacks only.[26]

Of course, one of the great theaters of all time was the Apollo. This theater was to Harlem what the Palace was to Times Square. Though the shows were primarily done for blacks, many whites appeared on the Apollo boards. When they did, the Harlem audience did not want the white act to treat them condescendingly. At the Apollo, whether it was morning, noon, or night, the audiences were alert and extremely enthusiastic. The great blues singer, Billie Holiday, asserted, "There's nothing like an audience at the Apollo."[27]

Downtown, however, matters were a bit different. The same medium that provided black performers the opportunity to earn handsome salaries still threw obstacles in their paths. It was not until 1918 that the blacks were seen onstage at the Palace without the use of levee sets, torn overalls, or Uncle Tom accents. The pioneers in that respect were Noble Sissle and Eubie Blake, who played and sang their songs in dinner jackets. Their act was a far cry from the likes of Irving Jones, who included in his repertoire a song entitled, "Saint Patrick's Day Is No Day for a Man with a Face Like Mine." Even a respected black headliner like Ernest Hogan was unable–some say unwilling–to break from the "coon" personality. Hogan, in fact, was one of the originators of the coon songs, writing the first really popular one, "All Coons Look Alike to Me." In later years he was ashamed that he had written the song that more than anything else had made him famous.[28]

Coon songs were not only sung by blacks, by any means. Perhaps the most famous of all such singers was Sophie Tucker. In the early part of her memorable career, she employed blackface and was billed, at one time or another, as the "World-renowned Coon Shouter," the "Ginger Girl, Refined Coon Singer," or as the "Manipulator of Coon Melodies."[29]

Had Sophie Tucker been black instead of white, it is questionable whether she would have become a major headliner as early as she did. Though talent was reputedly the only important factor in selecting a vaude act, it was mysterious that no black woman received top billing as a single at the Palace until Ethel Waters did in the fall of 1924. Buster Keaton also commented that he remembered very few Negro women performers in vaude during his younger days. He also related that he never saw whites and Negroes onstage at the same time.[30]

Despite contradicting testimony which tends to weaken the claims that no prejudice existed in vaudeville, the entire matter must be placed in context. The years in question were years that included the "Jim Crow" laws, a revitalized Ku Klux Klan, a wave of race riots, a national hatred of the black heavyweight boxing champion, the absence of any blacks in major league baseball, the furore over the President's having Blacks in the White House as guests, and a race's frustration that contributed to the rise of Marcus Garvey. Since vaudeville claimed to give the public what it wanted, then the black entertainer had no choice but to present himself as a caricature, at least until pressure groups demanded change. In vaude, the black performer could quickly gain recognition and good money. Backstage the black was respected for what he was and what he did.

"WHEN YOU LEAVE NEW YORK, YOU'RE JUST CAMPING OUT."

◆ ◆ ◆ ◆ ◆

IF THAT GREAT METROPOLIS OF NEW YORK CITY SUPPLIED VAUDEVILLE'S pulse, then the one and only Palace Theatre was its heart. Descriptions of the Palace are a veritable vaudeville bill by themselves. It has been called the "Taj Mahal of vaudeville" and the "Mecca of every vaudevillian," "the Seventh Heaven of the vaudevillians' dream," show business' "nirvana," and "the temple of vaudeville." Pat Rooney, Sr., called it "the home plate of show business." A booking at the Palace was considered "a diploma of merit," the "*magna cum laude* degree in show business."[1]

The Palace was also termed "the proud pillar of vaudeville," an institution that, like "Niagara Falls, would always be there." Fred Allen said that "a week at the Palace to a vaudeville act was like the Good Housekeeping Seal of Approval." For Sophie Tucker, playing the Palace "was to American performers what a command performance is to a British actor. Something to live for. Something to boast about all the rest of your days." The authors of *Show Biz* wrote, "What the White House represents to a political hopeful, a Palace booking signified to an actor."[2]

Marian Spitzer insisted that by 1918, the Palace was "unquestionably established as *the* great variety theater of the world. War or no, performers came from near and far for a chance to be seen there. For once seen–if liked–their future was assured." Ken Murray said, "I was pretty jittery because I knew it took everyone in show business a long time to forget a flop at the Palace."

Jack Benny referred to the Palace as "the theatre every actor was nervous about. . . ." Benny's statement may have been in memory of the time he was part of the team of Benny and Woods. In 1916 they were booked for a week at the Palace. They flopped so badly that they nearly lost a year's bookings. More often than not, though, Palace acts were well received and benefitted greatly thereafter. Success at the Palace meant at least a year's tour of the best vaude houses in the nation. A Palace booking was so important that very often vaudevillians would ask for postponements so that they could sharpen their acts to perfection.[3]

The opinion of most was that the Palace audience was easy. George Burns believed the Palace Theatre had the easiest audience in the world, primarily because the audience was filled with show business people, "and everybody knew your life was at stake, so whether you were funny or not they would scream at you." At the Palace it was smart to ad lib, or at least appear to be ad libbing. The ad lib gives any audience the feeling that they are getting a bargain, something extra. Some who were adept at this found that away from the big cities, these "asides" were rarely comprehended.[4]

The opening day matinee crowd at the Palace was a show in itself. There was even a spotlight which shone on such leading personalities as Alfred Lunt and Lynn Fontanne (who never missed an opening day at the Palace when they were in New York), Flo Ziegfeld, Charles Dillingham, and Charles Dana Gibson. The audience was jammed with agents searching for new talent, producers looking for new stars for their upcoming musicals, rival vaude managers, those looking to steal material, and whatever entertainers around town who were free, especially young aspirants. Always there was Father Kelly, "an engaging, personable, and high-minded young priest who, among other things, served as a watchdog for the Archdiocese and was known irreverently in some quarters as 'Cardinal Hayes' yes man."[5]

Despite its predisposition to be generous, even so, the challenge posed by such an audience was viewed as a nightmare. Charles Bickford maintained that the Palace provided "what was perhaps the most critical audience in the country." Rudy Vallee said, "It was about as tough an audience of 'pros' as you could find under one roof." Bernard Sobel, familiar to the scene, called the opening day matinee audience "tough, but ungrudging with applause."[6]

Prior to the opening matinee came the Monday morning rehearsal. At this rehearsal the performers learned the order of appearance. Some tried to wedge their way into certain positions, but the bookers made the final decisions. The bill often changed after the opening matinee, however, the juggling of positions sometimes going on for several days. There were times, too, when an act was cancelled after its first performance. Marian Spitzer wrote of that, "To call this a fate worse than death is hardly exaggerating. It was about as disgraceful as being drummed out of the army for dishonorable conduct. If you flopped at the Palace, there was nowhere to go but down."[7]

That statement, "there was nowhere to go but down," may offer the primary key to understanding the vaudevillian, his own aspirations, and his effect on America. The Palace was the top rung of the ladder. To play there usually represented an apprenticeship filled with rigorous travel, refinement of one's act, years of sacrifice and drive. Only then could the vaudevillian appear on the stage of the Palace. At that point in his career, a vaudevillian could wield only limited influence. Success at the Palace often led to performances in the same cities the actor had been playing all along except that he might play to a reserved-seat audience. The chance of expanding his influence, therefore, was not comparable to what one can ascribe to today's top movie or television personalities.[8]

When the vaudevillian played the Palace, he knew he had achieved the pinnacle of success. To escape the trap the Palace and syndication had created for him, the vaudevillian had to look to musical comedy, the great Broadway revues, and later, radio and movies for satisfaction.

Paradox in being number one meant that though the zenith was reached, the trail ended. From there life would either go in circles or plunge downward. The desperate scramble for the top once over, is replaced by a new feeling: overwhelming fear. Once he had reached the top, the vaudevillian had no peace of mind.

Since he depended upon one short sketch he never believed that his act was as good as it should be. He would brood over the gags and his delivery in his hotel room and train car. If the audience was unresponsive, he would perspire till he was wringing wet. He had to make good.

The Palace building itself was tall and narrow, towering over its Broadway neighbors. On West 47th Street the Palace stage door stood near the Somerset Hotel. Rudy Vallee said, "The theatre itself is just another theatre; in fact, as far as modern conveniences and comfort both for audience and actor go, the Palace would not even be considered third rate. . . ." Vallee also cited its "little old rickety elevator [and] the little, old-fashioned but clean dressing rooms," and added that the backstage help, though easy-going, were "very wonderful and co-operative."[9]

The sidewalk outside the Palace was nearly as famous as the theater itself. This stretch of Broadway was dubbed the Palace Beach, usually shortened to Beach. Some also referred to the location as Hope Island. There one could see big names—Jolson, Cantor, Jessel, Rubin, Blue (pick your headliner)—and many small ones. They all spent time on the Beach, swapping stories, showing off their diamonds, or just plain gossiping. On that pavement "there was no billing. . . . If he was a performer, he belonged." The area, including the Bond Building next door, where many agents were to be found, served as a kind of clearinghouse for out-of-work acts. Another group congregating on the Beach created a problem for the Palace management. These were the ticket scalpers who made immense profit peddling their wares. Even a sidewalk patrol which warned the public of their presence and the illegality of such speculation, could not eliminate them. The Beach, indeed, was "the crossroads" of show business.[10]

The neighborhood of the Palace was important to the vaudevillian, too. In the nearby restaurants, such as the St. Regis Cafe and the Somerset Coffee House, new routines were often tested and the cluster of comedians always trying to top each other probably led to many new gag lines. At some of these restaurants, a few performers, among them Jack Benny, Jimmy Durante, and Benny Rubin, would give the cashiers fifty dollars or so before going on tour, to take care of "broken guys." Cafeterias in the area also got a heavy play from the vaudeville crowd. Three of them, Kellogg's, the Palace, and the Theatrical Drugstore, were referred to by Joey Adams as the Corn Exchange for comedians, especially for those who were not yet headliners. "There," he said, "you could swap two Berle blackouts for one Red Skelton's Guzzler's Gin routine or twelve Bob Hope jokes for a Willie Howard sketch." Of Kellogg's, he termed it a place "where the little people of show business told their lies and laid their plans for headline booking."[11]

However, it was what went on inside the Palace that was most important. On the sixth floor the vaudevillian's fate was dictated. Here Albee and his executive staff had their offices. Marian Spitzer, who worked there for years, and Max Gordon, who was an agent familiar to the scene, wrote that there was "something sacred" about that floor. On the sixth floor the bigtime was booked. Smalltime was booked one floor below. The Palace was a virtual auction block. Performers there were exposed to the eyes of every New York booker, and even some from London, as well as the Ziegfelds, Carrolls, and the like. Though the Palace paid top dollar for its talent, many performers accepted a lower salary than they were used to in order to get on the Palace stage and the future it offered.[12]

Though every day was important at the Palace, three days of the week proved especially so. One was the opening day for each new bill. The second would be Wednesday, when the bookers gathered together to decide which acts went where, or if they were to go anywhere at all. Albee was the key figure, described by Marian Spitzer as "omniscient [and] omnipotent," a czar ruling over his kingdom. Without his permission, no agent was allowed on the sixth floor. The procedure for booking was to have an act's name called out and then to have the bookers respond. There were three possible answers: "No interest," which meant no one wanted the act, "Pick up," which meant someone was willing to give the act a chance, and "Give him a route," the signal that an act had earned one to two years of steady work.[13] The careers of countless vaudevillians hung on those three phrases.

The third special day at the Palace was Thursday morning, when week after week, auditions were held. Performers flocked to them, both smalltimers expecting to jump into the bigtime and rank amateurs. The audience was composed of bookers and other executives, a group that rarely showed any warmth. Yet the chance was there and the Thursday morning auditions never lacked a generous turnout. "We cannot afford to turn down anybody without a hearing," said Albee. "The person to whom we might deny a chance to show his goods might be the greatest potential headliner of all time." Though the Thursday auditions must have resulted in *some* finds, Marian Spitzer concluded that Buck and Bubbles, a top-flight dance team, was the only headline act discovered in that fashion.[14]

The Palace was so special that each bill had at least two headline acts, as contrasted to other vaudeville, where one headliner held forth. Since there was but one "star dressing room," there were times when rivalry caused problems. When trouble was anticipated, the chief booker, Eddie Darling, always made sure there was painting equipment all over the room. The headliners would be told the room was being refurbished. In this way, no one used the star's dressing room and no one was offended.[15]

Prior to the Palace's grand opening in 1913, New York's greatest theater was Hammerstein's Victoria. Since it was located at Broadway and 42nd Street, it was called the "Corner." Vaudevillians loved to play there because it drew a show-wise crowd considered superior to any. Buster Keaton termed the Victoria as being "in its day everything–and perhaps a little more–than the Palace became later." He asserted that "any old timer will tell you, Hammerstein's Victoria was vaudeville at its all-time best." Will Rogers also called it "the greatest Vaudeville theatre of that and all time" and George Jessel described it as "the most glamorous vaudeville theatre in all the world." Prior to the Palace, the vaudevillian knew that the best billing he could get was "Direct from Hammerstein's, New York."[16]

Atop the Victoria was its glass-walled Paradise Roof. Part of the roof could be rolled back on hot summer nights. Shows were played both there and downstairs. Oscar Hammerstein opened the theater on February 8, 1904, and became accustomed to a $4,000 weekly profit from its operation. In the theater itself he maintained a two room suite for himself, one an office, the other a combination bedroom and living room. He thought it would be bad luck if the magnificent building were ever renovated, so not one coat of paint was ever applied–once the theater began its run.

The Victoria's bill was a lengthy one, from 1:45 to 6:00 in the afternoon and from 7:45 to midnight. Few patrons stayed for an entire show, so the vaudevillian tried his best to be placed at or just past the middle of the program, when the fewest number of people were likely to be shuffling in or out.[17]

As important as Oscar Hammerstein was, his son Willie became the key figure in the theater's success story. He, too, held forth at the Victoria, in what came to be known as his "throne-room." Portrayed as "the most eccentric of the show business entrepreneurs of the day," Willie looked to sensational current events for beefing up his programs. Lillian Graham and Ethel Conrad, who had shot a prominent society figure, played for Hammerstein, billed as "The Shooting Stars." One woman, acquitted of a murder charge, came to Oscar Hammerstein at the end of her week at the theater and asked to be held over. The elder Hammerstein, who detested sensational acts like hers, curtly replied, "No, madam, not unless you shoot another man." Cap Anson, a great baseball star, Frank Gotch and James J. Corbett, the wrestling and boxing champions of the world, and Sandow "The Strong Man" were all thrust profitably onto the Victoria stage. At a salary of $3,500 a week, Evelyn Nesbit Thaw, who was scandalously associated with her husband's killing of Stanford White, appeared at the Victoria. For eight weeks she drew standing room crowds.[18]

It was at Hammerstein's that the Cherry Sisters made some of their best money. Billed as "America's Worst Act," these Iowa girls made a fortune being laughed at and insulted because they were so bad. Each turn was a virtual guarantee of a bombardment of rotten eggs and spoiled vegetables. Hammerstein shielded the sorry quartette with a screen drop. Their voices, it was claimed, sounded like "the rattle of an empty coal scuttle." Another good draw at the Victoria was an elderly woman known as "Sober Sue." The Victoria offered prizes to anyone who could make her laugh. Those comedians already on the bill were sure that a laugh from Sober Sue would get them a raise in salary. Others, some of the best of their time, reacted to the challenge and mounted the Victoria boards without pay. Paid only twenty dollars a week, Sober Sue packed the house for weeks. After her final appearance and not a laugh all season, she revealed her secret to the actors on the bill. Not only was she deaf, but she was near-sighted, as well. She had not seen or heard any of the attempts to make her laugh.[19]

Before the Victoria and Palace ventured on the scene, the leading theater was owned by Tony Pastor, called "the godfather of vaudeville." He owned an "intimate showhouse in the Tammany Building on East 14th Street," a vaudeville spot described as a "cosy and never-to-be-forgotten little bird-cage of a theatre." Pastor moved into the small theater in early 1881. The building itself had been constructed in 1868 and was not what could be called a showplace. The nearby Harrigan and Hart Theatre Comique at 514 Broadway, a superior building, was Pastor's chief rival. Pastor was a devout Catholic who had a prayer room built in his theater. He transformed his beer hall from an establishment that booked variety acts that were the ultimate in vulgarity when they were not actually obscene, into a respectable vaudeville house, the first to give attention to "clean" entertainment.[20]

Pastor's Music Hall was a three-a-day theater. There were morning, afternoon, and evening shows, though he later changed it to the standard setup where the third show was the detested supper show. No matter the hour, the Music Hall always had a good audience. Though all vaudevillians of the time aimed at Pastor's, they hated having to go on when Bill Brody was at the piano. Though Pastor received protests about Brody's ineptness, he remained loyal to his poor pianist. Pastor "never fired anyone in his entire career," according to reports. He even tolerated the numerous song pluggers and allowed them to sit where they wished.[21]

The Union Square area where Pastor's Music Hall was located made quite a name for itself in show business history. Throughout that section of New York were beer halls, burlesque houses, penny arcades, restaurants, and other vaudeville theaters. The Union Square Theatre was there, a Keith house, which opened under the management of J. Austin Fynes in 1893. A later manager was Abe Jacobs, "a little fellow with a cap on the side of his head, a dingy sweater, a cigar in the corner of his mouth . . . and a voice like Uncle Tom calling the bloodhounds. He didn't talk, he barked." It was at the Union Square that an unusual turnabout occurred. Instead of the Keith chain claiming exclusive contract, a rival, Hurtig and Seamon, did the claiming. During the performance of Nat M. Wills, "the happy tramp," a man in the front row stood, shouted, threw what "looked like a legal document" at the actor, and "was promptly escorted to the door and steered in the direction of the cable cars." But a temporary injunction had been served which forbade Wills to appear on the Keith stage.[22]

Also in Union Square was the Academy of Music. Originally an opera house, "an enormous barn of a theater," it was awkwardly converted into a vaudeville hall. Nearby was the City Theatre, considered by the Keith office as competition to its own Jefferson Theatre,[23] located on the same street. At the City, many Keith performers changed their names and appeared on its stage. A Jefferson usher was given the duty to list the acts that played the City, and to turn it in at the main Keith office. Any act on the list was thus automatically blacklisted. Since the usher never went inside the City but just copied the names from the sign, the Keith offices kept a substantial record of nonexistent names on its blacklist. At the City, too, a young pianist named George Gershwin was given the supper show job. He replaced the usual orchestra and proceeded to miss cues and play the wrong music. When the bill's comedian used Gershwin's ineptness as a subject for laughs, the musician fled the theater in embarrassment.[24]

Yet, if there was one theater that vaudevillians hated, it was the Colonial. Originally a Percy Williams house, it became part of the Keith-Albee circuit. "The Colonial was murder," Benny Rubin testified. "There was a certain type of audience in there who came in and dared you–let's call 'em a wise guy audience. And it was known–and, believe me, this is true–that if you paid a certain guy, he would bring people in to laugh and applaud." Sometimes the "applause" was anything but, for the gallery was proud of its "Colonial clap," when they derided the performer by applauding in a "clap, clap, clap-clap-clap" unison. They also threw pennies whenever they disliked a performer. Easily the toughest gallery in town, it finally took concerted police effort to suppress the rowdyism.[25]

F. F. Proctor owned a group of important New York theaters which retained his name after the ever-absorbing Keith chain absorbed them. Though he was tough-minded, Proctor was the first manager to put table tennis in theaters, placing three tables in his Fifth Avenue Theatre, so that "lady patrons may while away the time between acts in pleasant diversion." Each Thanksgiving he brought together the staffs and performers of his four theaters, seated them onstage at his Fifty-Eighth Street Theatre and provided them "a bounteous feast." Proctor also resorted to giveaways to lure patrons to his theaters. When toys were presented at Saturday matinees, *Variety* commented, "Santa Claus, like most everybody else, appears to have gone into vaudeville."[26]

The Proctor houses served as "show houses." Bookers regularly attended the performances to see the many new acts that were deliberately put on. Ethel Waters remembered her joy when two Orpheum bookers caught her act at the Fifty-Eighth Street Theatre and signed her to an important contract. But even more important as a show house was the Fifth Avenue, named that despite its location at Broadway and Twenty-eighth. Split weeks were common there. The theater also served as the scene for amateur jazz-band contests during the twenties.[27]

A very interesting neighborhood theater, played by headliners, was the Paradise in the Bronx. Eddie Cantor recounted the time that he and George Jessel finished a run at the Palace, then went up to the Paradise:

> What a contrast in audiences! Only the best play the Palace, so this is a sophisticated audience; but playing the Paradise is like playing in a big kitchen, a strictly homey place where the audience doesn't merely applaud, they virtually clasp your hand. . . . Some of the women brought us homemade soup! . . . A woman would come backstage and say, "Mr. Cantor, do me a favor. My two children have been in the theater since twelve noon. They haven't eaten for six hours. Will you give 'em these sandwiches?" So I'd call their names and they'd come up on the stage and get their dinner.

During their stay at the Paradise, the overfriendly atmosphere backfired. While they were onstage, a man down front got their attention and asked if he could have Cantor's autograph. Cantor, not wishing to do anything to upset the sensational rapport that he and Jessel had developed with the audience, assented and beckoned the patron to join them, and gave him his autograph. Before Jessel had time to wonder why only Cantor had received the flattering request, the fellow walked over to Jessel and handed the perplexed comedian a subpoena.[28]

On Sixth Avenue, between Forty-third and Forty-fourth, stood the coliseum of vaude theaters, the famed Hippodrome. It was a monster, with 1,202 seats in the orchestra, 2,008 in the balcony, and an additional 1,468 in the gallery. Each dressing room bore the name of one of the states in the Union. Though acoustically poor, its stage was immense, a fact which allowed for spectacles rarely seen in the normal vaude theater. The great size of the stage also allowed for "an occasional smashing historical saga, like the version of the Russo-Japanese War that was better staged than the war on which it was founded." Perhaps it was the very majesty of "the Hipp," as it was called, that impressed a Brooklyn woman to write to Albee that she could see a show there "on the Sabbath and still feel . . . in direct communication with God."[29]

The Loew chain of eleven theaters was booked out of the American Music Hall building at Eighth Avenue and Forty-second Street. Despite its ugliness outside, it was a typical Loew's theater inside, fitted with an ornate ladies' room. According to one of his former aides, "beautiful ladies' rooms were a fetish with Loew. The first thing he did when he bought old theaters or built new ones . . . was to order the ladies' rooms sumptuously decorated. It was said at one time that many ladies paid the ten cents' admission fee to his theaters simply to use his ladies' rooms." The same observer then made the devastating comment, "But Loew's vaudeville offerings never matched his ladies' rooms."[30]

Loew specialized in finding chasers, one of his best being a man who used clay to mold the faces of famous people. His sculpting was poor, yet "he never had to worry about being laid off because he was the best chaser in vaudeville." The main Loew building until the construction of Loew's State, was the American Music Hall. It held two theaters, "a dilapidated room on the ground floor and an equally battered roof garden." One especially busy Labor Day, "the inept clay modeler spent his entire day going up and down in the elevator chasing out the customers after each show." The American Roof was an important tryout spot for new acts.[31]

Loew's State, which became the showhouse of the circuit, was often called simply "the State." The theater became one of the foremost in the city, despite its awkward inauguration. On opening day it was discovered that there were no dressing rooms in the building. For a time the actors changed in the New York

Theatre, across the street. Then Loew purchased the building at 160 West Forty-sixth Street, built dressing rooms, as well as offices, into it, and connected it with the backstage area of the State by means of a bridge.[32]

Another Loew theater was the Delancey Street, "a grind house" located on the Lower East Side. It played five vaude acts along with movies, three times a day. Typical of an audience in that part of the metropolis, it consisted "mostly of bovine-appearing women, screaming babies and yelling kids." Charles Bickford, later an outstanding Hollywood actor, recalled that no attempt was made "to quiet the kids who, during the fourteen minutes we were on, seemed to be playing football in the aisles." The comedy drew no laughs and they finished their turn to no applause. Since the Delancey Street freely cancelled acts, Bickford and his partner dreaded the worst. Instead they were congratulated and it was pointed out to them that most of the audience did not understand English.[33]

At the Greeley Theatre, a Loew house in the garment district, an unusual attempt was made in order to better the attendance for the opening day matinee. The theater manager invited the public to attend the morning rehearsal. These rehearsals were problem enough without an audience to see the mistakes and arguments that generally ensued. But the idea drew a crowd, however, and the actors had to abide by the manager's wishes or face cancellation.[34]

Uptown, at 107th and Lexington, stood the Star Theatre. When an act played the Star, they said they were trying their material out "on the dog." If the response was good from the tough audience there, it was confident of being a hit just about anywhere. Also uptown was the 81st Street Theatre, a compact neighborhood theater. Unlike the Star, its audiences were noted for their receptiveness. Once, though, the audience reaction was so harsh that *Variety* observed, "Never was a tougher audience than the one at the 81st Sunday night." The occasion was an appearance on the bill by Ted Lewis, so loved by the throngs that crowded the theater, they gave a rough time to the other acts. The trade weekly's summation was: "Everything comes under the head of Ted Lewis here this week–bill, business and value received. It has been shown before that Lewis can't be followed, that nothing but a final curtain can get him off the rostrum. It now looks as though Lewis hardly can be preceded."[35]

In the later years of vaude, the most noted of the downtown theaters was the Capitol. Joey Adams referred to it as the Palace of his headline days. At the time it was built (1919), its 5,300 seats made it the world's largest theater. Despite its cavernous size, vaudeville played there and Ken Murray claimed he developed a voice that can still boom powerfully because he worked the Capitol without microphones.[36]

Across the East River was Brooklyn, chief among its vaude locations the E. F. Albee Theatre. Praised often by the vaudevillians who played there were its dressing rooms, alleged to be "as luxurious as an exclusive hotel room." Like Brooklyn itself, the theater was known for "cool receptions." Rudy Vallee, while breaking records at the Albee, still advanced the opinion that, though his group was received courteously, the audience's "fervor was judiciously restrained. . . . Brooklyn (and I say this with great affection) is a country unto itself!"[37]

Brooklyn had its share of unusual theaters, too. There was the part of the Percy Williams' string called the Greenpoint, which had once been a church. Another was Fox's Folly. This was a theater run entirely by members of the Fox family, with people in the immediate neighborhood filling the few spots that the large Fox clan could not fill. Its orchestra leader, for example, was Ben Oakland. According to Tin Pan Alley expert and ex-vaudevillian, Wolfie Gilbert, the only reason Oakland held that post was that he lived near the theater. Fox insisted on one of the terrors of a vaudevillian's life, the supper show. Gilbert learned that even someone as bad as Ben Oakland could be viewed as a shining light. When he stepped out onto the stage for the hated supper show and its sparse, dull audience, his depression plummetted when he heard the music for his act. For the supper show a lone pianist took over for Oakland and his orchestra, and Gilbert bemoaned, "She was bloody awful." When the act concluded, the theater manager, Al Lefkowitz, a Fox son-in-law, inquired, "How did you like my daughter? She is the piano player. Isn't she swell?"[38] Gilbert, like countless others who were booked into Fox's Folly, had to grin and bear it.

Wolfie Gilbert also played a Brooklyn house belonging to the Loew chain, the Royal Theater. He described it as "a dingy spot."[39] The theater was not too fondly remembered by Harpo Marx, either. The Marx Brothers proved to be "a dismal flop" when they appeared there. According to Harpo,

> The audience was predominantly Jewish. They had come thinking we were a Jewish act. From the moment Groucho came on and made jokes in English instead of Yiddish, they sat on their hands. All of our relatives turned out to see us, too. When not one of them was mentioned once in our act they all got sore, and when we came out for bows they sat on their hands.[40]

Brooklyn had many more theaters, of course, such as the Gotham, Novelty, Crescent, Prospect, the topflight Orpheum, and the appropriately named Flatbush, and many vaudevillians spent weeks, and even months, circulating among them.

Sunday vaudeville shows were illegal in New York, a law which, even in 1900, was recognized as being "practically a dead letter." Theaters circumvented the law by renaming their vaude bills "concerts" and lowering the curtain between acts. Oscar Hammerstein went so far as to name his programs "sacred concerts." Vaudevillians, though losing a day's rest because of the loosely worded and enforced law, were glad for the extra day's employment and, more importantly, the exposure. Flo Ziegfeld was the biggest among many Broadway producers and bookers who regularly scouted the Sunday concerts. For many, too, they got the chance to appear, if only that one day, at higher class theaters.[41]

The managers, while abusing the intent of the Sunday law, often abused the vaudevillian, as well. Since the concerts were presented only in New York City, many an actor was hurt when ordered to fill in, despite his having just played a week well outside the city. This meant that the vaudevillian might have had to return to the city from some distant point at his own expense. If he refused, he was immediately placed on a blacklist. *Variety* protested management's highhandedness, while at the same time ridiculing the restrictions being placed on the Sunday concerts. They pointed out that New York City was "not a city of homes but of flats and boarding places, and there are few who are content to remain at home on Sunday evening." They feared that if the concerts were hit with strict law enforcement, "many young men who might pass a pleasant evening at some concert [would] be driven to saloons and pool parlors."[42]

Vaudevillians did not confine their efforts to theaters when in New York. At the turn of the century, an "in" thing in high society was to put on a vaudeville show at dinners and parties. The leading exponent of this practice was "Mrs. Stuyvesant Fish, who [was] one of the swellest of the swell." And when a labor union went on strike against a cigar factory in 1900, the two thousand strikers requested that performers belonging to the union entertain them at the hall where they congregated. In 1914 steamship companies offered special travel rates to vaudevillians if they entertained the ship's passengers.[43]

Broadway has been described in a multitude of ways. A visitor to the United States called it the "strangest of all streets" and added that if, as he had been told, "New York is a miniature world, [then] Broadway is a miniature New York." Another visitor remarked of Broadway, "What a glorious garden of wonders this would be, to any one who was lucky enough to be unable to read."[44]

To American performers, Broadway was "the end of the tanktown rainbow." Eddie Foy said of this most important of all show business thoroughfares, "It may be only a street to most people, but to some of us it's a religion." Gene Fowler has colorfully portrayed it as "a Babylonian mirage at night, with hanging gardens of electrical bombast," while Allen Churchill called it "The Street of the Midnight Sun." Regardless of the description, Broadway was the center of New York, and as George M. Cohan said, "When you leave New York, you're just camping out."[45]

The road to Broadway was one that required all the help an entertainer could muster. A common aid was a claque, a hard core group that would applaud, laugh, even scream uproarious approval, if necessary, to make a performer look sensational. (The practice was not limited to vaudeville, for one of the best known claques held forth at the Metropolitan Opera House.) Samuel Marx, the father of the Marx brothers, was invaluable to the act because of his ability to "organize a larger claque for a smaller sum than any other claquer in the business." Though most claques were paid, a few artists managed to recruit enthusiastic receptions without paying a cent. Belle Baker was one. She would inform a small army of music publishers and song writers that she was going to sing their songs at her next performance. This always guaranteed her a generous audience, each music man applauding loudly, wanting her to be a great success, while at the same time wondering when she was going to get to his song. Most went away disappointed.[46]

Aside from talent the greatest help to a vaudevillian was an active agent. Agents were rough and tough competitors, sparing little in their efforts to get the best bookings and top dollar for their clients. The livelihood of the agent depended on the routes he gained for the acts he represented. When a vaudevillian felt he could have a better itinerary, he changed agents, so agents were constantly in motion. Their "offices" often were their hats, for the nature of the agent's business made the inner bands of their hats ideal for tucking away memorandums.[47] Like everything else in vaudeville, the best agents were in New York.

The place to be, then, was New York City, and any performer who had any real aspirations for himself sooner or later made his way there. This meant the obvious–where did one live?

The worst life was that where, from one day to the next, the player did not know where he would sleep. Al and Harry Jolson went through a period like that, when living "seemed to be a continual round of borrowing and lending, of desperately trying to raise money for board bills and a place to sleep." They even went out "busking," which meant they went from restaurant to restaurant, asking if they could sing songs for the patrons. It was like high-class begging and was considered "the last step downward for a would-be actor." Many restaurants barred their doors to buskers. Yet, a hard evening usually drew enough tips to cover the price of a bed and some food till the next day.[48]

The better the tips, the better that night's fare, but often actors in dire need put up at places for men only, "where cells cost only ten cents a night." These establishments were depicted as "something between a public toilet and . . . a jail," and the rules forbade the taking of anything to bed except what one was wearing. Any baggage was checked in a locker in the lobby. Seven o'clock was the waking hour for everyone, for the sheets were yanked from the beds then, and at eight o'clock, the water in the washrooms was turned off.[49]

The next step up were the boardinghouses, some cheap, some good, some excellent. Highly praised was Mrs. Charles' on East

Fourteenth Street, though most of the noteworthy ones were closer to the Times Square area. On West Thirty-eighth Street there were several good places; the Keaton family's favorite boardinghouse was the Ehric House. It was managed by a German family which provided good food, large and comfortable rooms that catered to an actor's needs, ample storage space, and a friendly atmosphere.[50]

One of the best detailed descriptions was Fred Allen's recollections of Mrs. Montfort's, at 104 West Fortieth Street. New owners had retained the well-known Montfort name but had unfortunately discontinued the meals. Fred Allen's first impression of the place was that it "smacked of the crab." Soiled windows faced the street, the hallways were long and dark, so much so that when Allen walked down the one on his floor, he said he felt he "was walking down a giraffe's throat." No telephones were in any of the rooms, but they were not to be expected, since the rooms cost only four dollars a week. When the light was turned on and he saw his room for the first time, "the darkness brightened a shade into gloom." The room had no window. "The single bed looked like a frozen hammock." A battered wardrobe replaced a missing closet. Typical of many roominghouses, the bathroom was down the hall. The clientele was entirely smalltime actors and those with children used nearby Bryant Park as a playground. Food was not allowed inside the Montfort, but vaudevillians knew all the techniques and the rule was easily bypassed. Typical of many such places, many acts rehearsed in their rooms. Allen recalled, among others, the Texas Tommy Dancers. When they "ran through their violent dancing routines, chandeliers swung like tassels, and when the plaster stopped falling, it was impossible to tell the floor from the ceiling."[51]

Leo Carrillo once rented a small room in an old stone house on Forty-third Street. Equipped with one "luxury," a tiny gas jet stove, he paid only six dollars a month. On the same street, Joe E. Brown and Emmett Callahan paid three times as much at the Yandis Court. However, they had a completely furnished apartment, equipped with linens. Every piece of linen was marked, "Stolen from Yandis Court." Charlie Chaplin and Stan Laurel got accommodations just off Forty-third Street, in a "dismal and dirty" brownstone house. The basement of the building was occupied by a cleaning and pressing business, and the "fetid odor of clothes being pressed and steamed wafted up" through their entire stay there. No cooking was allowed but Laurel used a gas ring, anyway.[52]

On West Forty-fourth Street was Mrs. Martin's Theatrical Boardinghouse, one of several situated in a neighborhood that "had the feeling of small town." Mrs. Martin was noted for her kindness and had a good reputation among vaudevillians. On Forty-eighth Street was Mrs. Lowery's, owned by a legless man the actors called "the Seal," because he literally bounced around the house on his stumps. The inner rooms had no windows, so that the boarders living in those rooms never knew what kind of weather awaited them outside. Before dressing, therefore, these actors dashed down the hall, hollered down to the lobby, and got a quick weather report shouted back. The home-cooked meals were good and Mrs. Lowery's had an active business.[53]

From the boardinghouse, the vaudevillian graduated to hotels. Benny Rubin related, "We lived for that day." In the Union Square area where vaudeville had its first prominence, were "two dilapidated hotels, the Trafalgar and the Academy." They were frequented not only by show people, but by "ladies of questionable profession, the men who lived off them, and some other phonies." Both hotels had huge front porches, "perfect spots for actors to show off." The Trafalgar and Academy were popular stopping places for vaudevillians.[54]

On the way toward Times Square, a one-time "high class theatrical hotel" was the Seville, located at East Twenty-eighth Street. Farther up was the Jefferson, a 60-room theatrical hotel at Broadway and Thirty-eighth. Among those who stopped at the Jefferson were Jack Pearl, Ed Wynn, and Bert Lahr, although Lahr much preferred the Forrest eleven blocks farther north on Broadway, a favorite hangout for bigtime acts. On West Forty-ninth Street, too, was the Markwell, which became a haven for down-and-out performers during the depression in the thirties. A "well-known hotel for the vaudeville performer" was the Mansfield Hall, at Fiftieth, just off Broadway.[55]

Just a few blocks away, on Forty-seventh Street, between Sixth and Seventh Avenues, eight theatrical hotels did business. Next to the famed Palace was the Somerset Hotel which, according to Fred Allen, catered to "high-class clientele," including many acts featured at the Palace and other bigtime houses in the vicinity. Yet, Leo Carrillo wrote that he and Will Rogers got a double room there for fifty cents apiece. Carrillo had heard the Somerset was "cheap." The Stanley was another hotel in that cluster. The Stanley, declared Fred Allen, "solicited the actor's patronage. Some of the Stanley's lady guests weren't so particular." Allen wrote a letter to his agent which mentioned the Stanley as the hotel where the "lost monkey" of Ted Healey had a room. The monkey yelled "like Hell" every morning, "but the guests all owe so much back rent that no one can complain to the management."[56]

Ted Healey, a vaude comedian, once owed a bill at the Lincoln Hotel that was so large he knew he could not meet it. Healey used three men as stooges in his act. At the Lincoln they served as his stooges, too. Each put on "two or three sets of his underwear, two complete suits of clothes, and an overcoat. Healey followed the stooges out of the Lincoln lobby wearing three suits and one topcoat, and carrying a raincoat with every pocket bulging."[57] Healey was undoubtedly not the only one who left an empty trunk in lieu of an unpaid hotel bill, for *Variety* reported at the beginning of 1929:

> Hotels in the Times Square district are bearing down on the actor, especially the newer hostelries operated on the chain system. These hotels are making the actor "lay it on the line" with a week's board in advance before accepting him. . . .
>
> Vaudevillians coming into New York without any immediate work in sight are the hardest hit by these stringent regulations. They are bluntly informed their trade is not wanted, no matter how much baggage they check in with.[58]

So, as late as 1929, there were still significant elements in American society which viewed the vaudevillian as unsavory.

Though in the Times Square area, one hotel that definitely could not have even considered participation in such an anti-actor scheme would have been the Bartholdi Inn. This was a large and "screwy theatrical hotel" which extended credit freely. Located at Broadway and Forty-fifth, the "Bartholdi was a rendezvous for actors and chorus girls out of work, and another kind of lady who was never out of work." The proprietess was known affectionately as Mama Bartholdi, a huge woman "with a heart to match her size." Joe Laurie, Jr., called Bartholdi's "the greatest of all theatrical hotels in America!"[59]

Well out of the Times Square area, near Central Park and the famous Carnegie Hall, were a series of hotels on Fifty-seventh Street. Fred Astaire liked the area of the Calumet Hotel, where he lived. It was located between Eighth and Ninth Avenues and Astaire stated, "It was a wide street, pleasant and residential when we were there." Just two blocks away stood the St. Hubert and Great Northern, hotels not strange to show folk. The Great Northern was especially popular with musicians, though it was a musician who said of it, "Unfortunately it's more northern than great."[60]

Every hotel had to abide by the Raines Act, which required guests to have some form of baggage or luggage. For the romantic vaudevillian, if he found a girl who was willing, the immediate problem was to locate a place to go. If the decision was to go to a hotel, "an old valise, with perhaps a few telephone books inside," allowed the couple to circumvent the Raines Act. Then came the hotel register, filled with "Mr. and Mrs. John Smiths." However, a small group of Harry Von Tilzer's friends always registered in his name, which caused a bit of difficulty on at least one occasion. Wolfie Gilbert related, "I boldly walked up to the hotel desk with my lady of amour and registered under this non de plume. The clerk glanced at the register, and said, 'Nothing doin', Mr. and Mrs. Von Tilzer are already upstairs.' "[61]

Though the possibilities seemed infinite, in New York City deciding where to eat was made on the basis of one's purse. Occasionally the vaudevillian was lucky enough to get a meal in a private home. Nick Lucas related that, when he sang Italian songs in areas heavily populated with Italian-Americans, the audience would not only "go wild," but once the show was over, "there would always be a crowd of Italian fans waiting to invite me to their homes for spaghetti." Lou Holtz remembered being an after-show dinner guest at several private homes. My father mentioned that "Many times people that seen us perform would invite us to their home."[62] Such invitations were unusual, however, and vaudevillians had to ever be on the alert to find hospitable eateries.

In the Union Square area was a restaurant run by a man

named Tysner. He went broke because he took too many IOU's from unemployed actors. In that area many landladies and restaurant owners were generous with the vaudevillians.[63] As the vaudevillian worked his way uptown, people were less trusting, the attitude though never entirely heartless.

Many vaudevillians enjoyed going to Brown's Chop House on Thirty-fifth Street between Fifth and Sixth Avenues. Located near the Harrigan and Hart Theatre, the restaurant was especially noted for its mutton chops and cream ale. At Thirty-ninth and Broadway was the Kaiserhof, a German restaurant considered to be the Sardi's of its time. Only the most successful players ate there. Three blocks up on Broadway was the bar of the Knickerbocker Hotel. Guthrie McClintic called it "the miracle of miracles" when he found the place, a haven for the down-and-out actor. Tipping was discouraged, beer cost only a dime, and with the purchase of a beer came a free lunch, selected from "a mouth-watering buffet luncheon—sardines, pumpernickel, cottage cheese, ripe olives," a lunch that was both delicious and ample, according to McClintic, who returned many times to the Knickerbocker when his grouch bag held little.[64]

In the same vicinity, Fred Allen went to the Olive Lunch on Sixth Avenue, where for ten cents one could have a large bowl of pea soup and three thick slices of bread with butter. He also ate at a self-service restaurant located next to the Union Dime Bank. There, for fifteen cents, a patron could enjoy liver and onions, rolls, butter, and coffee. For Allen and many others, there was always Mr. Dickinson's saloon on Sixth Avenue. Because so many vaudevillians frequented his place, Dickinson was always ready to extend credit. Allen remarked that "Mr. Dickinson never wanted any vaudeville actor to go hungry."[65]

Then there were always the automats. Across from the Fitzgerald Building on Forty-second Street, which was the hub for smalltime booking agents and chain managers, was one. Here the young aspirants congregated, ready to use chewing gum and other ploys to outwit the Automat system. By Bert Lahr's report, the Automat represented an unlimited source of food to the younger set. The Automat was also a source of typical vaudeville conversation, where each unemployed artist tried to top his neighbor. Vaudevillians boasted about the jobs they had refused just that day, giving all sorts of standard excuses. One vaude artist observed, "But the jobs which seemed so plentiful at midnight seemed to melt away with the morning sun," and the rounds of the offices that followed would ring with "Nothing today–nothing today."[66]

In a poem George Jessel paid tribute to James "Dinty" Moore's small saloon (next to the Gaiety Theatre) that expanded into a thriving stop for show people. And there was Lindy's, of course, an especially popular spot in later vaude days, when comedians would often gather together to hold court. Mother Gerson's Fudge Shop was also very popular. On West Forty-seventh, there was Shulem's, a favorite hangout of Max Gordon's. For many, the Friars was a common meeting place. Wolpin's, next to the Palace, was well populated with vaudevillians. In later years, the St. Regis was where actors swapped shop talk. And up in Harlem, on Seventh Avenue, between 123rd and 124th Streets, was Mrs. Frazier's Dining Room, where the cooking was better than "anywhere else in this whole world," judged Ethel Waters. Another restaurant she frequented was Welles'.[67]

To be sure, there were many more eateries and hangouts which vaudevillians visited regularly, (just as there were many more hotels, boardinghouses, and theaters that could have been discussed) but those cited provide an idea of the environment a vaudevillian had when he played the big city.[68] To play New York City, however, the vaudevillian would have done anything. In vaudeville parlance, New York City was "next-to-closing."

ın DiMeglio, ex-vaudeville magician billed as "Prof. John Ieglio," holding grandson, author John DeMeglio.

My father, Richard, at age of nine.

ıelia DeMeglio, my aunt, and Richard DiMeglio, my father. ›ther-sister song and dance act sometimes billed as "Miss ıelia and Brother Richard Montecristo."

Amelia and Richard DiMeglio.

Mitzi Goldwyn, Banjoist

WESELEY
VASSE
NAVY
PRINCETON
SMITH
Mitzi Goldwyn
ALEX and VIC HYDE
PRESENT
COLLEGIANA
Progress N.Y.

Jack Benny visits with Ted Lewis.
San Francisco Fair—1939

Benny Goodman visits Ted Lewis.
San Francisco Fair—1939

Ted was a great Ice Skater.
Central Park—Nov. 24, 1957.

Tony Martin, Josie O'Donnel, Ted Lewis
Latin Quarter, N.Y., October 17, 1965.

Ted Lewis. The Jazz King on Skates.

Estelle Major Hazel Blue

Albee Sisters (from left to right) Harriet, Ferne, Loraine, Aileene

The Fanton Trio.

The Fanton Trio.

Milton Berle, Joe E. Lewis, Sophie Tucker, Ted Lewis—all ex-vaudevillians.
Sunday Dec. 22, 1957. Friars Club. Party to Joe E. Lewis.

FRANK SENNES
PRESENTS

Mr. & Mrs. Show Business

★ Sophie ★ Ted

TUCKER • LEWIS

with TED SHAPIRO and COMPANY

Plus

FABULOUS PRODUCTIONS – BEAUTIFUL GIRLS

Opening! August 4th 1959
LIMITED ENGAGEMENT

Together For The First Time!
Make Your Reservation Now!

Call HOllywood 9-6333

FRANK SENNES' MOULIN ROUGE 6230 Sunset Blvd., Hollywood, California

World's Fair, San Francisco, California, 1939. Ted in center of stage.

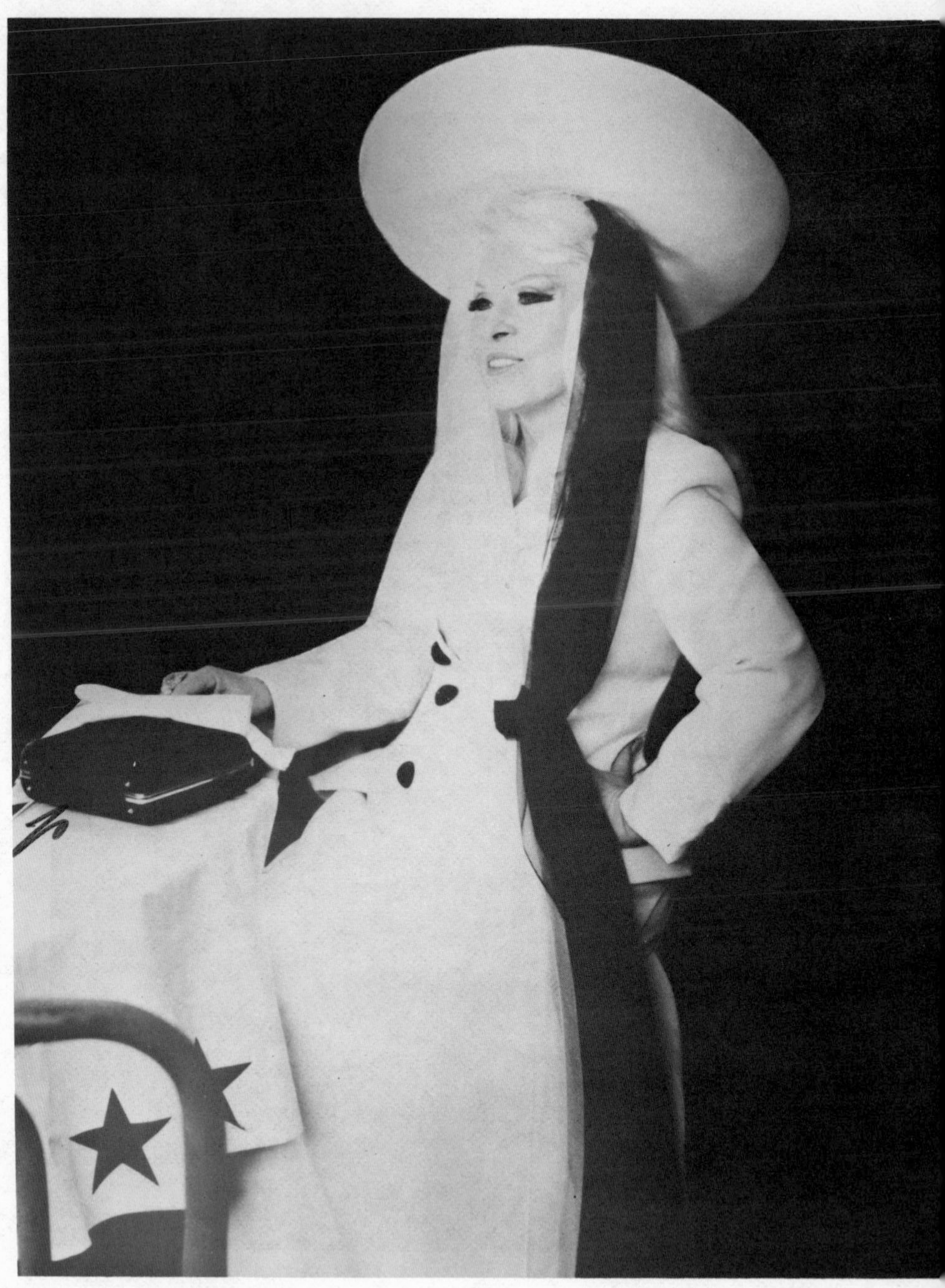

Mae West, star of "Myra Breckinridge"; taken on the set.

Nick Lucas

Joan Blondell

EAST COAST, WEST COAST, EVEN AL CAPONE

◆ ◆ ◆ ◆ ◆

SECOND ONLY TO NEW YORK IN IMPORTANCE WAS CHICAGO. THIS WAS DUE not so much to its huge population, but rather to the fact that major circuits, plus numerous small ones, booked their talent there. There were such booking agencies as the Bert Levy circuit, Gus Sun Booking Exchange Company, Webster Vaudeville circuits, Lester Bryant Booking Exchange, and others. The largest group was the Western Vaudeville Managers Association. It had agreements with the B. F. Keith and Orpheum chains and formed "a combination whose strength might easily be compared with that of the famous Rock of Gibraltar." They booked smalltime houses in eight midwestern states and split their week three ways: Monday through Wednesday in the first split, Thursday through Saturday for the second, and Sunday for the third. Fred Allen observed, "The Bible tells us that on the seventh day God rested, but the Bible had never been the Book-of-the-Month with the Western Vaudeville managers."[1]

The scattering of the theaters in that and other circuits required the use of different railroads. In Robert Conkey's informative pamphlet, a host of railroad fares were listed, specifically to benefit the vaude artist. A sampling of arrivals and departures indicates the breadth of a vaudevillian's travel: Bad Axe and

Dowagiac, Michigan; Baraboo, Wisconsin; Brazil, Mishawaka, and Warsaw, Indiana; Farmer City and Mattoon, Illinois; Oskaloosa, Iowa, and Yankton, South Dakota. Railroads that had to be used included the New York Central, Chicago and Alton, Santa Fe, Chicago and Burlington, and Union Pacific. According to Fred Allen, there never seemed to be a way of getting from one town to another on the W.V.M.A. (Western Vaudeville Managers Association) network without a train change or two during the night, accompanied by "endless hours at abandoned junctions waiting for connecting trains."[2]

Chicago itself had enough theaters, especially when its suburbs were added, to keep a vaudevillian acting for two seasons. Neighborhood theaters, as in New York, freely dotted the map. But of all the theaters the city had, the good and the bad, none gained more notoriety than the Iroquois, a theater that advertised itself as "Absolutely Fireproof," and which had done business for little more than a month when it was engulfed in flames that resulted in nearly six hundred deaths. The day after the tragedy, the Chicago *Tribune* condemned the city for its shortcomings and criminal neglect that led to the fire, under a banner headline which proclaimed, "God Damn the City of Chicago!" Eddie Foy, the headline clown who played such a dramatic part in the tragedy, described the Iroquois as one of the finest theaters he had ever seen, "a palace of marble and plate glass, plush and mahogany and gilding," which backstage was "far and away the most commodious" of any place he had played.[3]

The theater had opened on November 23, 1903, and was destroyed on December 30, five weeks later. On the day of the tragedy, the house was overflowing because of a bargain price matinee and a show, headlined by Foy, that had done excellent business before that. In a theater designed for 1,600, Foy and others believed over 2,000 were present when the fire started. Foy was in his dressing room when the blaze broke out, one which two stagehands at first tried to extinguish. No alarm box was near the theater, which added significantly to the delay in firemen getting to the scene. Foy's oldest boy, six-year-old Bryan, had accompanied him to the theater and was backstage. After Foy made sure Bryan was safe, he ran onto the stage, right through the eight trembling girls who were still bravely doing their act, even though the scenery above them was afire. The gallery audience was in panic but it was still relatively calm on the ground floor. Foy shouted to the crowd to take it easy, that there was no danger. But when the asbestos curtain went up in flames, its roar added to that of the clamoring theater mob. Foy painfully wrote, "In the upper tiers they were in a mad, animal-like stampede–their screams, groans and snarls, [the] bodies grinding against bodies merging into a crescendo half-wail, half-roar, the most dreadful sound that ever assailed human ears."[4]

A macabre sense of humor evidenced itself a few years after the Iroquois tragedy. Dressing rooms throughout the country bore signs that blared, "No smoking–Remember the Iroquois Fire." Below one of the signs, someone printed what, though witty, was nevertheless gruesome: "Don't spit–Remember the Johnstown Flood."[5]

Had there been no Iroquois fire, the most famous theater in Chicago's vaude history would have been the Majestic, with the Palace a close second. Jack Benny called the Majestic "the most beautiful, perhaps the most dignified theater in the world." The Majestic was definitely bigtime. An interesting description of it was Elbert Hubbard's, to the effect that it was run like a battleship and had the discipline of the German Army. He observed that there were no loafers anywhere, onstage or off. To him, the Majestic combined "order, system, regularity, cleanliness and effectiveness in rare degree."[6]

The Palace was bigtime, too, a very important date to any vaudevillian who played Chicago. Fred Astaire, as a typical vaude artist, detested the opening position on the bill, but when he and his sister, Adele, were assigned that spot at the Palace, it was all right. For one, it was a great house, and two, the Palace showed a newsreel before the opening act, so that the audience would be seated by the time the bill started. He also praised their orchestra and singled out the conductor as an "extra-fine musician" who gave them confidence from the start. The stage manager, too, received Astaire's plaudits as a result of his allowing the dancer to put some rosin down. Adele and Fred Astaire "stopped the show" and were moved to number three, so that they came directly before the hit team of Cantor and Lee. Astaire would never forget the Chicago Palace, for it gave Astaire and his sister "the first real feeling that [they] were finally catching on."[7]

Sophie Tucker fondly recalled the American Music Hall, located at Peck Court and Wabash Avenue. She compared it favorably to Hammerstein's in New York, "a long, narrow theater, very intimate, and a very warm house." When an act proved to be a hit at the American Music Hall, it was automatically booked into the suburban houses like the President, Kedzie, Wilson, Willard, and Circle. A hit at the Music Hall meant eight to ten weeks of employment at excellent theaters. Sophie felt that Chicago audiences were easy as pie, a friendly, wonderful gang. She said of them, "If they like you they let you know it, and no halfway about it, either."[8]

The Wilson Avenue Theatre, under Albee management, paid the same scale as the Chicago Palace and was one of the best showcases in the city. A good showing at the Wilson could net a long route on the Orpheum circuit. The Kedzie was the first bigtime theater that Ethel Waters ever played. From forty dollars for three days, which she was getting in the Black theaters, she jumped to $350 a week. Nobody stomped or screamed or jumped up and down, as in the circuit she had left, but she got generous applause and the manager was elated.[9]

The Chicago Opera House was "an awfully big place [that] had what they called 'nigger heaven.' " The audiences there were good and acts enjoyed playing there, despite the "scrubby looking" dressing rooms. One reason why many top acts liked a booking at the Opera House was that it afforded them a chance to make a second salary. The alleyway behind the Opera House also served as the alleyway for the Sam T. Jack Theatre, a burlesque house. The Jack would book the headliners playing at the Opera House, who would do their act for the vaude audience at more expensive vaude prices, then throw a coat over their costumes and dash to the Jack to do the same act for the burlesque audience at cheaper burlesque prices. The only difference in the act was that it changed its name and may have thrown in some blue material.[10]

Leo Carrillo, for several reasons, never forgot the Haymarket Theatre. It marked not only his first Chicago booking, but his first visit to the Windy City, as well. Calamity was involved in both. Carrillo, then only in the beginning of his illustrious show business career, was warned by his father, before the performer left California, that Chicago would have snow and cold winds. Then Carrillo paid the "immense sum" of forty dollars for his chair car ticket and boarded the train for cold and bleak Chicago. The trip was a typical one, big cinders coming through the unscreened windows, hard and uncomfortable seats, and the huge sack of food that so many travelers took with them on long hauls. For Carrillo, that meant a large supply of tortillas, fried chicken, chilis, oranges, and cookies. The sack lasted him until the Illinois line where, at a station restaurant, he "splurged a quarter and enjoyed a hot meal consisting of two kinds of meat, mashed potatoes, cornbread, gravy, beans, corn, squash, three kinds of pie and white and chocolate cake."[11]

Finished with his meal, he "staggered" to the rest room and, though the weather was hot, he trusted to his father's words about Chicago and changed to long red underwear. Indian summer greeted him in the huge metropolis. Carrillo stated, "Hounds lay panting in any spot of shade they could find. As for me, I felt as if I were in a Turkish bath." He walked to the Haymarket Theatre and was shown to a dirty room backstage that was to be his dressing room. He shared the area with a monkey act and a burro. He sorted out his equipment, familiarized himself with the theater, and left to find a place to stay. The weather had abruptly changed and it was snowing. "My wet underwear began to congeal. I thought I was going to freeze into a sort of walking icicle," he recalled.[12]

The snow was part of a blizzard which provoked the theater manager, who complained it would kill his business that night. The manager then remembered there was a Sioux Indian convention in town and, after a hurried call to the theater owner, an official invitation was given to the Indians to attend the show. When Carrillo came onstage before the full theater of Indians, he discovered quickly he was to get no laughs from them. He said, "I might just as well have been preaching a funeral oration for Sitting Bull." But, from a box where four regular patrons sat, there came some applause. Carrillo directed his act to them and got more applause and a shout of "Bravo!" The shout acted as a signal to the Indians. One began to dance in the aisle, another waved a tomahawk, war whoops resounded through the audience, then more were dancing, till finally one swung from a cut-glass chandelier. It developed that the cry of "Bravo!" had been yelled by James J. Corbett, former heavyweight boxing champion of the world, a great vaudeville fan and vaudeville performer himself. The reaction of the Indians and the praise of Corbett brought Carrillo instant recognition and he was booked for six weeks in New York's bigtime.[13]

Among the other theaters in Chicago were Shindler's and the Great Northern Hippodrome. Vaudevillians hated the manager at Shindler's because he walked down the aisle when he canceled an act and yelled, "You are shut!" The Hippodrome was a "shift" house, which meant it used two separate units of shows on shifts of four performances each, daily. For the first three days of the week, one group worked from ten to five, then the other worked from five till midnight. The groups then exchanged time slots for the last three days of the week. Top salaries were paid, however, and bigtime acts played there.[14]

In the Chicago theaters, too, vaudevillians and other show folk learned that Al Capone liked entertainment. Capone often attended performances and was always good for sixteen tickets, two for himself and the rest for bodyguards located at strategic points. Entertainers were often called upon to appear in Capone's own nightclubs and some became very friendly with the gangster crowd.[15]

Chicago was also the site of a classic example of the philosophy of "the show must go on." Al Jolson and Eddie Cantor were headlining at rival theaters and both were extremely sick. Neither knew of the other's illness and both dragged themselves onstage time and again, despite excruciating pain. Finally, Cantor was so weak he had to cancel. Immediately after Jolson heard the news, he cancelled, too.[16]

Chicago's theaters had also gone through a "frenzied purge" in 1910, when "impure" songs were banned from their stages. Songs that were censored included "Without a Wedding Ring," "Her Name was Mary Wood but Mary Wouldn't," and "I Love My Wife, but Oh, You Kid." Sophie Tucker was stopped by Chicago police from singing "Angle Worm Wiggle" and took the censorship matter to court. The judge decided in favor of the police.[17]

Chicago itself? For Benny Rubin, it meant "the best meat in the world, bar no place at all." Charlie Chaplin spoke of its frontier spirit and its grimy industrial atmosphere, which made it "attractive in its ugliness." He also had the impression the city was full of burlesque shows and their "smutty harem comedies." Chaplin noted, too, the House of All Nations, highlight of the city's red-light district. Two middle-aged spinsters ran the establishment, which was "notorious for having women of every nationality." Rooms were decorated in the style of various countries, even to an Arabian tent motif. Chaplin claimed it was the most elaborate and expensive house of its kind in the world.[18]

Chicago also had a Board of Health which took an interest in the city's continuous performance vaudeville theaters at the start of the century. The Board wanted the theaters closed at least two hours during the day in order to replace the "condensed atmosphere," that usually developed in those theaters, with fresh air. A trade paper sarcastically commented that the theater managers were "at their wits' end, trying to find out where they are to obtain the fresh air. This commodity," the journal claimed, "was unknown in the 'Windy City.' " A Chicago citizens' group also made an effort at using the vaudeville stage to bring about improved civic intelligence and social betterment. The Calumet Juvenile Protective League, an organization in South Chicago, worked out an agreement with a 1,000 seat vaudeville theater which gave them a place on the bill. Their contribution was a series of lectures, which started with a stereopticon talk on the history of steel, as presented by Professor Paul Goode, of the University of Chicago. The first audience to see it was the matinee crowd, made up almost entirely of steelworkers assigned to the night shift.[19]

When in Chicago, vaudevillians on the smalltime generally stayed at the Hotel Grant, the Revere House, or the Saratoga. The manager of the Grant, Leonard Hicks, was very popular among vaudevillians. The hotel's small lobby and basement bar served as a rendezvous for both after-show gatherings and girl-hunting. The elevated ran by the Grant, shaking the beds and making for a disquieting night. The Revere was described as "a superannuated hotel whose guest list contained the names of characters ranging from the nefarious to the negligible." Fred Allen claimed there had been a rumor that so much opium was smoked at the Revere that a new arrival would fall asleep while crossing the lobby. The Saratoga was so rundown that no headliner would stay there.[20]

Offering a turkish bath was the Palace Hotel, owned by H. B. Humphrey. It advertised rates of $3.50 per week, seven dollars with private bath. Charlie Chaplin lived in a small hotel uptown on Wabash Avenue, next to the elevated. As the trains flashed by at night, he recalled that they caused flickering on his bedroom wall "like an old-fashioned bioscope." Though the hotel was "grim and seedy," the fact that it was heavily populated with burlesque girls made it a hotel he "loved." Chaplin related, "In each town we always made a beeline for the hotel where the showgirls stayed, with a libidinous hope that never materialized."[21]

One fascinating boardinghouse in Chicago was a home known as Mrs. Keller's. It was a haven not only for vaude artists, but for many "freak" museum acts. At a typical meal the vaudevillian would have George, "the turtle boy," on one side of him, Eli Bowen, "the legless wonder," on the other, and scattered around such acts as the fat lady, the bearded lady, and the glass eater.[22]

As much as the great majority of show people loved Chicago, San Francisco was probably the favorite city of all. It was described as an actor's paradise, where people could never get enough entertainment. Leo Carrillo's first impression was that "everything seemed cloaked in magic. I was looking for the blue beyond the blue and the hill beyond the hill." Carrillo's impressions after that dealt a great deal with a Swedish restaurant across the street from the California Theatre. For twenty cents he got a breaded veal cutlet with all the trimmings, including coffee, and because the meal was such a bargain, he ordered the same thing day after day. He summarized, "I have never been able to look a veal cutlet in the face since."[23]

Fred Allen declared that San Francisco was a revelation to him. His impression was that every city west of Chicago was really just another Hackensack, but San Francisco changed his mind. The city appeared to him to be a "New York with a hill in the middle of it." Joe Laurie, Jr., called it "the New York City of the West." He emphasized that the city loved actors and actors loved the city. James Weldon Johnson was "delighted" with the city. He signalled the fact that it was a "freer city than New York" with respect to the Black, and said, "I encountered no bar against me in hotels, restaurants, theaters, or other places of public accommodation and entertainment."[24]

Sophie Tucker pronounced San Francisco to be "a great town" and stated that, just as the average American living west of Yonkers wanted to visit New York, the New Yorker wanted to visit San Francisco. When he did, he returned "feeling that he has been to Paris, Rome, Honolulu and Hong Kong, all at the same time." She remembered her own first trip there, when they hired a guide because they had been told it would be unsafe to go to the Barbary Coast without one. She mentioned a club located there, called the Cave, which San Franciscans claimed was the toughest place in the world. And in a city filled with "wonderful eating places," a particularly attractive eatery to her was Coffee Dan's, located across from the Orpheum Theatre.[25]

The gateway to the Orient, a city of good food and cheap prices, was how Charlie Chaplin saw it. His first time there was in 1910 and he stressed that the natives referred to the fire, and not the earthquake, of 1906. Though he noticed a few cracks in the streets, he praised the brightness and newness of the city that had so remarkably recovered from disaster. The spirit of San Francisco, to Chaplin, was one of optimism and enterprise. Al Jolson had been booked into San Francisco very soon after the April 18th tragedy. The downtown section, especially the Market Street area, was still a shambles, although reconstruction was proceeding full force and theaters were springing up almost overnight. Though these theaters were temporary and make-shift, they were always filled to capacity.[26]

Vaudeville became a heavy favorite in San Francisco during the first decade of the twentieth century. When it was housed principally in the Orpheum and the Chutes, a theater in an amusement park, vaude got about 10 percent of the city's audiences. By 1909, however, the medium was commanding approximately 50 percent. By then there were four chief theaters, the Orpheum, Empire, Wigwam, and National. The Orpheum was a new building, erected on the site of the old Orpheum, which had been destroyed during the great quake. When the new theater opened, just three years after the disaster, the longest box-office line in the city's history was seen.[27]

The new Orpheum left out a few things the old theater had. There were no shelves on the backs of the seats, and no waiters serving beer. The old theater had really been a "high-class honky-tonk," but the new Orpheum was simply high-class. The new Orpheum also had strict censorship and not even "cockroach" could be uttered on its stage. And the theater had the typical stage door tender, in the Orpheum's case, "Old George." All vaudevillians knew that "Old George" would let them know that, without him, the theater would be a sure failure.[28]

Leo Carrillo broke into vaudeville at the Orpheum, so much a novice that Pat Rooney and his wife had to put on his makeup. When Carrillo saw rouge on his face for the first time, he felt uncomfortable. He debuted at a special Sunday matinee, the audience composed of "gamblers, bartenders, stockbrokers, newspaper people, and livery stable owners; all the people who made up old San Francisco." There were also several vaudevillians from the theater across the street. And, just before his act, the "supreme tribute" was paid him. Doty Valencia, "the most fashionable madam in all of San Francisco," walked in with all her girls and took the entire second row. "I plunged into my act with new inspiration," recounted Carrillo. His debut was so successful that he was moved from the number two spot on the bill to next-to-closing. During the three weeks he played at the Orpheum, Carrillo not only gained confidence and experience, but also discovered what so many other entertainers have found. He explained, "The feeling that I was lifting people out of their humdrum existences for a few minutes and giving them a laugh was the greatest thrill I ever had."[29]

Dave Grauman owned the Unique Theatre, a house that was L-shaped. Early arrivals sat in the part of the L that faced the stage. Latecomers waited in the part of the L that faced a blank wall. The theater did a good business, often so good that Grauman would pare the length of the show. In this way, audience turnover would be better. However, the hurry-up system could not be used unless the acts were readily available. Grauman made sure they were. Whereas in other theaters a vaudevillian could leave the theater to get something to eat, at the Unique, he was fed. Grauman at first served sandwiches in the wings, but subsequently hit upon a better scheme. Joe E. Brown described the new practice as Grauman's "taking a lesson from the zoo." A new act was added, one which featured every performer on the bill. A huge table was placed center stage, loaded with food, and when the curtain was raised, the audience was treated to the sight of actors having their meal. While the vaudevillians ate voraciously, Grauman commented to the audience about the table manners onstage and got in all the necessary advertisements. The meals never cost Grauman a penny. The meats were from Samson's Market, the vegetables from Wong Song's Vegetable Market, the pies and bread from Schultz's Bakery, and the preparation and catering by the Market Street Cafe. All got repeated plugs from Grauman. The meal thus not only added a terrific attraction to the Unique, but enabled Grauman to put on an extra show. As for the onstage eating, many may consider that humiliating. But the vaudevillian was very often not used to the steaks that came from Samson's or the great variety of other foods from the rest of the establishments. Humiliating to the vaudevillian? As Joe E. Brown expressed, "For a meal like that I'd have done half a dozen more [shows]."[30]

As for places to stay, the big headliners could live in style at the St. Francis Hotel, where Lou Clayton stayed when he hit the top, but most vaudevillians were not in that category. For them it could mean the Continental Hotel, with its slogan, "We get the stars on the way up and on the way down," a hotel that was very popular among the vaude crowd. It could also mean the Golden Gate, a hotel that offered special rates to performers, in itself a most unusual practice in the early days of vaude. But in the first decade of the twentieth century, eight dollars a week netted a private room and excellent meals for the actor who stopped at the Golden Gate. If vaudevillians shared a room, the individual rate was even lower.[31]

The Five Marvelous Ashtons, a standard acrobatic act, always stayed at the Turklu Apartments on Turk Street whenever they played San Francisco. Joe E. Brown, a member of the troupe at that time, described the Turklu as "a fifth-rate rooming house." Nearby was a small cafe where the act always ordered curried lamb, a meal they selected because it was served with a great deal of gravy and a huge stack of bread. On one particular stay, they were playing the Haymarket Music Hall. Their act had gone onstage at one in the morning and by the time they had performed and changed, it was well after two. Brown recalled their trudging their weary way up the hill to the Turklu, where he and another acrobat "practically fell" into their double bed. About two hours later, he was awakened by what he thought was someone shaking him. "I opened one eye enough to see the wall outside our window. It was weaving back and forth, so I knew I needed more sleep. I turned over and immediately dozed off again." Brown thus became one of the few who slept through the San Francisco earthquake of 1906.[32]

San Francisco was also the site of Bushnell's, probably the most respected professional photographer in the United States, as far as vaude was concerned. Bushnell's was rated more highly than New York's fine photographers not only because his work was excellent, but because a picture from Bushnell's was proof positive that a vaudevillian was important enough to travel.[33] As its expert photographer, San Francisco, too, ranked number one.

A city with a particularly bad reputation among vaudevillians was Cincinnati. Elbert Hubbard had seemingly made a successful transition from the dramatic stage to vaude and was salaried at $1,250 a week. Then he played Cincinnati for the first time. A heckler drove him from the stage and he never participated in vaude after that.[34] Harry Richman's home town was Cincinnati, but every appearance he made there flopped. A great actor, Richard Bennett, starring in a play at the same time as Richman was in town, knew of Richman's tremendous worry over his failures in his own home town. Bennett told Richman to be at his theater for the final curtain of that play. Richman was present and, along with an audience of Cincinnati theatergoers, heard one of the classic curtain speeches in theater annals. Bennett carried a chair to center stage, held up his hand for silence, sat down, and said:

> One minute of your time, ladies and gentlemen. Please be seated. For forty years I've been an actor on the American stage. My entire family is well represented in the entire field of show business. I've played this very city of Cincinnati for thirty or forty years. I've never had a decent reception here. I've been waiting all this time, ladies and gentlemen, to say to you that you, you people of Cincinnati, are the greatest morons, the most unintelligent, illiterate bastards I ever have appeared before in my entire life. Take a good look at me, because you'll never see me again. Thank you.[35]

Many a vaudevillian would have applauded that speech had they been present. Cincinnati, the town known for sitting on its hands, had only one good thing, as far as vaudevillians were concerned.

That was the Strauss, a hotel which had the American plan, and where performers got clean rooms and very good food.[36]

There was a saying that the worst weeks in show business were Easter, the week before Christmas, and Salt Lake. Charlie Chaplin summarized it by writing, "Like the Mormons, the city is aloof and austere–and so was the audience." Joe E. Brown was in a vaude unit that "went like wildfire everywhere," although the veteran troupers kept warning Brown and the other younger performers about Salt Lake City, a town that would take the wind out of their sails. The unit finally played the Utah capital and Brown's summary was, "They are good people in Salt Lake City. They are right people, liberal, God-fearing, and honest. But they didn't laugh." Brown, however, was kinder than most. He felt the show itself was to blame.[37]

As for black performers, Salt Lake was definitely not one of the best. James Weldon Johnson was playing the Orpheum circuit and was making the jump from Denver to San Francisco. Wishing to see the Mormon Tabernacle and the city itself, he decided to stop over in Salt Lake City. At the "best" hotel in town, he heard the words, "I'm sorry, but we haven't got a vacant room." Attempts to register at two other hotels resulted in the same treatment. When he tried to get service in a restaurant, he was refused and ordered to leave. When he asked his cab driver if he knew of a Negro family in town which might feed him, the driver knew of none. The driver did, however, locate a "saloon and chophouse" where Johnson was served. Then the driver took him to a "lodging house for laborers." The woman who owned the "shabby place" took a long time before she agreed to let Johnson stay overnight. She finally assented when he said he would be out of the house before her regular lodgers awakened.[38]

Vaudevillians claimed Kansas City was "murder." Benny Rubin said, "Here sat the nicest people that you ever saw in your life, in their reserved seats, ladies and gentlemen, and you heard no laughter and very little applause." In Rubin's opinion, to be successful in Kansas City, a comic had to be down-to-earth. Sophisticated humor would not work. Rubin stated that "Chic" Sale was the only act which ever drew hearty laughter there. Bert Lahr, however, once claimed to have received five curtain calls in Kansas City. He made the claim at the Friars Club, in the presence of Eddie Foy, Jay C. Flippen, and Joe Frisco, all top acts in vaude. Frisco, who had never met Lahr before, found the claim very difficult to believe. Lahr, wishing to treat the group to drinks, asked, "What would you like?" Foy and Flippen ordered beer. Frisco, a noted stutterer, replied, "I–I'd like to see your act, you bastard!"[39]

Kansas City also happened to be where Eddie Jackson, Dot Taylor, and her young son were stranded while playing in vaude. For three days they ate popcorn. The city was also the site of one of the first experiments in theater air-conditioning. John Considine put tons of ice in the air shafts of his theater and "cold storage vaudeville" came into being. The most important development in Kansas City theatrical history, however, may well have been a hearing that was held before a Police Magistrate. A vaude patron had hissed during a performance and had been arrested. The man was released, however, and the statement was made that "if a person has the right to applaud in a theatre he certainly has a right to dispraise a performance by hissing."[40]

Variety called Philadelphia "Sleepyville" in a headline. Fred Allen gave an example of what life would be like if people became extinct: "It will be like Philadelphia on a Sunday."[41]

The most difficult cities for vaudevillians, however, were probably just across the river from New York City. Jersey City and Hoboken were especially noted for tough audiences. According to Ben Blue, Jersey City got a reputation for being tough, then decided it would really live up to the reputation, which made it even tougher. Amy Norworth felt it was the worst town to send anybody to, especially comedians, because of its large foreign population. She recalled her first husband, Bert Swor, demanding to be placed in a theater where people would understand what he was saying, after he had experienced difficulty in Jersey City. Even a dancing act was not safe. Fred Astaire recalled the behavior of the gallery during the opening day matinee at the Monticello Theatre. They threw pennies at the Astaires and made "occasional noises like cats." The Astaires learned afterward that the theater "was noted for its roughhouse opening matinee gallery."[42]

Hoboken was even rougher than Jersey City. The Lyric Theatre was especially notorious. Thinking he was a "dumb hick," its audience booed Will Rogers from the stage. The Lyric was a tryout house for the Loew circuit. When a new act went well at the Lyric, which could mean simply being able to last through its turn, it was booked at the American Music Hall in New York. The Lyric itself was a dilapidated building on the Hoboken waterfront, in a slum neighborhood. Nils Granlund, a Loew executive who often previewed acts there, claimed it was one of the worst theaters in the world. Granlund said, "The customers didn't always throw things, but few acts lasted more than two or three performances. It was not unusual for us to send over three or four replacements after a matinee."[43]

In comparison to Jersey City and Hoboken, Newark was not a feared booking. Eddie Cantor suggested that, while Newark was a large city, it had the warmth of a small town. He believed a lot of "back fence" advertising took place.[44]

A very active vaudeville town was Boston. The Drama Committee of the Twentieth Century Club there had given its views of Boston and vaude:

> The worst criticism that can be made of the average performance at these houses is that at least half, often more, of the acts on the program are just plain "padding," pure and simple, inexcusably dull and mediocre. This condition reflects more on the taste of the audience than upon the lack of enterprize [sic] of the management, for it is axiomatic that so long as the attendance is satisfactory there is no inducement to furnish better (and necessarily higher-priced) acts. The audiences are too good-natured, too easily satisfied.[45]

Boston was the home of the "coast defender," a name given by bookers to Boston actors who never left the area. However, bookers were always on the lookout for out of town talent and just about any act, if not a coast defender, could gain instant booking. The coast defender was used as a "convenience" and found bookings fairly difficult to procure.

Scollay Square itself was the center of activity for the entertainer in Boston. Smalltime vaude played two theaters there, the Beacon and the Palace, and three other theaters offered either movies or stock productions. There, too, was the Old Howard. The Old Howard was a legendary burlesque house, but played vaudeville in between its burlesque shows. The theater, not far from the Charlestown Navy Yard, got a lot of business from sailors. A "burly special policeman carrying a billy club" was assigned the task of maintaining order in its gallery and, with energetic zeal, carried out his duties. Before each show, he stood in the first row of the gallery and forcefully ordered the patrons to remove their hats, not to smoke, and to keep their feet off the rails. Then he would slam his billy club on the iron rail next to him, as a final reminder of his sincerity. "Metallic reverberations ensued, and for minutes no galleryite could hear a thing," reported Fred Allen. Despite the presence of the special officer, there were moments of trouble in the Old Howard. One involved the Marx Brothers, then billed as the Four Nightingales. Three drunks were seated in an end box which over-hung the stage. During the act, they were noisy and abusive, and one announced that he was going to "get the second kid from the end!" Harpo Marx was that kid and he got it—"a jetstream of tobacco juice, smack down the front of [his] white duck jacket." A chronicler of the Marx Brothers wrote that the Old Howard was "a hoary institution [and] no place for the fastidious and sensitive."[46]

The major theater in the city was Keith's. It, too, suffered trouble, though far more serious than drunks spraying tobacco juice. For several weeks, three to four times a week, people in the audience were brutally injured by being struck by large iron bolts. No fatalities resulted, but there were some very bloody scenes. All sorts of measures were taken to find out what was happening: private detectives were hired, carpenters and engineers inspected the house, renovations were made. Yet, the bolts continued to find unsuspecting targets. Finally, the mystery was solved, when a house policeman was caught throwing bolts in the darkened theater. He was judged insane and placed in an asylum. Probably, the most amazing part of the story was the fact that the Keith-Albee combine was able to keep the scary news out of the newspapers.[47]

The Keith audience was judged to be a "wonderful" one. The same was not said for its manager, Robert Larsen. Larsen was the type who fit the title vaudevillians gave to managers—"Big Noise." He scrutinized the acts and his reports to the central New York office were among the most important they received. He also booked for many other theaters and his practices in this respect led Wolfie Gilbert to say that Larsen's name was probably a derivative of larceny. Gilbert stated that a booking at Keith's was given only if the act played other houses in town for a cut rate.[48]

Other theaters included the Colonial, "where anything could happen," the Old South, and the Boston. The Colonial's management did its best to maintain decorum in their theater, although one of their practices was unique. Whenever a member of the audience became too loud and boisterous with his laughter, an usher handed him a card which read, "Please do not laugh too loud." The Old South was a quality theater that all vaudevillians hoped to play. An engagement there was a guarantee of bookings in any Boston house. Will Cressy remembered the Boston stage door tender, "Con" Murphy, a man he had come to know over a period of eighteen years. Murphy, like most of his kind, worked from nine in the morning till eleven at night, "with an hour off for dinner and an hour for supper."[49]

Summer in many locations meant the closing of theaters and the opening of amusement parks. This was especially true in the greater Boston area. For vaudevillians, this was a boon, since each of the leading parks had a "rustic" theater that played six or eight acts of vaudeville twice daily. The parks were owned and operated by traction companies and the companies recognized quickly that top vaudeville attractions helped fill the parks. Full parks meant full trolley cars, so the trolley lines were very interested in securing the best acts they could. Regardless of the theater location, however, Boston censorship was Boston censorship. *Variety* referred to Boston Mayor James Curley as "The Strictest Censor of Morals in the United States." Edwin Royle recalled one line in his act: "I'll have the devil's own time explaining." In most cases, for "devil" he substituted "dickens." In Boston, however, even "dickens" was out; Royle was requested to "soften the asperities."[50]

As for places to stay, a notorious hotel in Boston was the Rexford. "Property of the Rexford" was printed on the blankets, sheets, and pillowcases. There were bars on the windows, which gave the building the appearance of a jail. No one ever seemed to sleep at the Rexford. At three a.m. a bell rang, which meant one thing–go to your *own* room. A massive and rundown affair, the girls from burlesque made the Rexford their headquarters which in turn guaranteed its popularity with male vaudevillians.[51]

Equally as notorious but not as large was the Higgins Hotel. Fred Allen's description was classic: "There were thirty-five rooms in the hotel, and many days five hundred were rented. . . . [Its] slogan was 'Your grandfather dined here.' The slogan didn't mention what else your grandfather might have done there." The Higgins also had a favorite vaude hangout in its basement, the Bucket of Blood, a poolroom and betting establishment. Across the street was the William Tell House, which charged five to six dollars a week, room and board. The William Tell also had a favorite hangout in its basement, Hamm's Periodical Store. If nothing else made it popular, the fact that Mr. Hamm "extended credit" guaranteed the presence of many actors.[52]

Eateries in Boston were plentiful. Full-course meals could be had for a quarter at such places as the William Tell House (guests of the hotel paid nothing) and the Daisy Lunch. A tiny alehouse next to Hamm's was a meeting place for older performers. And, there was a woman who owned a grocery store who, after every Saturday matinee, came backstage and handed out small bags of rock candy.[53]

A full continent away was Los Angeles. Here was the community that would absorb many vaudevillians in their post-vaude days, a community that would become "home." One of the places that made it feel like home was the Continental Hotel. Like its counterpart in San Francisco, it advertised, "We get the stars on the way up and the way down," and it was reputedly run like a "fun-house," with performers continually playing jokes on one another. Not all the hotels, however, had the "heart" that the Continental did. Joe Frisco, "in his later and leaner days," lived in a Los Angeles hotel and let a down-and-out friend of his sleep on the floor in his room. The management learned of Frisco's action and informed him that an extra guest meant two dollars more a day. He replied, "All r-r-right, but s-s-send up another Gideon B-b-bible, p-p-please."[54]

Los Angeles was compared unfavorably to its northern California rival, San Francisco, by most vaudevillians who played the West Coast. Charlie Chaplin, destined to make a fortune because of the southern California movie industry, candidly appraised Los Angeles as "an ugly city, hot and oppressive, and the people looked sallow and anemic."[55]

The Astaires played the Orpheum where he recalled the people "made a fuss" about such small children being on the bigtime. The Orpheum was the best vaude house in the city, one that Benny Rubin ranked as second only to the Palace. To him, the Orpheum had a great audience, composed of motion picture people who wanted to be entertained after their own very long entertainment work day. "They screamed and they hollered and they applauded," said Rubin. The Orpheum also had an excellent boss, Clarence Drown, so good that W. C. Fields praised him in the pages of *Variety.* Drown ordered all his employees to get the vaude artist everything he asked for, emphasizing that the performer was coming in after a long, tiresome journey from San Francisco and deserved special consideration. Fields also praised the theater itself, one with well ventilated and sanitary dressing rooms, excellent lavatories, and "shower baths for both sexes." The best thing about the Orpheum, though, could well have been Drown's policy of not seating late arrivals while an act was in progress.[56]

More important than the Orpheum or any Los Angeles vaudeville theater was Hollywood. The big industry was motion pictures and vaude never forgot it. The kingpin of the silent days was Charlie Chaplin, who had starred in vaudeville, and whose success served as the prime example for other vaude players. When Al Jolson, a bigtime vaude star, proved a sensation in the 1927 production of *The Jazz Singer,* vaudevillians recognized the advantages that films offered. During the late twenties and through the thirties, vaudeville artists were cast in wholesale lots, Hollywood taking full advantage of the show biz knowhow vaudevillians had acquired in their craft.

A partial listing of vaudevillians who became movie stars illustrates the importance of vaude to the screen, while showing that vaudevillians themselves, via motion pictures, contributed very significantly to bigtime vaudeville's finish. Jolson added to his success by making *The Singing Fool, Sonny Boy, Say It with Songs, Mammy, Hallelujah, I'm a Bum,* and *Wonder Bar.* Eddie Cantor brightened the nation's screens in such movies as *Glorifying the American Girl, Whoopee, The Kid From Spain,* and *Roman Scandals,* the last a film which also featured Ruth Etting, a lovely vaude singer. The great vaudeville team of George Burns and Gracie Allen starred in *The Big Broadcast of 1932, College Humor,*

College Holiday, which also starred Eddie Foy, and *The Big Broadcast of 1937,* the last pair of films also featuring Jack Benny. Benny was also cast in the *Hollywood Revue of 1929*, a film which resembled a vaudeville show in format, with Benny acting as a Master of Ceremonies. Other vaude performers in the same movie were Marie Dressler, Buster Keaton, Stan Laurel, Cliff Edwards, and Gus Edwards.

Chasing Rainbows, Medicine Man, Broadway Melody of 1936, and *Artists and Models* were also Benny vehicles. Ben Blue, the great vaude pantomime and dance star, appeared in *College Holiday* and *Artists and Models,* while Buddy Ebsen, still another vaude dancer, had parts in *Broadway Melody of 1936, Born to Dance,* and *The Girl of the Golden West,* a 1938 MGM production which also included vaudevillians Cliff Edwards and Leo Carrillo. Carrillo had enjoyed earlier roles in *Mr. Antonio, Girl of the Rio,* and *Moonlight and Pretzels.* Best known as the Cisco Kid's sidekick, he also had a feature part in the 1940 production, *Lillian Russell,* which starred Don Ameche and included in its cast Weber and Fields and Joseph Cawthorne, the last a vaude star who had been a contemporary of Lillian Russell's and who played in many movies, including *Gold Diggers of 1935* and *The Great Ziegfeld.*

The Great Ziegfeld, a 1936 spectacular, was a good property for other vaudevillians, as well. In its cast were Fannie Brice, Ann Pennington, Ray Bolger, William Demarest, and Leon Errol, all veterans of the vaude boards. Ann Pennington had starred earlier in the 1929 film, *Gold Diggers of Broadway,* which also featured Nick Lucas and Nancy Welford, the latter a great star of musical comedy who had served a vaudeville apprenticeship in her teens. Lucas, who appeared on the last two-a-day Palace bill in 1932, also appeared in *The Show of Shows,* along with fellow vaudevillians Bea Lillie, Frank Fay, and Ted Lewis.

A classic of the mid-thirties was Warner Brothers' *A Midsummer Night's Dream.* Joe E. Brown, James Cagney, and Mickey Rooney, vaudeville blood all, were among the film's stars. Brown had already starred in other popular movies, *Painted Faces, Maybe It's Love, Fireman Save My Child, Elmer the Great,* and *On with the Show!* Cagney, under contract to Warner Brothers, made a series of films, including *Blonde Crazy* and *Footlight Parade,* a pair of flicks which also featured Joan Blondell, who had been a child vaudevillian.

Still other vaude stars who made it big in Hollywood were Fred Astaire, W. C. Fields, Jack Haley, Will Rogers, Ed Wynn, and the dynamic Mae West. Astaire was in such films as *Dancing Lady, Flying Down to Rio,* which featured a prominent star of black vaudeville, Clarence Muse, *Swing Time,* with Victor Moore, a vaudeville veteran, and *Roberta,* which also included vaude banjo comic, Gene Sheldon. W. C. Fields was in a host of comedy classics, including *Her Majesty Love, Million Dollar Legs, If I Had a Million, Tillie and Gus,* and *The Great McGonigle,* using his juggling skills in many instances. Jack Haley was in *Alexander's Ragtime Band, Pigskin Parade,* which featured in its array of stars vaudeville stars Patsy Kelly, Judy Garland, and Julius Tannen, *Wake Up and Live,* yet another film with an abundance of vaudevillians, Patsy Kelly, Walter Catlett, William Demarest, Ben Bernie, and Walter Winchell, and the great history-making film, *The Wizard of Oz.* This annual television Easter show stars vaudevillians Judy Garland, Bert Lahr, and Ray Bolger.

The films of Will Rogers included *They Had to See Paris, Happy Days, So This Is London, State Fair,* which also featured Louise Dresser, a magnificent singer in vaude, *Doctor Bull,* and *Steamboat 'Round the Bend,* which included in its cast Roger Imhof, who had spent many a vaude season as part of the headline act, Imhof and Corinne. Ed Wynn starred in *Follow the Leader* and *The Chief* and later became a major television hit, utilizing to the utmost his enormous vaudeville repertoire. Mae West starred in film after film in the thirties, including *Night After Night, She Done Him Wrong, I'm No Angel,* and *Belle of the Nineties.*

No movie list centered on vaudevillians would be complete if it eliminated the fabulous film successes of the Marx Brothers. A list of their movies is an imposing one. *A Night at the Opera, Animal Crackers,* which included Lillian Roth, a child vaudeville attraction, *Duck Soup, The Cocoanuts, Monkey Business, Horse Feathers*—all these and more contribute heavily to the movie enjoyment brought to the nation by vaudevillians who had converted to the new medium. They had joined the ranks of Buster Keaton and his *Free and Easy, Parlor, Bedroom and Bath,* and *Sidewalks of New York,* of Marie Dressler and her *Tillie's Punctured Romance, Anna Christie,* and *Min and Bill,* of Fred Allen and his *Dinner at*

Eight. Vaudevillians had their impact on filmdom, an impact felt crushingly in their former vaudeville world.

Never forgotten, too, were the times that the President of the United States showed his appreciation to vaudevillians. Of the occupants of the White House during the best days of vaude, apparently the best fan was Woodrow Wilson. He felt it served as a valuable relaxation from the pressures of the office and Keith's Theatre kept an upper box available every Thursday night for Wilson and the guests he brought with him. Wilson particularly enjoyed comedy and song-and-dance and was called "a great audience." He especially loved May Irwin and once asked her to accept "the portfolio of Secretary of Laughter." Wilson even managed to take in vaude during the trying days of World War One, on one occasion inspiring Louise Dresser and George Gershwin, appearing together at Keith's, to march in a Preparedness parade. Wilson also enjoyed treating various acts, sometimes taking them for drives around the Capital, other times inviting them to the White House. Milton Berle remembered playing Keith's when he was twelve years old and being invited to the White House for lunch. Estelle Major Smith also recalled sitting next to President Wilson at a lunch where she was the guest of Joseph Tumulty, the President's secretary. Wilson's successor, Warren Harding, also greatly enjoyed vaudeville and often went backstage after the show for friendly conversation.[57]

Other Chief Executives mixed with vaudevillians, too. Will Rogers was challenged by Alice Longworth to make Calvin Coolidge laugh. Rogers had never met Coolidge before but accepted the challenge. The meeting of the two occurred at the White House and Rogers succeeded with his first try. Immediately after he was introduced to Coolidge, Rogers asked, "What was that name again, please?" Franklin Roosevelt proved to be a hit with vaudevillians. Joey Adams was thrilled when he was summoned to meet FDR and overjoyed when he was asked to tell stories that made Roosevelt the butt of the joke. And for George M. Cohan came an even greater thrill. Cohan's authorship of "Over There" and "A Grand Old Flag" moved FDR to grant him the Congressional Medal of Honor.[58]

FDR was not the only Roosevelt who showed a special interest in show business. Theodore Roosevelt was approached by

William Morris when Albee threw a roadblock in Morris' way. Morris wanted to have Sir Harry Lauder perform in Washington but, because of Albee's interference, was unable to get a theater. Roosevelt not only interceded and got a theater, but attended Lauder's performance, as well.[59]

Presidents were not the only political figures to draw notice. Ken Murray related the time that he was playing Keith's. Murray, at that time, used to go through the theater during the opening act and greet members of the audience. He had found that his "getting-to-know-you bit" worked best when he could single people out before they sat down. Then came the "very dignified gentleman, with his wife and daughter." Murray confronted them in the aisle, offered his hand, and was not only ignored, but threatened with, "Young man, you'll regret this." Murray did not retreat and instead called for the show to start over so that the latecomers could see it from the beginning. That turned the patron around and, to the tune of much laughter, he stormed from the theater. The man, Murray later learned, was Vice-President Charles Dawes.[60]

Another performer who encountered difficulty with official personages was Violet Dale. World War One was being fought and the United States was still neutral. The Chase Theater's boxes were generally filled by personnel from the embassies, which caused a bit of tension for Miss Dale, who was doing an act called "War Brides." The act contained reference to "brood mares," meaning the peasant women of Germany, who were "producing cannon fodder." When she did those lines the German diplomat "deliberately stood up in the stage box, turned his chair around and sat down, with his back to the stage."[61]

W. C. Fields felt that Washington was the toughest city a vaude comic had to play. For years, he analyzed the problem and determined that politics was undoubtedly at the root of it all. To him, the citizens of Washington were not going to laugh at an ordinary stage comic when so many better comedians populated Capitol Hill. Men from Capitol Hill were also pretty lively characters at Mother Irish's, a favorite theatrical boardinghouse in the city, for there resided the transient chorus girls and actresses.[62]

When Mother Irish's did not suffice, Baltimore was just up the road. Baltimore was called by a British tourist a cheerful city where the people laugh at everything, though in fact, that was hardly the case.[63]

One of the best boardinghouses in the United States was in the city, Mrs. Howard's, or as many referred to it, Mother Howard's. Joe Laurie, Jr., in fact, claimed that the two best boardinghouses in the country were in Baltimore. He added Sparrows to Mother Howard's. The food at Howard's was excellent and there was always a friendly atmosphere.[64]

Baltimore also had a cafeteria-style restaurant called Buck's, which had a policy that perfectly suited down-and-out show people. As the patrons left the cafeteria they told the cashier what they had eaten and he charged them accordingly. This afforded the opportunity to have a solid meal "costing as much as 35 cents," then telling the cashier, "Cup of coffee and a piece of pie," pay a dime and leave.[65]

Violet Dale commented sharply about two annoyances she encountered in Baltimore. One involved the society women of the city. They sat front center and talked throughout the show. Representatives of the French legation who had come up from Washington "chattered like magpies through the entire performance," said Miss Dale, "and as each act left the stage the actors were deeply distressed because they had not been able to hold the attention of the audience." When she went on, she kept asking the orchestra conductor to play her introduction music, while she stood staring at the unmindful legation. After the fourth introduction, they finally quieted down and turned their attention to the stage. She threw them a kiss and announced, "Now we'll go on," a statement which drew hearty applause from the audience.[66]

In Cleveland, the Palace's facilities were opulent. Opened in 1922, the theater was part of a twenty-one story building, sat 3,680 patrons, had a lobby of marble, paintings by Corot and others scattered around, plush rugs, a private kitchen and poolroom for the actors, and private dressing rooms and bath not only for each name act, but for each chorus girl, as well. It ranked as one of the finest theaters in the world.

Cleveland also boasted a stage crew at the 105th Street Theatre which, like many other crews, prevented as best as possible the stealing of an act's material. The first step was to tell the thief that he "lay off." If he chose to continue to use pirated material, a blunt reminder would be given him by the stagehands, perhaps in the form of a crashing sandbag. Dangerous, too, were poolrooms, if the vaudevillian tried to pull a fast one. Chico Marx, an expert at pool, had beaten just about every local Cleveland player, but had done so without incurring bitter resentment. Then "a sharpie turned up and clipped him for twenty bucks." Chico decided to get even and got Willie Hoppe to go to the same poolroom. Hoppe ran 220 balls and someone recognized him. As his brother Harpo said, "Chico felt that Cleveland was no longer where he wished to be."[67]

Pittsburgh had long been known as a tough place for show people.[68] The house manager of Pittsburgh's Davis Theatre, Eugene Connolly, was described as "a man gifted with both superior taste and a reputation for being hard to please." Sophie Tucker declared, "It's not going too far to say that the Davis Theatre was hated by every performer in the business. Lots of them refused to play it, knowing that a date there let you in for a hell of a time." Connolly's word was law. The only way out was to quit—and to quit was to be banned from Keith time.[69]

The "Prince of Buffalo" was the big vaudeville noise in that city, a man described as "a grand old fellow, and an actor's friend." The man was Mike Shea, whose "word was as good as the Bank of England's." Vaudeville was so extremely popular in Buffalo, that Shea had to have ticket speculators arrested. As for the audience, Ken Murray always looked forward to Buffalo, a great town for him. On the other hand, Benny Rubin found it tough "at that time" because of a large foreign population that he felt did not understand what was being said onstage.[70]

A town that drew mixed reactions from Rubin and many vaudevillians was Minneapolis. He loved the "great audience" at the Orpheum Theatre, until they stopped adhering to their reserved seat policy. After that asserted Rubin, "they were but lousy. They were awful."[71]

But one who pronounced Minneapolis to be "a great town" was Lou Clayton. Eddie Jackson, his partner, felt the audiences were "a little tough." Jimmy Durante had never been to the city, so when Clayton said it was great and added that George Burns and Gracie Allen were in Minneapolis and might stay over to see them if they played there, Durante assented and the trio took the vaude booking offered them. The result was a gigantic flop, with one critic writing, "Minneapolis can sure do without Clayton, Jackson, and Durante." Durante came away with two conclusions about "Minneanapolis." One was that an enemy must have booked them there. More importantly, the second was that, "Broadway and New York ain't the whole world. There's a great big country outside of it, and each place has a solid humor of its own, and you got to have an act that is right down to earth."[72]

Neighboring St. Paul meant to the vaude artist the Lowry Hotel which served excellent popovers. It also meant Mrs. Qualey's boardinghouse, which served stew on Monday, corned beef on Tuesday, hash on Wednesday, and then started over with a stew on Thursday, week after week, year after year. Monotonous as it was, it was good food. Vaudevillians got a "big kick out of Mrs. Qualey," who was considered by some their favorite landlady of all. She maintained an autograph album and wanted all her show business guests to sign. One signature became legendary: "To Mrs. Qualey–Hebrews 13:8. Julius Tannen." Whether Mrs. Qualey understood or not, every vaudevillian did. Hebrews 13:8 was: "Jesus Christ, the same yesterday, today, and forever."[73]

Unlike Mrs. Qualey, who was greatly concerned for her guests, no matter their creed, Dallas' George Woods, who ran the Camp Street Theatre, as well as the hotel the actors stayed in, disliked Jewish performers. At the theater he had no recourse, for his audiences liked Jewish comics. At his hotel, however, his dislike manifested itself in the meals. Practically every meal was pork.[74]

Dallas and Fort Worth were part of the Interstate circuit. Fort Worth provided a valuable lesson to Bob Hope. He "was doing a brash type act and working fast and making it the audience's problem whether they got the jokes or not." The style worked very well in Chicago. Then he went to Fort Worth "and laid the biggest bomb in the world." The manager of the circuit advised him to slow his pace. Though Hope was not sympathetic to the idea, he gave it a try. Indeed, he got laughs and gained some insight.[75]

Ken Murray discovered, too, that a successful routine in New York did not necessarily mean success elsewhere. His first show in Montreal got no laughs at all and put him in a state of depression, until he learned it was a French-speaking audience and they had not understood a word. The evening audience was a good one. The fact that Montreal was "very Frenchy" made it a very attractive city to many vaudevillians. Whereas the comedy and dialogue acts bombed with the matinee crowds, musicians, singers, magicians, acrobats, and similar acts, were unaffected.[76]

At the other end of Canada, Vancouver was usually a welcome date for performers, especially during prohibition. Groucho Marx stated a general vaude opinion: "Canada, being a civilized country, was never taken in by the will-o'-the-wisp promises of prohibition." Vancouver, like any Canadian location near the border of the United States, served as a liquor port for its southern neighbors. "Almost every vaudeville actor who played in Canada," related Groucho, "managed, one way or another, to sneak a few bottles back to the land of the free and the home of the bootlegger."[77]

South of Vancouver sat the "Queen City of the West Coast," Seattle, the port city with its "smell of pine woods, spiked with the salt air of the Pacific." Guthrie McClintic remembered, too, its "fast women." He made clear, "A fact the Chamber of Commerce neglected to publicize was that Seattle had one of the biggest and most flourishing red-light districts in the country." For two leading vaudevillians from the East, Seattle meant memories of food and landscape. Jimmy Savo stated the hilly city would always be for him, "the place where you could buy a whole salmon for twenty-five cents." Crawfish came to Sophie Tucker's mind. She ate too many of them, became "sick as a poisoned pup," and missed two shows. Seattle also meant to her "a tangle of queer-looking ships in the harbor."[78]

As the twentieth century began, vaudeville was already underway on the West Coast, Seattle playing a very significant role. Both the Pantages and the Sullivan-Considine circuits started in Seattle. Joe E. Brown remembered the time he played for Pantages when the vaude impresario had but two small houses. Not only were both in Seattle, but they were next door to one another, former stores converted into vaude theaters. The stages were small enough that Brown occasionally banged the theater wall on backward swings required to perform an aerial act. Playing for Pantages also meant four shows a day, with five on Saturdays and Sundays. The strain worked hard on the young acrobat, especially his wrists. Brown recounted, "The skin wore off and the blood would run worse than perspiration."[79]

Seattle also showed the effect a locality could have on a performer's material. Edward J. Fisher had come to Seattle as an actor and went onstage at Considine's People's Theatre, billed as a Hebrew comic. The area, however, had hardly any Jews and the stereotype fell flat. The area did have a heavy Scandinavian population, though, and when Fisher switched to Swedish characterization, he became a hit.[80]

The existence of rival circuits in Seattle benefitted vaudevillians, for each circuit grew to hate one another and went to extremes in bidding for actors' services. One time, however, a xylophone trio got caught in the middle. They had an agreement with Pantages but the Sullivan-Considine circuit offered double salary. The trio argued with Pantages that their agreement was not airtight and announced they would play for the opposition. Pantages phoned his stage manager and asked if the xylophones were still in the theater. When he was told they were, instantly he ordered: "Take them out in the alley and burn them." When the trio protested, Pantages barked his order again. The trio got the message. They played for Pantages. The xylophones were not burned, but neither was Pantages. The feud between the two circuits ended when Considine's son married Pantages' daughter.[81]

An audience which went from boredom to anger was in New Orleans, when Duffy and Sweeney flopped badly. When the act ended, Duffy bowed and made a classic speech: "Thank you, ladies and gentlemen, for the way you received our act. To show our appreciation, my partner will now pass among you with a baseball bat and beat the bejesus out of you!" Vaudevillians playing New Orleans also could involve themselves in an interesting set of contrasts. The old Orpheum had once been a church, so that its dressing room windows were still stained glass. Then, after changing beneath the old church windows, the performer could hop "over the tracks" to one of the world's largest and most notorious sporting house districts. Several of the madams and their girls regularly attended the vaude shows and the entertainers were always welcome to return the visits. Particularly attractive to the vaudevillians were the "palaces" run by Lulu White and Jesse Arlington, with their "mirrored bedrooms and girls from all over the world."[82]

Not all prostitutes were found in palaces, however. Most were found in tiny houses or shacks, hardly big enough to hold the bed, chairs, and washstand which were its only contents. Many of the prostitutes put their names on their doors. Their usual practice was to stand in the doorway, very scantily dressed, and solicit the men walking by. The wise vaudevillian, however, knew that venereal disease was easily contracted in the cheaper parts of the vast red-light district of New Orleans and he made every effort to find his women in the high-class sporting houses.[83]

Upriver was St. Louis, home of Dave Rilling's boardinghouse, one of the better ones in the country, the Brevoort Hotel, a typical theatrical hotel, and Babe Connors' place, a brothel which was known over the vaude circuits and which imported many of its girls from New Orleans. The Brevoort had a rehearsal room in its basement, not uncommon with hotels which catered to show people. It was dingy, with broken-down furniture, many yellowed theatrical photographs on the lobby walls. June Havoc remembered it as "a heavenly place." Her older sister recalled that they played in the hallways, the elevators, on the stairs, and searched for unlocked broom closets. These closets "were a special treat. The sharp evil smells of the disinfectants in the large drugstore-like bottles were dangerous and exciting." Sometimes they found empty liquor bottles in the broom closets, which they filled with water and drank from, making believe they were drunk. Only the lobby was off-limits as a playground, as their mother wanted to maintain a good impression.[84]

St. Louis was a memorable city for Bobby Dillon and Bing Crosby. Dillon appeared at the Columbia Theatre and the audience reaction made him think he was an outstanding success. The next day's newspaper, however, panned him. He remained dismayed until he met the critic. One of Dillon's songs was a stuttering song. The critic stuttered. As Dillon accurately summarized, "It just goes to show that whatever we do on the stage, someone always takes it personally." With Crosby, St. Louis' remembrance would be a theater manager. Crosby was a member of the Rhythm Boys and Paul Whiteman had booked them over the Keith-Orpheum circuit. As Crosby himself admitted, the group was less than conscientious and missed some dates, went to a wrong city, and changed their act. The theater manager in St. Louis balked and demanded that the act be presented in its original form or suffer cancellation. The Rhythm Boys agreed but kept their promise for only three shows. Then they drifted from their original act. As they were performing, the curtain closed in front of them. They were cancelled on the spot. Thereafter they did only their original act.[85]

The big cities offered their peculiar challenges to vaudevillians. Minneapolis meant one thing, nearby St. Paul something else. Baltimore accepted what Cincinnati denied. Boston laughed at material which Kansas City accepted soberly. And the kingpin, New York? It was a nation of big cities in itself.

GUS SUN, DEATH TRAIL, BORSCHT, AND KALAMAZOO GARBAGE COLLECTORS

♦ ♦ ♦ ♦ ♦

*AS TOUGH AS PLAYING CITIES COULD BE, HOWEVER, IT WAS MUCH PREFER*able to the small towns of America. The cities offered a variety of hotels and boardinghouses, of restaurants and stores, of theaters where, with luck, one could get to see other shows. Rarely was any of this possible in the small towns. But it was in the small towns, in the Keokuks, Mankatos, Bangors, Bethlehems, and Aberdeens, that many of the bigtime headliners learned their trade. The small towns were an indispensable and fascinating part of a vaudevillian's America.

Smalltime theaters were not necessarily so small that the vaudevillian felt his efforts went for naught. It was difficult to predict just when someone with influence would see a show and lift a performer from the doldrums to the bigtime or to Broadway. Yet, there were some towns so remote and small that the theaters were known as hideaways, where nobody of importance could ever see an act. And there were the "cake-and-coffee houses" where an act booked an engagement simply because it was better than nothing, even though the engagement itself hardly paid enough to cover expenses.[1]

Regardless of town or theater, however, the act had to be good. Any act's strength was in its universal appeal. Parts could be changed here and there, depending on locale, but the core of the act, including its "wow finish," had to prove as successful in Macon, Baton Rouge, and Ypsilanti as it would in New York.[2] Prior to the days of radio and television when a national taste could more easily be projected, when a new song could become a hit overnight, its melody and lyrics known even in the smallest village, the challenge of vaudeville was extraordinary.

It helped little when theaters were rundown. Benny Rubin remembered the theaters that had no dressing rooms: "You'd come into a basement, a stinking, lousy basement, one toilet, with one bowl to wash up in, and more or less a blanket or a big sheet, the ladies on this side, the men on that side." Where there were separate dressing rooms, other problems could exist. According to Fred Allen, "a few depraved actors carried gimlets and bits around with them, and drilled holes in the walls to watch the sister act or the single woman in the next room undress." Sophie Tucker pictured some of the theaters she played: "Drafty old firetraps, no toilets, filthy dirty cracked walls that let in the wind and the rain, old broken floors. . . . One hard jump and down into the cellar you went. Never enough heat." She helped to sustain her spirit by carrying in her trunk cretonne hangings, wall sheets, table covers, a rug for the usual cold cement floor, and a chair. Once she had arranged her own furnishings, she felt her "dressing room" was always clean and neat, with no mess on the floor.[3] For her, the gigantic theatrical trunk was indispensable.

W. C. Fields also had a trunk that was no less indispensable. His was a miniature bar, brass footrail and all. The trunk helped him break the standing rule against liquor. But it helped him little when he was in the mood for tomfoolery or when he worried about any reasonable sums of money that he so often had. Occasionally, Fields put on a stage beard, perhaps an opera cape, and went to whatever social functions he could find, pretending to be Oglethorpe P. Bushmaster, or something equally grandiose, just back from the Antarctic. Fields also opened bank accounts wherever he toured, sometimes using assumed names and keeping the bank books in his trunk. He estimated that he once had accounts in seven hundred banks.[4]

"Jumps" from one booking to another were a headache most vaudevillians could easily have done without. Violet Dale recounted how she would perform every day of the week, travel Sunday night to her next engagement, go straight to the theater for rehearsal, getting nourishment from a sandwich sent backstage, giving the matinee performance, and only then being able to search for hotel accommodations. Once a room was found, it was usually less than perfect. Joey Adams said, "I lived in rooms so small that if I dreamed, I had to dream about midgets."[5] Big city hotels were sometimes good, often poor, as portrayed on earlier pages. Small town hotels were even less attractive.

In every town that vaudevillians played, another feature they could never escape was the theater alley. Groucho Marx insisted that one way to find the stage door of any town's theater was to seek out the dirtiest alley in sight. June Havoc commented about the alleys, too, writing that "it was traditional for all vaudeville theaters to release the actors into a dark, wet, garbage-strewn alley. I don't know why, but that's the way it always was. I was quite used to those alleys. . . ." It must be remembered that she was a young girl when she played vaude and that when she saw "a rat the size of a toy poodle,"[6] it was a tiny girl's eyes seeing it, a tiny girl alone in a horrible environment.

Small towns also presented the constant possibility of being stranded in remote areas. For many it meant a long walk home. For others it meant borrowing on whatever collateral they had available, or simply making a "touch." Some even took jobs. There were those, however, who reacted with a touch of genius. Joe E. Lewis was teamed with Johnny Black in vaude and they were frequently without work. Black then got out his surveyor's outfit, he and Lewis would find a suitable rural location, and they would expertly act out the parts of a railroad or highway surveying crew. Black was well-researched in the field and would manage to tell bystanders, in the strictest confidence, just what the new project would be. The ploy would garner numerous invitations, as people vied with each other to get the pair in favorable conference circumstances. Abundant food kept Black and Lewis healthy and well-fed until they managed a new booking.[7]

Dancers also faced constant problems, for most small town theaters, as well as some big city houses, contained the terror of all dancers–slippery stages. Worse, practically all stage managers refused to allow the use of rosin. Fred Astaire would often sneak into the theater before the start of the show and try to put rosin on the floor under cover of darkness. Even then he was detected many times. Astaire referred to the whole matter as the "Battle of Rosin," which he said he fought from Maine to California.[8]

Thousands of theaters across the country awaited the vaudevillian, each with its own peculiar baptism. There was a New England circuit of Hathaway theaters which played such towns as Malden, Brookton, Lynn, New Bedford, and Fall River. The Gus Sun circuit covered well over one hundred theaters in Ohio, Kentucky, Pennsylvania, Michigan, Virginia, West Virginia, New York, Indiana, Illinois, and Canada. The Wells circuit controled eleven theaters in the South. A booking on Hodkins Lyric Vaudeville Circuit meant twelve to fourteen weeks in the Southwest. The Interstate Amusement Company, called simply "the Interstate time" by vaude artists who played it, had sixteen cities in Texas, Oklahoma, Arkansas, Illinois, Kansas, Kentucky, and Missouri. Wisconsin had its own circuit, the Cone, which played six cities. Circuits were in existence everywhere, the Allardt in the midwest and Canada, the Theilen in Illinois and Iowa, the Delaney in Pennsylvania, the Delmar in the deep South, the Poli in New England, Sullivan and Considine, known mostly for its West Coast rivalry with Pantages, but which had thirty-two cities from Cleveland westward, including sites in Canada, the Finn and Heiman time, which booked only eight midwestern cities, the Finkelstein and Rubin (or F&R time), in the midwest, and many more. The Theatre Owners Booking Association, or T.O.B.A., was a busy Negro vaudeville circuit which stretched from New York to Florida, Chicago to New Orleans. Performers referred to it as Toby, or Tough On Black Actors. Then there was Sablosky and McGurk in Pennsylvania and Fally Markus in and around New York, described by Benny Rubin as the smallest of the smalltime. Fally Markus, stated Rubin, booked one, two, and three day appearances. As for the salary, Rubin said, "We used to express it this way: he paid you off in the dark, paid you with old programs and baked apples. You know, he didn't pay much money." Rubin also cited the Butterfield time, which "was as low as you could get," and the Crescent circuit, which he termed a "big nothing. Nothing, nothing. It's somebody stuck a name on some toilets, as we called it."[9]

A coast to coast tour of small town vaudeville could easily begin in Bangor, Maine. Here was a town that Charles Bickford claimed was populated by "uncritical show-hungry natives." Bickford also described the trains in Maine, the locals that were always late and which usually were made up of both passenger coaches and freight cars. The show people would often find themselves in a passenger car with a carload of potatoes in front, and a carload of hogs in the rear. Heat was supplied by a wood-burning iron stove. Bickford did, however, praise the people and the food. As he put it, "the food was . . . wholesome [and] the people were . . . Down-Easters." Ed Wynn remembered Bangor for quite other reasons. At the age of sixteen, he found himself stranded there. To earn enough to take him back home, he played piano "in a whorehouse, practically."[10]

Maine and snow are inseparable, or at least it seemed to many vaude performers. Even Ferne Albee Burton, native of Minneapolis, laughed when she recalled the wintertime they found in Portland. Snow also greeted a troupe of vaudevillians during the depression years who responded to a request from fifteen C.C.C. camps, to come to "the northern part of Maine in the dead of winter," to a location forty miles from the nearest railroad station. Maine was also the site of a novel approach to bolster attendance figures for vaude shows. The manager of the Scenic Theatre in Westbrook gave away trading stamps and, as a result, drew 25 percent more patrons to his shows.[11]

George Jessel recalled the "SheedyTime," a circuit he played which covered upper New England and Nova Scotia. He opened in Gloucester, Massachusetts, in a small theater set out on a pier. It was winter, the actors found water in the dressing rooms, and were forced to place boards and boxes on the floor in order to change into their costumes. Fred Allen vividly remembered a theater in Gloucester, too. It had no plumbing or any kind of lavatory facility. A coal and lumber yard stood across from the stage door. That yard served as the rest rooms for the vaudevillians. Female performers entered the yard through one gate, while the men used the only other gate. Allen also wrote of a theater in Dorchester, an upstairs movie house called Winthrop Hall. Harry Norton, a piano player, was its manager, a one-man gang. He sold the tickets, turned the job over to a girl when it was time to start the picture, then played piano through the several reels of film and the "three acts of underpaid vaudeville." When the lights came on for the intermission, Norton rushed to the top of the stairs to ask the patrons how they had enjoyed the show, and to advertise the forthcoming presentations.[12]

Harry Norton, though cheap, was an active manager, at least, and did have helpers. Allen told of another who hired only one vaude act to supplement his movies and who could not see why stagehands were necessary when there was just a lone act. At this theater in Yarmouth, Nova Scotia, the vaudevillian himself had to pull up the movie curtain and operate the switchboard to turn the lights on and off.[13]

The most talked about smalltime appearance in New England was the one at Poli's Theatre in New Haven, Connecticut. Here were the Yale students who would occasionally riot and even tear the theater apart. Though the Yale students constituted a fearsome threat to many entertainers, the Poli date was still looked forward to with eagerness. The reason was the "superb plank steaks" that were the mainstay of the menu of the hotel across the street from the theater. Good and bad memories came from appearances in New Haven. Already alluded to in an earlier chapter was the episode where Buster Keaton was thrown by his father at an unruly member of the audience. Wolfie Gilbert remembered being next-to-closing and going over "like an iron balloon." He appraised the collegians as a tough audience: "If they didn't like you, brother, they let you know it–audibly!"[14]

The Yale crowd could be a tremendous boost, too. Adele Astaire was the object of admiration for Yale students when she and her brother appeared with their dancing act. Fred recalled being hounded by students seeking an introduction to his sister and mentioned the same type of reception was accorded by Harvard students in and around Boston. "Those college audiences could really whoop it up if they liked you," he observed. "They'd arrive at the theatre in masses of hundreds." For Fred Allen, too, the Yale undergrads proved hospitable. Allen played New Haven no less than four times one year, the last three appearances at the specific request of the students.[15]

Perhaps the most popular entertainer to ever play New Haven, not to mention other towns, was Mae West. The students reacted to her turn in wild fashion. She related how the audience, "made up mostly of young bloods," shouted and applauded so vigorously that Poli became quite concerned. He had received protests from some "local blue-noses" about the impropriety of Miss West's act and was determined that the rest of her performances must be beyond "any criticism, even from the most morally sensitive." But Mae West was Mae West at the next two performances and she again had the students in an uproar. In addition, fifty of the students had purchased a block of seats down front, but stayed out until Miss West's spot. Then they marched down the aisle, singing, "Boola Boola." The empty seats had done little to buoy the spirits of the other acts, but had served notice that Mae West was doing something special. Poli refused to tolerate either the continued West wriggling or the boisterous aisle-marching. He cancelled her act. The Yale crowd then proceeded to wreck the theater. Mae West declared their actions, done in her behalf, "a charming gesture."[16]

Another interesting town in New England was Newport, Rhode Island. The audiences there were a wealthy, cosmopolitan lot and generally very receptive to vaudeville entertainment. Newport was also the scene of an occasional "vaudeville dinner," where the members of high society would entertain their fellows at a sumptuous banquet, accompanied by vaude acts. The New England atmosphere generally proved pleasing to actors, if for no other reason than that the food was the kind that sustained a touring body. Benny Rubin said that very little food was fried and that the New England boiled dinners and lobster were "just out of this world."[17]

The small towns in New York seemed little different from those of New England, though the food was never particularly praised. One of the favorite stops was Elmira, considered "a great show town." Despite its size, the populace supported two vaude theaters, the Mozart and the Majestic. Elmira's people made the town a good date. They liked going to the theater and openly displayed their enjoyment.[18]

Usually, however, the vaudevillian made his few dollars and gained experience in circumstances quite unlike Elmira's. Nancy Welford Morris recalled a "two by four" theater in Poughkeepsie which had a sign backstage that read, "Please don't flush the toilets while the act is on."[19] Ken Murray described the Gaiety Theatre in Utica, New York, one he played in his very early days in show business:

> [It] was really smalltime. In fact, it was a carry-over from the nickelodeon days—a dismal wooden structure with a narrow front that looked like any other small store along the block. Backstage was equipped with a big, live, ferocious-looking bat which would sometimes swoop down through the spotlight during the show and scare the hell out of the girls working on stage. . . .[20]

Working upstate New York could also mean doing a Christmas Day show for the convicts at Sing Sing, perhaps the best audience any performer ever had. As reported, "even the 'chasers' were encored vociferously and not a patron left his seat or even manifested disapproval of the old gags."[21]

New York State also provided summer employment for many vaudevillians in the very time it was needed the most, the dying days of the great medium. The work was in the hotels and resorts scattered through the Catskill Mountains, an area that became known as the Borscht Circuit to performers. The usual lineup for a show in the Catskills had a dance team, a female singer, and a comedian. A salary of $350 a week was considered good, although there were headliners who traded performances for a week's vacation. Joey Adams, in the midst of the depression, worked as "Social Director" at the Plaza Hotel in Fallsburgh, got room and board, plus $1,500 for twelve weeks, although that had to cover seven others who worked for him. The Borscht Circuit became so important that, by Eddie Cantor's definition, Grossinger's became the Palace of that day.[22]

New Jersey meant Atlantic City, a top date for vaudevillians. George Jessel declared, "Oh, what an Atlantic City it was in those days! Nothing perhaps but the promenade at Cannes had its style." Eddie Cantor also praised the city highly, addressing himself chiefly to the type of audience to be found there. He believed the audience to be "truly representative of America," since its makeup included people from all over the nation. He also praised the Atlantic City audience as the best in the world, basing his view on the fact that the crowd was a vacationing one, carefree, so full of "a gala spirit [that] every hour of every day is Mardi Gras."[23] There were those, however, who had quite other memories of the shore resort. Groucho Marx painted this picture of his stay, when he was part of the Four Nightingales:

> For two dollars and a half, a boardinghouse could buy a week's supply of fish, and in Atlantic City only the very rich had meat on their tables.
>
> We ate fish for breakfast. We ate fish for lunch. And that night, just to vary the monotony, we had crabs. We had bluefish on Tuesday, whitefish on Wednesday, and on Thursday we had red snapper for lunch and fried eels for dinner. By this time, two of the Nightingales were growing fins.[24]

Among the circuits that operated in Pennsylvania were such as the Aborn Circuit of Polite Vaudeville Houses, which included Scranton, Wilkes-Barre, Erie, Harrisburg, and Reading, the Feiber and Shea chain, and a group of theaters owned by Edward Mozart, who also owned the Mozart in Elmira. Mozart was an industrious impresario, to say the least. Less than four months after *Variety* had reported his Pennsylvania holdings as four theaters, they were to print that he had increased his Pennsylvania circuit to fifteen. In the same year, the trade sheet wrote that vaude managers saw Pennsylvania "as a possible gold mine for their amusement ventures, which will outrival any coal field that has been located there." Mozart must certainly have felt so. He developed a trolley car circuit, making it possible for acts to play his theaters, with each of their jumps via cheap trolley transport. As well, the houses were close enough together that Mozart sent an agent by automobile to all fifteen theaters every week, his job to do the billing and oversee business matters.[25]

Mozart's first theater was opened in Lancaster and proved an immediate hit with vaudevillians. The new Lancaster location served as a convenient stop going from Philadelphia westward, so that the previous long jumps were no longer necessary. Mozart, though breaking in vaudeville in a fresh locale, was almost immediately challenged by another vaude house. The competitor was F. W. Woolworth, who brought in some of the outstanding performers of the time to appear in his theater, built atop the roof of his store. But Mozart perservered, and while Woolworth concentrated his attention on developing a chain of stores, Mozart did the same with theaters. In addition to his large assortment of Pennsylvania houses, Mozart also opened theaters in New York, having more than twenty altogether. Lancaster was also big with two sports. One was pool, a game vaudevillians loved and played wherever they could. The other sport, bowling, caused many performers great consternation, at least when in Lancaster! One of the bowling alleys was on the floor directly above one of the vaude theaters.[26]

Ken Murray's memories of Pennsylvania were keyed to train rides. The jumps between towns were on trains that had hard, rust-colored, reversible seats, so that "if you were lucky, maybe you could switch one over, put your feet out straight, relax." The trains had no dining cars and allowed only five minute stops at various stations. So the vaudevillian had to dash into the station, do his best to get a sandwich, and run back out to the train. Eating on Pennsylvania trains was made even more unpleasant by the numerous turns. He ticked off the towns, among others, that he toured: Carbondale, Lancaster, York, Easton, Allentown, Reading, and Shenandoah.[27]

Shenandoah had a special meaning to Eddie Cantor. In his very early career, he was booked to open on Christmas Eve. According to him, no one came to the theater, not even the manager, who had departed for New York. Cantor and the rest of the small-time troupe were, as he put it, "left . . . to fold in the snow." His grandmother rescued him by sending enough money to get him back to New York City. Easton was one of the early experiences for the Marx Brothers. They were booked to play the Arcade Theatre, which turned out to be a reconditioned storeroom. The act went well enough that the manager congratulated them on their accomplishment. Groucho pressured him into putting that in writing. The letter was then used by the group to get a booking in neighboring Bethlehem. There the boys met a rowdy and unsympathetic gang of Lehigh University students. No letter was forthcoming from the manager of that theater.[28]

Bethlehem produced a unique circumstance for the Albee Sisters. In their entire show business career, only one hotel ever had bedbugs and that hotel was in the Christmas City. The city was also the site of one of the legendary vaude tales. A great vaudeville monologist, also noted as a great drinker, was James Thornton. Booked to play Bethlehem, he arrived in the town and became enraged at his billing and the spot assigned him on the bill.

He refused to appear and announced he was quitting. The manager bellowed, "You can't do that. You can't walk out!" Thornton, who worked deadpan almost exclusively, cast a baleful, alcoholic stare at the manager and stated, "Christ walked out of Bethlehem. So can James Thornton!"[29]

George Burns considered Wilkes-Barre and Scranton good towns for breaking in new material. In vaudeville, so strictly timed, the insertion of a new joke meant an old one had to be deleted. New York was not the place to experiment. According to Burns, the two mining cities of Pennsylvania were. He clarified, "If we went to Wilkes-Barre and did a joke, whether it got a laugh or not wasn't the point. We wanted to *know* the joke and *know* the line so that when we got to New York we could tell it and get a fair reaction."[30]

Just to the west of the Pennsylvania line was one of the roughest vaude towns in America, Youngstown, Ohio. Whenever vaudevillians encountered difficult audiences, they would say it was another Youngstown. Ben Blue ascribed the poor reaction to the fact that steelworkers, most of whom did not know English that well, simply did not comprehend the comedy. Acrobatic acts, however, "would always stop the show."[31]

From Youngstown westward to the foothills of the Rockies was the great Middle West, as full of vaudeville lore as any other section of the United States. That lore included many a tale of Midwestern weather, especially the glories of winter. Fred Allen summarized:

> . . . the snowstorms were frequent and severe, trains were late, and baggage was lost, but neither rain, sleet, hail, snow, lack of sleep, nor empty stomachs kept the Western Vaudeville acts from making contractual rounds. The show must go on. Through the years I have spent a hundred nights curled up in dark, freezing railroad stations in the Kokomos, the Kenoshas, and the Kankakees, waiting for the Big Four, the Wabash, or C.&A. trains to pick me up and whisk me to the Danvilles, the Davenports, and the Decaturs. Most of the actors playing the Western Vaudeville theaters looked as though they hadn't been to sleep for many months. They looked that way because they hadn't.[32]

Among those who had little praise for Mid-America were the Marx Brothers. Groucho recalled the towns he played for the Western Vaudeville Circuit, including many college towns. They performed before tough student crowds from such schools as Michigan, Purdue, Indiana, Ohio State, Illinois, Northwestern, and Notre Dame. Groucho remarked that, when the students disliked the act, they often threw things at the performers, even parts of seats. The students also harassed the female troupers outside the theater, so that the male entertainers generally escorted them between the hotel and theater, "armed with the customary blackjacks." On one occasion, the Ann Arbor, Michigan, fire department had to use hoses to disperse several hundred students who refused to leave the stage door area.[33]

Describing his early days in vaude and referring to the Midwest, Groucho said, "We played towns I would refuse to be buried in today. . . ." The typical town had one or more national chain stores, "the threadbare hotel, and the restaurants that dish out grub so far removed from food that it's a wonder we're still alive." Brother Harpo held the same opinions: "Looking back, I simply don't know how we survived it. Those early days on the road were sheer, unmitigated hell. They made my earlier days on the streets of the East Side seem like one long recess period."[34]

Harpo clarified a very important point, one that applied to many vaudevillians, not just the Marxes. When they played towns in the Midwest or South, they figured they had "three strikes" on them before they started. "One: we were stage folks, in a class with gypsies and other vagrants. Two: we were Jewish. Three: we had New York accents."

An interesting contrast to the critical remarks of American vaudevillians was provided by Charlie Chaplin's statements about the Midwest. "In those days the Middle West had charm," he claimed. "The tempo was slower, and the atmosphere was romantic; every drugstore and saloon had a dice-throwing desk in the entrance where one gambled for whatever products they sold." Very pleasing to Chaplin, too, was the low cost of living, which enabled him to save two-thirds of his salary. He summarized:

> At a small hotel one could get a room and board for seven dollars a week, with three meals a day. Food was remarkably cheap. The saloon free-lunch counter was the mainstay of our troupe. For a nickel one could get a glass of beer and the pick of a whole delicatessen counter. . . . Some of our members took advantage of this and piled up their plates until the barman would intervene:

"Hey! Where the hell are you tracking with that load–to the Klondike?"[35]

The largest smalltime circuit in the Midwest, the Gus Sun chain of theaters, had its home offices in Springfield, Ohio. Sun, portrayed as a "nice guy" by Joe Laurie, Jr., was the originator of a few ideas that were far from popular with vaudevillians. He introduced split weeks, which forced an extra jump from one town to another in the middle of the week, and also paid an act six-sevenths of its salary when they had Sunday off. Undoubtedly, the most unpopular innovation tied to Sun was the cancellation clause. That allowed any manager to cancel an act after the first show without paying the vaudevillian anything. Sun may also have been the first to make a special effort to bring women to the theater, by offering free dishes and silverware.[36]

The Marx Brothers played five shows a day on the Sun time, plus one or two extra, but at no extra pay, if the business was really good. Despite less than bigtime treatment, however, bigtime performers were happy to have Sun time to play. It meant additional work and pay. Sun advertised in trade papers that any bigtime act wishing to could work his theaters at a guarantee of three weeks' booking. In order to avoid the wrath of the Keith-Albee office, bigtime acts with open dates changed their names and appeared on Sun stages.[37]

One who changed his name, but to fool Gus Sun, not the Keith time, was Ted Lewis. Years before he became a star, Lewis suffered repeatedly because of Sun's cancellation clause. He reported, "I'd been cancelled so many times that each week I had to wire Gus Sun under a different name in order to get some towns to play in."[38]

An Ohio manager who was far more compassionate supervised the theater in Sandusky. He knew the patrons who came to his theater were not a good audience, so he built an applause machine. By slapping a series of wooden paddles together, the machine rendered a facsimile of applause. Placed in the rear of the house, the machine was used repeatedly.[39]

Terre Haute and Evansville, Indiana played by vaudevillians in the same week on a split week contract, should have been, at most, three hours apart by direct train connection. Instead, the trip took eight hours, for there was no direct connection which could be used. The midnight train was taken from Terre Haute and ridden for only one hour. Then the actor had to get off and make connections with the train to Evansville. That train did not pick up its passengers until five a.m., making for a miserable middle-of-the-week jump.

Fred Allen commented on other Indiana locales, as well. In Logansport, the theater manager doubled as drummer. Because he made numerous visits to Chicago to book his acts, the theater patrons believed he was "the smartest man in town." Since the drummer sat very high in the orchestra pit, whenever comedians played Logansport they directed their material to him for they knew the audience would laugh as soon as they saw the drummer laugh. The Orpheum Theatre in South Bend was managed by a man who did not talk to the vaudevillians, but who was respected because he kept the dressing rooms clean and employed an orchestra that stayed in tune.[40] South Bend also had a newspaper which kept a sharp moral eye on the vaude stage. One editorial stated:

> Vulgarity is the crying evil of the vaudeville stage. The managers recognize it and fight it. The audiences dread it and endure it. The vulgar minded expect and applaud it. The performer resorts to it to raise a laugh and get a hand. . . . This class of performers is an incumbrance which keeps the standard of the profession far below the point it should be. . . .[41]

Discussed as much as any other midwestern state, Iowa was viewed with as jaundiced an eye as either smalltown Indiana or Ohio. Even their homebred performers found fault with the Hawkeye State. Booked to appear at Marshalltown, the Cherry Sisters proudly anticipated their engagement, until they saw their billing. Then they threatened to sue. The billing read: "Iowa's Famous Song Birds! Bad Eggs, F'ack Powder, and Ten-gauge Guns Barred!"[42]

If there were any dates feared by vaude artists, however, high on the list would have to have been appearances at Jack Root's theaters. Root, a former middleweight boxing champion, owned houses in Burlington and Ottumwa.[43]

In Cedar Rapids, the vaudevillian had to face the possibility of a different kind of punishment. The manager there, William J. Slattery, not only advertised in the local newspapers, but paid to have a byline column, in which he reviewed the acts playing his

Majestic Theatre. Slattery was anything but a shill for his own business and gave very honest and objective, often cutting, reviews. Fred Allen stated that Slattery did this because he was an oldtime showman, feeling a genuine obligation to his community instead of to his pocketbook. The community itself was a conservative one and knew they could depend on Slattery to maintain high standards on his stage. The Marx Brothers once limped across the stage in a parody of "The Spirit of '76," and members of the community protested that they were insulting the American flag. Despite Slattery's columns and close scrutiny, the Cedar Rapids' date was considered one of the better ones on Western Vaudeville time.[44]

If anything was really wrong with a Cedar Rapids' booking, it was the jump afterward, the typical complaint of road entertainers. Fred Allen wrote of leaving Cedar Rapids at 3:45 a.m., arriving in Mason City at 6:15 a.m., getting his luggage in order, then hoping the 6:45 train for Clinton would be on time.[45] One can imagine the sinking feeling that must have seized vaudevillians when seven theaters in Iowa and Nebraska combined to form one night stand houses. Despite the New York *Clipper*'s hailing the setup as very good,[46] it is doubtful that the performers enjoyed the arrangement.

The rest of Middle America seemed no better or worse. Fred Astaire could speak highly of his hometown, Omaha, emphasizing its neighborliness and smalltown feeling, while the objective eye of Violet Dale pointed to one of its theaters where the dressing rooms were in the cellar. She also saw what many others saw in many theaters throughout the country, a large rat, accompanied by "Mrs. Rat and some little rats." Fred Allen described a theater in Centralia, Illinois, as "a freight car minus wheels." The theater had no running water and only two toilets, both located in the dressing rooms. The latter fact prompted Allen to write to his booking agent, "Any act you like that's booked here, advise them to get rooms 1 or 4 unless they would rather get constipated and dress in rooms 2 and three."[47]

The vaudevillian could have been in Duluth, Minnesota, in the dead of winter. Eddie Cantor was there when it was twelve degrees below zero, staying in a small and cheap hotel because he could afford nothing better. The beds had "blankets you could read through." Or he could have been in Grand Rapids, Michigan, where "the better class of people" never attended vaudeville. Violet Dale avowed, "The result was that our audience consisted of groups of undisciplined people. If they sat in a box they put their feet up on the rail, or if they sat in the front row they put their feet on the orchestra rail, and always laughed in the wrong places." And though it could have happened anywhere, in Kalamazoo, Michigan, in the Marx Brothers' act, Groucho asked Harpo, "And who might you be, my good fellow?" Harpo, not yet the mute character, replied, "Why, Patsy Brannigan, the Garbage Man," to which Groucho cracked, "Sorry, we don't need any." Backstage afterward, the theater owner came to them and shouted the words no vaudevillian ever wanted to hear: "You're shut!" What the comedians did not know was that the local scandal in Kalamazoo concerned the theater owner's wife, who had run away with a garbage collector.[48]

The vaudevillian might have been booked into Kansas, where the new century's excellent crop enabled farmers in the southern part of the state to "import vaudeville into their midst." Schoolhouses became makeshift theaters and farmers could enjoy vaude in their own community. The setup was dubbed the "potato bug circuit."[49]

The South, trouble enough for black vaudevillians, was no cinch for white performers, either, although some enjoyed it immensely. Bert Swor, a blackface comedian who was a Southerner, was very popular in the South. "They just loved him down there," stated his widow. She related that she and her husband were "entertained royally" wherever they went. In every town there were "friends waiting at the station for him."[50] But not everyone was a Bert Swor.

The South, to vaudeville actors, meant poor boardinghouses and bad food, especially in the earlier 1900's. Vaudevillians had a saying about their tour of the South: "Just saving enough dough to have an operation on my stomach when I get back North." Harpo Marx said he and his brother survived on "boardinghouse spaghetti, chili and beans." He remembered complaining about some food they had purchased from a pushcart vendor at a railroad station. When it was pointed out that the food was cold and caked with dust and crawling bugs, the vendor told them to go to hell, that if his food was good enough for "white folks," it was good enough for "New York Jews."[51]

Of the audiences, Harpo stated that if they disliked the act they threw "sticks, bricks, spitballs, cigar butts, peach pits and chewed-out stalks of sugar cane." When checking into hotels, they never asked to see any accommodations, for they knew what they would be like, "gritty, smelly, either stifling hot or freezing cold, and infested with vermin." Harpo thought that the cheap hotels of the South and Southwest must have been intended as "bug sanctuaries." He portrayed the conditions:

> Fleas, ticks, bedbugs, cockroaches, beetles, scorpions and ants, having no enemies, attacked with fearless abandon. . . . After awhile you just let them bite. . . . In one hotel the ants were so bad that each bed was set on four pots of oxalic acid. This kept the ants off. It also kept them from competing with the fleas and the bedbugs, who had the human banquet all to themselves.[52]

As anywhere else in the hinterland, the less sophisticated audience could present peculiar problems. In Arkansas, a rider on horseback came to the stage door and asked which of the brothers carried the basket of sausage on stage. When he learned it was Groucho, he threatened, "That's mah sister who plays the pi-anna in this yere the-ayter. Ah don't want to hear you makin' that kind of talk to her agin, or I'll blow your Yankee brains out. You hear?" The "talk" that was referred to was Groucho's onstage line, "I love my wife, but oh, you kid!"[53]

Harpo spoke, too, of the dressing rooms. Screens were never in the windows, so that if they were kept shut, "you could suffocate," whereas if they were open, "you could be bitten to a red pulp by mosquitoes." Violet Dale told of a dressing room in Knoxville, Tennessee, that had no window. The room was constructed of corrugated iron and she recalled that "it was like walking into an inferno." The dressing area so sapped her of energy that she collapsed after one of the performances.[54]

Rough times were to be had in the West, too. The Ackerman and Harris "Death Trail" was there, with its extremely long jumps that often permitted only three days of performing in a single location. One of the roughest circuits was George Webster's, based in Fargo, North Dakota. This smalltime had houses scattered through the Dakotas and into Canada and sometimes demanded ten shows a day, for Webster often booked only one vaude act with a movie. Playing the Webster chain, Harry Richman said, "it was pioneering time." At the same time, though, Richman talked of some of the good things connected with playing for Webster. Prices for hotel, transportation, and "good solid western food" were low enough that he was able to rent a horse and buggy and take the local girls on rides. However, once it was discovered that he was a vaudevillian, the parents refused to allow their daughters to see him.[55]

There were other memories of the Dakotas, too. In Jamestown, North Dakota, Grandma's Pantry Restaurant served a special chicken dinner for forty cents, which was popular with the actors. The theater they appeared at, however, was quite something else. The team of Wishbone and Chessy, blackface comics, avowed, "Dat's the wus orchestra I evah saw." In Grand Forks, North Dakota, one vaudevillian was particularly impressed by the Indians who walked the streets. The same observer remembered, too, the train she took from Grand Forks. "Some of the Indians from town were on it," she said, "along with some careless passengers. I could smell feet and lunches and babies' diapers. I sat down by a big foreigner's straw hamper with some fish hanging out." Nancy Welford Morris also remarked that train rides would always mean to her the "smell of orange peel and babies."[56]

The trains in the West were the subject of lore among actors. Guthrie McClintic said there were three types of train travel one could get west of Chicago: Pullman, tourist, and day coach. Only the Pullman class allowed use of the dining or observation cars. For most vaudevillians, therefore, it meant packing huge lunches, the main foods seeming to be cold ham, chicken, and potato salad. The stove in the railroad car allowed for the brewing of coffee or tea.[57] Food was not the only problem, however, Norman Bel Geddes depicted a trip he took as a day coach passenger, enroute from Chicago to Sheridan, Wyoming:

> The further west we went, the more barren everything became. The train itself was dirty, full of cinders, soot, dust, and drafts. There was no drinking water or washing water, and one lavatory served both ladies and gentlemen. Soon my hair was full of dust and my fingers were sticky and black. So passed almost three days.[58]

More than in any other section of the nation, travel in the

West was hazardous. For vaudevillians any delay was serious, so when trains were marooned because of snow storms or avalanches, the pocketbook was adversely affected. Nancy Welford Morris was once stranded in Missoula, Montana, because of a snow storm. Fred Astaire remembered a trip between Butte, Montana, and Denver, Colorado, where the train ran into a snowbank. While waiting for the tracks to be cleared, another storm hit and the snow reached above some car windows. Then the heating went out. They finally arrived for their date at Denver's Orpheum, but two days late.[59]

Where the route westward took the trains past ranches, many vaudeville performers supplied a unique service for the ranchers. They would wrap up newspapers and magazines into tight rolls and throw them from the train when they saw a nearby ranch house. It was never known if the ranchers ever read the content of the bundles, but vaudevillians felt the cowboys were so isolated that they probably did appreciate the reading matter.[60]

Charlie Chaplin commented that he felt better the farther west his train traveled. "Looking out of the train at the vast stretches of wild land, though it was drear and somber," he said, "filled me with promise. Space is good for the soul." Chaplin included towns like Denver, Billings, and Butte among those he stated "throbbed with the dynamism of the future." Butte was an especially interesting stop for the vaudevillians, primarily because of its array of prostitutes. Chaplin described its red-light district as "a long street and several side streets containing a hundred cribs, in which young girls were installed ranging in age from sixteen up—for one dollar. Butte boasted of having the prettiest women of any red-light district in the West, and it was true."[61] Harry Richman wrote of the "Bull Pen" in Butte:

> . . . a city block square, about four stories high, a hollow building around a courtyard. It had no stairs; you walked up ramps. There were little stalls on every floor, some facing the outside, the others facing the courtyard, and in each one was a whore. Their rooms were not more than about five feet wide and maybe ten or twelve feet deep. Just about big enough to hold a bed. There were over three thousand whores in the Bull Pen—all getting rich, they turned so many tricks a night. The price in the Bull Pen was three dollars top for one time. If you wanted to stay all night, that called for a few dollars extra.

> Competition was very keen in the Bull Pen. Some of the girls had adopted modern marketing methods. Not the Farmer's Market, the Flesh Market. . . . There were a couple who had globes of the world outside their stalls. The globe would revolve on its axis and the sign said, A TRIP AROUND THE WORLD–$3. Others wanted to take their customers out of the world. A sign said, COME TO HEAVEN–$3. The ones who weren't so agressive had signs that said, JUST LIVE A LITTLE FOR $2.50.
>
> If the girl was French, her sign would say, A TRIP TO PARIS FOR $1.50. There were other signs but few of them were printable.[62]

It was no surprise when Richman declared the city was wide open. Everyone was armed and Richman claimed it was rare that a miner was not shot by an officer. Chaplin, too, referred to Butte as a "Nick Carter" town and was witness to "a fat old sheriff shooting at the heels of an escaped prisoner." But it was the prostitutes, above everything else, that vaudevillians talked about when discussing Butte. The best audience was found every Monday night, when a special section of the theater was set aside for prostitutes and madams. Harpo Marx maintained, "With them, you could do nothing wrong."[63]

In Colorado efforts were made in many localities to attract show people. Telluride was one community where the owner of the New Sheridan Hotel built what he called an opera house next to his hotel. Special doors connected the theater to the hotel dining room and lobby on the first floor and one of the second floor rooms was converted into a connecting hallway. Cut glass chandeliers, private boxes with brass rails and velvet curtains, and ample storage space highlighted the theater. Used primarily for vaude and movies, the theater had a life span of little more than a decade, folding in the mid-twenties when the world seemed to sweep Telluride by.[64]

Traveling in the West also presented a unique problem to the vaudevillian. Early in the century, they were paid in gold. Buster Keaton depicted his ninety-pound mother who, "like every other woman in vaudeville . . . carried the act's cash in a grouch bag." The burden finally became an impossible one, so she purchased a money belt.[65]

The Southwest presented ticklish problems of its own, perhaps the worst for traveling actors being food. Benny Rubin put it, "And Texas is a question of if you liked fried and fried and fried and fried."

Rubin less than fondly remembered Amarillo, Texas. There were no streets, just mud chutes, so the vaudevillians had to change in a railroad car before going to the "stinkin', so-called theater." The procedure was to carry shoes, stockings, and towel, walking barefooted, arriving at the theater, then wiping the feet with the towel, putting the shoes and stockings on, and going onstage.[66] Small town Texas provided a turning point in the career of the Marx Brothers. They were playing Nacogdoches, a typical honky-tonk brand of theater "full of big ranchers in ten-gallon hats, and a few small ranchers in five-gallon hats," according to Groucho. The performance was going well until, to the consternation of the Marxes, the audience suddenly dashed out of the theater. When the performers discovered the cause, a mule creating havoc in the streets, they went wild themselves. When the audience finally returned they found the actors yelling and screaming, burlesquing their own act. Then the Marxes yelled insults about Texas, all the time racing about. The audience responded with tremendous laughter and applause, and it could be said that the Marx Brothers' style was born that day. Audiences in succeeding Texas towns, such as Brownsville and Denison, received the horseplay just as enthusiastically as had Nacogdoches.[67]

In El Paso, Gypsy Rose Lee appeared at the Colon Theatre, located in the Mexican neighborhood. The Colon booked Mexican vaude acts to supplement their Spanish language movies. Gypsy recalled that the theater "smelled of mildew and dirty clothes and bad breaths." The local red-light district was directly in back of the theater and the hotel where the performers stayed served as the neighborhood bathhouse. Most of the houses in the area had no bathrooms, so for twenty-five cents, people could bathe at the hotel. She said, "Saturday there was a line of people waiting with their own towels all the way down the hall. The hotel was shabby and not very clean but it was cheap. . . ."[68]

The Southwest was not the only region of the United States that featured a Mexican atmosphere. Joe E. Brown told of the "dumpy little theatre" he played in Vallejo, California. The theater shared the same building with a Mexican restaurant, a fact which Brown claimed disturbed his concentration. The odors of

Mexican food permeated the theater and Brown "drooled all through the act."[69]

The Sullivan-Considine circuit had a good reputation with actors. Their managers were noted for showing the vaude artists considerate treatment. Wolfie Gilbert remembered one incident on Sullivan-Considine time. He and his partner were performing as Hebrew comics and one night in Spokane, as they were bowing to the applause, they noticed four bearded men in the wings. Gilbert, thinking them to be angry Hebrews, described his reaction: "My heart went down into my shoes. Here were the crusaders on our trail!" Instead, the four turned out to be vaudevillians who "had all put on crepe-hair beards . . . to scare hell out of [us]."[70]

Other localities in that area of the Pacific Northwest that vaudevillians played included Kellogg, Idaho, and Walla Walla and Toppenish, Washington. Walla Walla was portrayed as a town that had tiny houses situated high on the hill. The hotel where the actors stayed included a large bowl of red apples in its rooms. At Kellogg, the drummer missed his cues, a detail very disturbing to certain types of vaude acts. He also liked to escort the performers through the mines. At Toppenish, an audience composed entirely of Indians was not unusual.[71]

The real cold country, though, was to the north in Canada. Here is where the "Death Trail" was traveled: Winnipeg, Regina, Moose Jaw, Saskatoon, Medicine Hat, Calgary, Edmonton, and Vancouver. Charles Bickford was in vaude and arrived in Winnipeg just after a cold spell had ended, so the temperature was "only" six degrees below zero. From Winnipeg, the next jump was to Regina. The jump was "one to remember." The day they were to leave it snowed long and hard. Dressed in "arctic clothing" and warmed further by "a few belts of potent Hudson's Bay Company whiskey," the troupe went to the railroad depot and boarded their assigned car, a tourist sleeper parked on a siding. Bickford referred to it as "a battered old relic . . . that belonged in the Smithsonian Institution."[72]

While parked at the siding the car had been warm and comfortable, since it was hooked up to a steam pipe. After its pickup, however, they traveled only three miles before being put on another siding to wait for their train. That siding was not equipped with a steam pipe and it soon became extremely cold in the car.

Bickford and an acrobat were selected to go for help, so they hiked the three miles back to Winnipeg. Bickford stated that every breath seemed to burn his throat and lungs because of the cold, sharp air. They were able to get help but not in time to prevent the sickness which caused the cancellation of the show the next day.[73]

Ted Lewis had memories of Winnipeg, too. He and his partner had been stranded "way up there in Alberta." Broke and wondering how they could get to Chicago, they sent a collect wire to their agent in New York. The agent refused to accept the telegram. Fortunately Lewis was a member of the Moose. Fellow brothers of the fraternal lodge came to his rescue, among them conductors and baggagemen on the Canadian Pacific, who let the two travel free to Winnipeg. For their "fare," the vaudevillians entertained the railroad employees on the train. Winnipeg was the location of the circuit owner's office, so Lewis and his partner went to find out why they were unpaid and stranded. It developed that their own manager had absconded with the funds. With the circuit owner out of town, the office secretary could offer no help. So Lewis helped himself. On the hall tree, just outside the secretary's door, was a beautiful raccoon coat. As Lewis depicted it, "So I put my arm out and this raccoon coat just seemed to get off the rack and come alive and got right ahold of my arm, and we went down to the pawnshop with it and got enough money to get to Chicago."[74]

Harry Richman had his difficulties on the "Death Trail," too. In Manitoba, he dated the daughter of the theater owner. The owner detested this, not wishing his daughter "to have anything to do with a cheap ham and bum." During the week of Richman's stay, there was friction between the two. At the end of the week, the owner withheld half of Richman's salary and gave the actor one hour to get out of town. Richman had no recourse. The owner was also the town's chief magistrate.[75]

"Death Trail" was not completely unpopular, however. Bobby Clark rated Moose Jaw to be an exceptionally cultured town, primarily because his act always went well there. A lot depended, too, on the type of act being presented. Fred Allen maintained that Canadian audiences appreciated acrobatic, dancing, and novelty acts more than they did talking acts. Mitzi Goldwyn, a musician, felt that Canadian audiences were marvelous.[76]

Canadian audiences, like any other nation's, could also be strange. In Victoria, British Columbia, "a colorful little seaport," numerous nationality groups gathered together. It was not unusual to find Hindus and Japanese peddling their wares at the theater. In Quebec, during a matinee at the Auditorium Theatre, Johnny Black, who was appearing with Joe E. Lewis, kept making remarks to two local lovelies seated in front. The remarks were rather clear, for Joe E. Lewis' biographer wrote that the subtlest one gave an assurance the vaudevillians would be very happy to entertain the girls privately later that afternoon. What Black did not know was that the husbands of the pair were seated directly behind them. Outside the stage door, the "two burly lumberjacks" confronted Lewis and Black, ready to beat the performers to a pulp. Instead, some fast talk by the comedians led to the four men making the rounds of some local bars, with the now friendly husbands picking up the tab. But the story did not end there. The next day Black answered the knock on his hotel room door. Standing there, apologizing for being a day late, was the wife of one of the lumberjacks.[77]

North, South, East, and West, the traveling actor served to bring big city glamour to the hinterlands of America. But no matter where he went, the traveling actor never really knew what to expect.

OLIO

♦ ♦ ♦ ♦ ♦

THE SCOPE OF A VAUDEVILLIAN'S TRAVEL MADE HIS AMERICA LARGER than anyone else's. The breadth of vaudeville's audience and the substance of its entertainment made it *the* comprehensive entertainment of its time. It was more popular than any other form of entertainment during this critical juncture of American history when the United States was going through a host of significant changes. While vaudeville supplied the nation's people with their favorite stage amusements, the country was growing into an industrial and economic world power, converting from rural to urban-centered interests, expanding its population and work force with hordes of immigrants, involving itself in serious world conflict and facing its first pangs of international leadership and responsibility. A rapidly changing social structure and titanic historical events affected the nation. The American public was expected to react with the utmost resiliency, sensibility, enthusiasm, and cooperation. In such crucial times, the release that entertainment provided cannot be underestimated.

Vaudeville maintained its status as show business' kingpin because it gave the people what they wanted. Its focus was the family. Strict censorship was exercised on its stages so that any member of a family could attend a show without risk of being offended. Though circumvention of the censorship codes was fairly common, the image of vaudeville as being "clean" remained intact. Vaudeville's pride was in offering family entertainment, and by extension, morality of the highest order was to be practiced by its performers.

The censorship that controlled vaudeville morality did not die when vaudeville died. Their code served as the core and example for similar practices in the motion picture, radio, and television industries. Prior to vaudeville and its clean presentations, the popular entertainment fields had been raucous, bawdy, and wide open, designed for anything but the family. Vaudeville reshaped the patterns so effectively that the American public clung to its moral views long after the medium expired, forcing those views to be accepted by the more powerful and more popular mediums that replaced vaudeville.

Assaults on the moral code have occurred periodically, and the current pornography battles centered on the recent wave of nude movies indicates that today's assault is the most serious to date. Yet, even in the midst of the permissiveness that pervades the entertainment fields today, the motion picture industry gives "X" ratings and "R" ratings, on down–or up–the line to "G." The ratings clearly are affected by appeal to the total family. With very few exceptions, the more permissive television shows–and even they are censored–appear late at night, when children are presumably asleep. Yet this small group of censors who virtually dictate a nation's morality claim their limitations are set by public pressure. This attitude can clearly be traced back to vaudeville.

Vaudeville, for better or worse, dictated morals and attitudes. True, vaudeville, like any entertainment mirrored the life led by the nation's people. While it reflected mass attitudes, it also exercised a considerable power in shaping its viewers' feelings. While musically extoling traditional American ideals of motherhood, clean love, America's virtues, and innocent delights, those songs became the hit songs of the day. When its jokes made ethnic groups the butt of their humor, its jokes helped sustain the stereotyped misunderstandings and mythologies that still plague the American scene. When good triumphed over evil in its sketches, when adversity was conquered by perseverance, with the help of a script writer, when children were presented as lovable brats, when hoboes were viewed with pathos, and on and on, if only subtly, the American public was being affected. If it is considered that vaude audiences contained great numbers of young minds easily influenced by amusements, it is no wonder that the influence of vaudeville on America is still great.

Vaudeville was a national entertainment, yet its power base and its greatest center of influence was New York City. Not only were its most important bosses, bookers and managers located there, but great numbers of its entertainers were born and raised there, as well. And of the many from New York who did enter vaudeville, the great majority of them came from underprivileged circumstances.

It would be virtually impossible to say how much a part the New York City influence in vaudeville affected the nation's sense of humor and sense of stagecraft, and how much that influence has carried over into movies, radio, and television. At the same time, vaudeville managers had to be responsive to each audience, so that outside of New York, local tastes definitely affected the medium. This effect, though, was more so in the use of questionable words in sketches or routines than in the more meaningful and influential content and purpose of the entire sketch or routine. Ideas were more difficult to censor. In this manner, big city mores penetrated the small town and rural areas of the United States. Audiences that would not tolerate hearing the words, "hell," "cockeye," "broad," or jokes as, "A girl taking a tramp in the woods" and "Lord Epsom, Secretary of the Interior," would absorb sketches that showed married men out on the town or certain immigrant groups in stereotyped urban situations. Vaudeville definitely brought the big city to the small town and helped create an American humor and taste for song and dance.

Another influence that vaudeville had on the American psyche is that connected with the low economic background of so many top artists. It should be questioned whether these stars who emanated from poor circumstance would include in their material a concern, a sensitivity, a compassion that transmitted itself to an audience which in turn would regard the problems of the poor with more understanding. On the other hand, did their very success, their conspicuous example of rags-to-riches, harden the audiences—and even the artists themselves—against the plight of the poor?

There is no question, however, concerning the major focus of vaudeville! That focus was money. Decisions were made with that foremost in mind. Syndicates fiercely competed with each other in the typically American fight for the dollar. Once an act proved a hit, vaudeville management did everything in its power to insure its continuing success. Management's conclusion was that an act must remain as is when successful. Experimenting with a sure thing was viewed as horrendous, an unnecessary invitation to disaster. Thus, in vaudeville, numerous acts went unchanged for years. This failure to experiment, this order by vaudeville management to its top acts to stay static, left a bad taste in the mouths of those in the legitimate theater, many reviewers, and even quite a few vaudevillians themselves. What was generally ignored by these critics, was that vaudeville allowed abundant experimentation, but of an innocent variety. There were a tremendous number of acts which tried to gain success in vaudeville through very original approaches. The vaudeville management slapped on its restrictions only when any act proved a draw. Then, no tampering was to be done.

In more serious experimentation, however, where social issues and original drama would appeal to the intellect, vaudeville maintained a hands-off policy. As the nation's most popular branch of entertainment, this neglect to deal with challenging matter deserves analysis. In effect, did vaudeville retard the intellectual growth of the nation? Vaudeville was a mirror image of its public, reflecting a country that was evidently content to be socially and intellectually mediocre, a mass population weary of the pressures of a long and hard working day, wishing only to relax and enjoy its leisure hours. The theatergoers, in the main, did not wish to think, to face still more pressures. They were passive, not active. "Entertain us!" they demanded, and vaudeville did just that.

Vaudeville, the kind that flourished till it was driven to the sidelines by radio and motion pictures, is obviously dead. But the vaudevillian is not dead, and neither is his America. It has transferred itself to radio, movies, and television.

Vaudeville, vaudevillians, and their audiences were America in microcosm. Unlike legitimate theater, opera, and concert halls, where patronage was smaller and socially more selective, vaudeville drew from all walks of life. A typical vaudeville audience covered the spectrum of American society. There were other forms of show business which could also claim that distinction, of course, burlesque being one of them, but none drew the attendance figures that vaudeville boasted.

The very nature of vaudeville, where anyone could get a tryout, if only at an amateur night, where the opportunity was available to rise as far as one's talent and Lady Luck could take him, was representative of the American mystique. The expansiveness of vaudeville, as well, where novelty acts, animal acts, impersonators, acrobats, variety acts, magicians, soloists, monologists, comedy teams, drama sketches, dancers, and even chasers, all got billing and did their separate, highly individual parts, yet all somehow integrating into the whole, served as a symbol of Americanism. In as much as each vaudevillian, with his unique contribution, could help the greater entity while retaining his own identity, so too could ethnic groups cling to their identity, while still working side by side with others in the cause of a greater America. And the headliners had, for the most part, worked their way up from the bottom, achieving their success only after struggle and fortitude. The individual vaudevillian stood as a prime example of what could be achieved in a land of free enterprise.

That country of free enterprise stressed the importance of the individual and the opportunities for him that abounded within its borders, yet at the same time, the individual was somehow to remain humble. Here, too, the vaudevillian helped the American public achieve its goal. It was relatively easy for the vaudeville audience to stereotype the vaudevillian as being supremely egotistical (and indeed in so very many cases this was absolutely true). But by typing the vaudeville performer as being so egotistical, the theatergoer could then readily cover up his own ego by observing that the vaudevillian had more than enough for everybody.

The vaudevillian's America included a most interesting paradox. People paid to see him entertain and applauded his efforts—sometimes out of sheer kindness—but still denigrated him as a person. Onstage he was one thing, offstage quite another in the public eye. They could laugh at him, awe at his achievements, thrill at his dancing and singing, cry because of his dramatic skills, but they could not accept him into their society. "Stay away from our daughters," they bellowed. "You're immoral and everyone knows it," they maintained. "You can't get a room here," more than a few shouted, as they slammed numerous doors in the vaudevillian's face. It was a thin but obvious line and both sides observed it. For the black vaudevillian, it was even worse in this respect, for he was often not even wanted in their restaurants, and certainly not welcome in just about any hotel or boardinghouse that his white colleagues were able to patronize. The same mythology about the morals of show people remain today, even more acutely because of the many yellow journals that sensationalize and distort material centered on the so-called private lives of entertainers. As for blacks, the story may have improved somewhat, if only because of legislation and a much broader public demand. But the black entertainer still is too often cheered for his performances, then told that a certain neighborhood really is not for him.

Vaudevillians traveled across America and they could not avoid gaining impressions, undoubtedly forming their own prejudices. In that sense, they contributed, and perhaps more so than anyone else, to the numerous stereotypes that tend to strangle efforts at understanding in America, where localism remains excessively strong, where Americans who move to other parts of the nation are so often viewed as outsiders, if not intruders. The vaudevillian, by inserting into his onstage material jokes or statements regarding various parts of the United States, helped to perpetuate myths and stereotypes, or to create new ones, more effectively than anyone else in the country could. When the black shuffled across the stage or showed fright at graveyards or ignorance in everyday situations, indeed that was everybody's black. When the Southerner was a plantation owner, surrounded by poorly dressed workers, or a hillbilly, slow to reason, slow to act, slow to do anything, with the humor built around his laziness, that was everybody's Southerner. The Yankee was always stern, exceptionally wise, able to outwit the city slicker. The city slicker image warned all small town dwellers to beware of anyone from large urban areas, and certainly to be especially on guard when traveling to any major city. On and on went the stereotypes and they still persist.

To Americans, the vaudevillian also typified the spirit of liberty. Was he not utterly free? He travelled across the expanses of the great land, and did as he wished on the stage. In the most mobile of all nations, that nation's most mobile citizen, the vaudevillian, represented something special. Vaudeville entertained the family, the sacred core of America's strength. Yet the nation had been founded by daring adventurers who challenged the unknown. The average American had to remain close to home, but not the vaudevillian. He was heroic in this sense, meeting the challenges of one town after another, one audience after another, his very career at stake each time he mounted the stage. The theatergoer could share in all this. The destiny of the lone figure onstage was in his hands. The American needed the vaudevillian, but no more than the vaudevillian needed him. The one big difference was that the patron was in competition with no one once he entered the theater, whereas the vaudevillian was always in competition. At the same time as he was in competition with every performer on the same bill, he was also in competition with every other act like his in the field.

The pressure on the vaudevillian was relentless. His one goal was the Palace in New York, or Hammerstein's or Pastor's in earlier times. To get there—and most never did—required an arduous journey for all but a very lucky few. The rites of passage for many was amateur night, facing a hostile audience. From there, the route could often lead away from vaudeville, encompassing carnivals, dime museums, circuses, burlesque, riverboats, minstrel shows, and other types of show business. But the road came back to vaudeville, to its numerous smalltime circuits, with basement dressing areas, poor lavatory facilities, battered boardinghouses and hotels, tough theater managers, grinding schedules, and ancient and uncomfortable transportation. The road was never secure. The word "security" simply did not fit into a vaudevillian's vocabulary. Pitfalls were everywhere. The vaudevillian had to be running scared, for even when he was on the bigtime, he was only as good as each show's applause rendered him. The pressure made many adhere to numerous superstitions, look for get-rich-quick schemes, gamble for high stakes, fight for better billing, and in general sweat profusely on a day-to-day basis. But every hardship was worth it when the goal, the Palace, was reached.

The Palace, vaudeville's highest honor, the end of vaudeville's glory road, was the top. Once there, he had to just as desperately as ever fight to keep his place. Audience acceptance was still the key to success. The only directions from the top were downward, or the more desirable alternative, to leave vaudeville and join the ranks of musical comedy, the great revues, the legitimate theater, or to enlist with radio and motion pictures and help sound the death knell of vaudeville.

The vaudevillian who did cross into another branch of show business did so with as thorough a training in stagecraft as any performer could have had. Unfortunately, this training-ground aspect affected the status of vaudeville detrimentally. Supporters of legitimate theater viewed vaudeville's service as a training-ground as its chief contribution to the entertainment field. Vaudeville was relegated to a second-class category in the theater arts. While many more people attended vaudeville shows than they did performances in the legitimate theater, the dynamics and influence of plays and their creators have been over-emphasized. Though meaningful to the development of American character and the arts, vaudeville has never received such attention. It is regrettable that this imbalance has occurred, for while great playwrights are studied and evaluated—and rightly so—for their meaning to Americana, vaudeville has received but scant attention. Once the most popular medium of its day, it is now reduced to a point where it is fortunate to receive more than a one or two sentence mention in the very works that stress the importance of the legitimate theater. The entertainment medium that was easily the favorite of the nation's people during so many critical years and the personalities who devoted long hours to perfecting that medium deserve more recognition than they have gotten. It is a distorted work of history which can only describe vaudeville as a collection of separate acts featuring jugglers, animals, and comics, and end its description by chronicling the fact that it was the most popular area of the entertainment media for approximately thirty years. The question as to why it was the most popular is left unanswered, leaving a huge blank in a so-called history of the United States.

In days only recently past, when a majority of the readers of an historical account could readily visualize vaudeville, since it was reasonably familiar to them, such meager accounts in history books may have been forgivable. But that day no longer exists. Vaudeville is no longer a byword. It is ancient history. It has gone the way of Hoovervilles, Merkle's boner, the Katzenjammer Kids, and twenty-three skidoo. Now these outdated terms need the clarification. Vaudeville and vaudevillians, in order to gain their deserved recognition in historical studies of America, need greater attention from the writers of broad, comprehensive works. Hopefully, this work will have helped to bring about a greater appreciation for the importance of vaudeville and a better understanding of a vaudevillian's America.

NOTES

PREFACE

[1]Groucho Marx, *Groucho and Me* (New York: Dell Publishing Company, Inc., 1959), 105.

[2]Larry Wilde, *The Great Comedians Talk About Comedy* (New York: The Citadel Press, 1968), 52.

[3]Joe Laurie, Jr., *Vaudeville: From the Honky-Tonks to the Palace* (New York: Henry Holt and Company, 1953), 9.

[4]For more detail concerning efforts to get help, see John E. DiMeglio, "Old Vaudevillians Fade When Invited to 'Tape' Their Memoirs for a Ph.D.," *Variety*, January 7, 1970, 153.

[5]Bernard Sobel, *A Pictorial History of Vaudeville* (New York: The Citadel Press, 1961), 10.

[6]"From Honky-Tonk to Palace," *Life*, XXXV (December 7, 1953), 38; Joey Adams, *The Curtain Never Falls* (New York: Frederick Fell, Inc., 1949), 25; Joe Laurie, Jr., "Vaudeville Dead? It's Never Been," New York *Times Magazine* (October 14, 1951), 67.

[7]John Lahr, *Notes on a Cowardly Lion* (New York: Alfred A. Knopf, 1969), 81-83.

[8]Franklin P. Adams, "Olympic Days," *Saturday Evening Post,* CCI (June 22, 1929), 18; Albert F. McLean, Jr., *American Vaudeville As Ritual* (Lexington: University of Kentucky Press, 1965), 39; "A King of the Vaudeville Stage," *Current Literature,* XLVI (January, 1909), 85-6.

[9]Mary C. Canfield, "The Great American Art," *New Republic,* XXXII (November 22, 1922), 335; Laurie, "Vaudeville Dead?" 70.

[10]Albert F. McLean, Jr., "Pilgrims and Palaces: The Meaning of American Vaudeville," (unpublished Doctor's dissertation, Harvard University, 1960), 24.

[11]Laurie, "Vaudeville Dead?" 25.

CHAPTER 1

[1]Arthur Prill, "The 'Small Time' King," *Theatre,* XIX (March, 1914), 140; Warren E. Crane, "Alexander Pantages," *System,* XXXVII (March, 1920), 501; Laurie, *Vaudeville,* 362.

[2]M. Willson Disher, "The Music-Hall," *Quarterly Review,* CCLII (April, 1929), 259.

[3]J. Odenwald-Unger, "The Fine Arts as a Dynamic Factor in Society," *American Journal of Sociology,* XII (March, 1907), 663-4.

[4]Marx, *Groucho,* 71-73.

[5]Otis Ferguson, "Daughters and Others," *New Republic*, XCVII (January 18, 1939), 97; Alexander Bakshy, "Vaudeville's Prestige," *Nation*, CXXIX

(September 4, 1929), 258.

[6]Father of Edward Albee the playwright whose work reflects the somewhat carnivalistic and vaudevillian aspects of life.

[7]Howard Taubman, *The Making of the American Theatre* (New York: Coward McCann, Inc., 1965), 127-8.

[8]Joe E. Brown, as told to Ralph Hancock, *Laughter is a Wonderful Thing* (New York: A. S. Barnes and Company, 1956), 165.

[9]"The Decay of Vaudeville," *American Magazine,* LXIX (April 1910), 842-3.

CHAPTER 2

[1]Arthur M. Schlesinger, *The Rise of the City: 1878-1898* (New York: The Macmillan Company, 1933), 301, footnote. Schlesinger also cited a Boston *Transcript* article of 1926 which had given the initial date as 1852.

[2]As good a definition as any for vaudeville's heyday was that by Joe Laurie, Jr., who believed it "started approximately during the McKinley Administration and lasted well into the Volstead Era." Laurie, "Vaudeville Dead?" 25.

[3]Abel Green and Joe Laurie, Jr., *Show Biz* (Garden City: Permabooks, 1953), 26; Allen Churchill, *The Great White Way* (New York: E. P. Dutton and Company, Inc., 1962), 197.

[4]*Variety,* December 20, 1912, 52.

[5]Transcription of tape-recorded interview with Benny Rubin, 5.

[6]Letter from Harry Houdini to Dr. Waitt, November 20, 1906, Harvard University Theatre Collection.

[7]Harpo Marx, with Rowland Barber, *Harpo Speaks!* (New York: Published by Bernard Geis Associates, Distributed by Random House, 1961), 113; Bob Shayne, "Vaudeville is Dead and Living on Vine Street," *A. C. T. Program*, performance of *Hair* at the Geary Theater, San Francisco, August, 1969, 8.

[8]Green, *Show Biz,* 14. Sime Silverman, for a time, actually ran three papers simultaneously—*Variety,* New York *Clipper,* and *Times Square Daily*—Abel Green, "Chas. Evans Hughes 'Saves' Albee," *Variety*, January 4, 1967, 196.

[9]Marian Spitzer, *The Palace* (New York: Atheneum, 1969), 15.

[10]*Variety,* January 3, 1919, 6.

[11]Harry Jolson, as told to Alban Emley, *Mistah Jolson* (Hollywood: House-Warven, Publishers, 1951), 114-15, 135-6.

[12]Marx, *Harpo,* 155-60.

[13]*Ibid.,* 148-9.

[14]Marx, *Groucho,* 138-9; Ethel Waters with Charles Samuels, *His Eye is on the Sparrow* (London: W. H. Allen Limited, 1958), 150.

[15]Buster Keaton, with Charles Samuels, *My Wonderful World of Slapstick* (Garden City: Doubleday and Company, Inc., 1960), 82-3, Bernard

Sobel, *Broadway Heartbeat: Memoirs of a Press Agent* (New York: Hermitage House, 1953), 236.

[16]Max Gordon, with Lewis Funke, *Max Gordon Presents* (New York: Bernard Geis Associates, 1963), 84-5; Robert Grau, *The Business Man in the Amusement World* (New York: Broadway Publishing Company, 1910), 315; Spitzer, *Palace,* 86.

[17]Sobel, *History,* 75, placed the Actors' Fund figure at one million. Laurie, *Vaudeville,* 370 set the figure at $100,000.

CHAPTER 3

[1]Gordon, *Gordon,* 185.

[2]Russel B. Nye, "Notes on a Rationale for Popular Culture" (pamphlet published by the Popular Culture Association, 1970), 8; Gordon, *Gordon,* 75.

[3]Transcription of tape-recording by Al Fanton, 5-6.

[4]New York *Dramatic Mirror*, January 31, 1903, 18.

[5]L. Wolfe Gilbert, *Without Rhyme or Reason* (New York: Vantage Press, 1956), 51; Marion H. Brazier, *Stage and Screen* (Boston: M. H. Brazier, Publishers, 1920), 72, also emphasized Eltinge's "utter manliness away from the footlights."

[6]Walter B. Gibson and Morris N. Young, *Houdini's Fabulous Magic* (New York: Chilton Book Company, 1968), 16-17.

[7]*Variety,* April 5, 1918, 3.

[8]Eddie Cantor, *As I Remember Them* (New York: Duell, Sloan and Pearce, 1963), 51; Transcription of tape-recording by Lou Holtz, 3; Edward B. Marks, as told to Abbott J. Liebling, *They All Sang: From Tony Pastor to Rudy Vallee* (New York: The Viking Press, 1935), 94.

[9]Cited in two works by the same author, James Weldon Johnson, *Along This Way* (New York: The Viking Press, 1968), 177; James Weldon Johnson, *Black Manhattan* (New York: Arno Press and The New York *Times,* 1968), 103. Johnson himself does not believe Hogan was better.

[10]G. K. Chesterton, *What I Saw in America* (New York: Da Capo Press, 1968), 113.

[11]Brett Page, *Writing For Vaudeville* (Springfield, Massachusetts: The Home Correspondence School, 1915), 7-8; Fred Astaire, *Steps in Time* (New York: Harper and Brothers, Publishers, 1969), 47. Gottlieb later changed his name to Godfrey. Spitzer, *Palace,* 65.

[12]In an article that decried the fact that comedians and singers were always the headliners, the "Brothers Rath" were singled out as the example of an excellent dumb act which should have been given headline billing. Marsden Hartley, "Vaudeville," *Dial*, LXVIII (March, 1920), 336-7.

[13]Murray, "Interview," 20-1; Rubin, "Interview," 13-14. Both men were limited in time in making their decisions and could well have named other acts if they had taken more time to analyze.

CHAPTER 4

[1]"Psychology of the American Vaudeville Show From the Manager's Point of View." *Current Opinion,* LX (April, 1916), 257.

[2]Caroline Caffin, *Vaudeville* (New York: Mitchell Kennerley, 1914), 20.

[3]Gordon, *Gordon,* 38-9.

[4]"Editor's Easy Chair," *Harper's Monthly Magazine,* CVI (April, 1903), 815; Adams, "Olympic Days," 18.

[5]Nora Bayes, "Holding My Audience," *Theatre,* XXVI (September, 1917), 128; Disher, "Music-Hall," 269.

[6]Mae West, *Goodness Had Nothing To Do With It: The Autobiography of Mae West* (Englewood Cliffs: Prentice-Hall, Inc., 1959), 49-51.

[7]Transcription of tape-recorded interview with Ben Blue, 1.

[8]Edward Reed, "Vaudeville Again," *Theatre Arts Monthly,* XVII (October, 1933), 803.

[9]Walter DeLeon, "The Wow Finish," *Saturday Evening Post,* CXCVII (February 14, 1925), 44; Eddie Cantor, edited by Phyllis Rosenteur, *The Way I See It* (Englewood Cliffs: Prentice-Hall, Inc., 1959), 100.

[10]Transcription of tape-recorded interview with Mitzi Goldwyn, 2; Rubin, "Interview," 10.

[11]Robert Lewis Taylor, *W. C. Fields: His Follies & Fortunes* (New York: Bantam Books, 1951), 129-30.

[12]Transcription of tape-recorded interview with Ted Lewis, 3-4; Eddie Cantor, with Jane Kesner Ardmore, *Take My Life* (Garden City: Doubleday and Company, Inc., 1957), 201.

[13]Sobel, *History,* 13; Cantor, *My Life,* 49.

[14]Marx, *Groucho,* 69.

[15]Sewell Collins, "Breaking Into Vaudeville," *Collier's,* XLII (March 20, 1909), 20; Marks, *They All Sang,* 127-8. One can only speculate on whether, because the entertainer was there in the flesh, a more intimate relationship prevailed between him and the audience, or whether, because of the mass audience itself, intimacy was lost. A person alone or in a small group watching television can establish an intimacy, on the other hand, that often amazes television personalities when they are greeted as friends by people they have never seen before.

[16]Lahr, *Lion,* 29. [17]*Ibid.*

[18]Constance Rourke, *American Humor: A Study of the National Character* (Garden City: Doubleday Anchor Books, 1953), 109; Sir Harry Lauder, *Between You and Me* (New York: The James A. McCann Company, 1919), 204.

[19]Lahr, *Lion,* 76; Robert Lewis Taylor, *The Running Pianist* (Garden City: Doubleday and Company, Inc., 1950), 66-7.

[20]Corey Ford, *The Time of Laughter* (Boston: Little, Brown and Company, 1967), 2; Cantor, *Remember,* 20.

[21]Ford, *Laughter,* 133. [22]Rourke, *Humor,* 231-2.

[23]Arthur S. Hoffman, "Who Writes the Jokes?" *Bookman,* XXVI (October, 1907), 171.

[24]Paul A. Distler, "Exit the Racial Comics," *Educational Theatre Journal*, XVIII (October, 1966), 249-51; "Enter the Italian on the Vaudeville Stage," *Survey,* XXIV (May 7, 1910), 198-9.

[25]Nye, "Notes," 5-6. [26]McLean, "Pilgrims," 29.

[27]*Variety,* January 6, 1906, 3. [28]Laurie, *Vaudeville,* 71.

[29]Marks, *They All Sang,* 190-1; Green, *Show Biz,* 172.

[30]*Variety,* March 15, 1918, 5.

[31]Marks, *They All Sang,* 191; Rubin, "Interview," 9. Rubin did say that there were some white Southerners on some bills who refused to mingle with black performers, but he "only saw this once or twice" and it does not represent a general "hate" factor in vaudeville, as did that brought on by World War One against Germans. *Ibid.,* 8.

[32]*Variety,* September 20, 1918, 5.

[33]Spitzer, *Palace,* 53; Nellie Revell, "Vaudeville Demands Cheerful Patriotism," *Theatre,* XXVI (December, 1917), 364; Nellie Revell, "Vaudeville Doing Its Bit," *Theatre,* XXVI (August, 1917), 90.

[34]Lyle Stuart, *The Secret Life of Walter Winchell* (Boar's Head Books, 1953), 22.

[35]*Variety,* August 20, 1915, 7; Green, *Show Biz,* 136.

[36]Spitzer, *Palace,* 53; Marian Spitzer, "The Business of Vaudeville," *Saturday Evening Post,* CXCVI (May 24, 1924), 133; Green, *Show Biz,* 128.

[37]*Variety,* December 27, 1918, 15.

[38]Nils Thor Granlund, with Sid Feder and Ralph Hancock, *Blondes, Brunettes, and Bullets* (New York: David McKay Company, Inc., 1957), 75.

[39]Green, *Show Biz,* 128. [40]*Ibid.,* 274.

[41]*Dramatic Mirror,* August 1, 1903, 16.

[42]Spitzer, *Palace,* 35.

[43]McLean, *Ritual,* 69; Albert F. McLean, Jr., "Genesis of Vaudeville: Two Letters from B. F. Keith," *Theatre Survey*, I (1960), 86.

[44]McLean, *Ritual,* 69; *Dramatic Mirror*, August 6, 1904, 15; McLean, "Pilgrims," 106-7.

[45]Edwin M. Royle, "The Vaudeville Theatre," *Scribner's Magazine,* XXVI (October, 1899), 487-8; *In Vaudeville,* November 13, 1909, 3.

[46]*Variety,* March 16, 1917, 5; "Playboy Interview: Mae West," *Playboy*, XVIII (January, 1971), 80.

[47]William Cahn, *The Laugh Makers: A Pictorial History of American Comedians* (New York: Bramhall House, 1957), 41; Robert Grau, "B. F. Keith," *American Magazine,* LXXVII (May, 1914), 87.

[48]Spitzer, *Palace,* 35-6; Marian Spitzer, "Morals in the Two-A-Day," *American Mercury,* III (September, 1924), 36.

[49]Harry Richman, with Richard Gehman, *A Hell of a Life* (New York: Duell, Sloan and Pearce, 1966), 40-1.

[50]From a handwritten commentary and letter sent by Benny Rubin to

the writer, Spring, 1969, 6-7.

[51]Green, *Show Biz,* 332-3; Douglas Gilbert, *American Vaudeville: Its Life and Times* (New York: Whittlesey House, McGraw-Hill Book Company, Inc., 1940), 201. The long Keith list is interesting to compare with a later 1942 handbook for the Motion Picture Association of America, which listed among its taboos, "Alley cat, chippie, God, Jesus, cripes, fanny, louse, lousy, toilet gags, whore, damn, and S.O.B." *Variety,* March 25, 1970, 1, 61.

[52]Fred Allen, *Much Ado About Me* (Boston: Little, Brown and Company, 1956), 246; *Dramatic Mirror,* January 7, 1905, 16.

[53]Charles R. Sherlock, "Where Vaudeville Holds the Boards," *Cosmopolitan*, XXXII (February, 1902), 420; "The Trend in Vaudeville," *Independent*, LIII (May 9, 1901), 1093; "Decay of Vaudeville," 840. Only a year before the condemning piece was published, another writer stated, "Vaudeville to-day is as 'clean' as a church sociable." Collins, "Breaking," 20. Either the articles were in total disagreement or else church sociables deserve re-examination.

[54]"Decay of Vaudeville," 842, 846, 848.

[55]Joe Laurie, Jr., "Vaudeville," *Theatre Arts,* XXXII (August, 1948), 54; Laurie, *Vaudeville,* 286. Marian Spitzer, "Morals," 36, felt the average vaudevillian was "burdened with very little sense of his high moral obligation to his public."

[56]Leo Carrillo, *The California I Love,* (Englewood Cliffs: Prentice-Hall, 1961), 191.

[57]Brown, *Laughter,* 279-80.

CHAPTER 5

[1]Gilbert, *Rhyme,* 49; Murray, "Interview," 4.

[2]Letter from Richard A. DiMeglio to the writer, [n.d.]; Lewis, "Interview," 8; Told often to me, my father finally put it in writing in a letter probably sent in 1966, a letter which also told of his father's and his own subsequent immigration to the United States: "My Father then in early 1902 came to USA for a vacation and believe it or not to see the streets that were paved with gold. [He] went broke in no time—then he send for me and Amelia [the author's aunt] as he felt we being so young and he had not seen any young ones on the stage here in N.Y.C., we would make a good go here." Once on the circuits, he wrote of the vaudevillians he met: "No matter where we went the stage people . . . were like a big good family one for all and all for one always ready to help."

[3]Laurie, *Vaudeville,* 6.

[4]June Havoc, "Old Vaudevillians, Where Are You Now?" *Horizon,* I (July, 1959), 113; Green, *Show Biz,* 200. Miss Havoc added that being a standard act also, of course, guaranteed years of work in the field. About her school: "My teachers comprised a faculty of clowns, female impersonators, and performing seals. My training was strict. 'Keep it neat, keep it clean,

keep it dainty.' "

[5]Havoc, "Old Vaudevillians," 114-5.

[6]Charles Bickford, *Bulls, Balls, Bicycles & Actors* (New York: Paul S. Eriksson, Inc., 1965), 91-2.

[7]Green, *Show Biz,* 202; Cantor, *Remember,* 52; *Dramatic Mirror,* July 5, 1902, 18, January 10, 1903, 18; Spitzer, "Business," 133.

[8]Jack Burton, *In Memoriam–Oldtime Show Biz* (New York: Vantage Press, 1965), 63.

[9]Jolson, *Mistah,* 70-3, 87-8. [10]Astaire, *Steps,* 5.

[11]Guthrie McClintic, *Me and Kit* (Boston: Little, Brown and Company, 1955), 82.

[12]In an article written by the Superintendent of the Boys' Club in Birmingham, Alabama, there is a warning that if a youngster goes too regularly to the vaudeville theater, among other dreadful effects, he will put "undue emphasis on self-importance." Maurice Willows, "The Nickel Theatre," *Annals of the American Academy of Political and Social Science,* XXXVIII (July, 1911), 98.

[13]Cantor, *I See It,* 101. [14]Cantor, *My Life,* 17.

[15]Wilde, *Great Comedians,* 55, 131; Lahr, *Lion,* 10, 13-14; Churchill, *White Way,* 28; Fanton, "Tape," 2.

[16]Allon Schoener (ed.), *Portal to America: The Lower East Side 1870-1925* (New York: Holt, Rinehart and Winston, 1967), 10, 12.

[17]Waters, *Sparrow,* 76; Rubin, "Interview," 3.

[18]Marx, *Harpo,* 27.

[19]William K. Everson, *The Art of W. C. Fields* (Indianapolis: The Bobbs-Merrill Company, Inc., 1967), 2; Ford, *Laughter,* 174; Ward Morehouse, *George M. Cohan* (New York: J. B. Lippincott Company, 1943), 15, 17.

[20]Speech by Sophie Tucker at the 1954 Golden Jubilee Dinner, 2, New York Public Library, Lincoln Center Branch.

[21]Shayne, "Vine Street," 8; George Jessel, *This Way, Miss* (New York: Henry Holt and Company, 1955), 6; George Jessel, *So Help Me: The Autobiography of George Jessel* (New York: Random House, 1943), 18; DeLeon, "Wow Finish," 47; Alva Johnston, "Those Mad Marx Brothers," *Reader's Digest,* XXIX (October, 1936), 50. Also appears by same author as "The Marx Brothers," *Woman's Home Companion,* LXIII (September, 1936), 12-13+.

[22]Maurice Zolotow, *No People Like Show People* (New York: Bantam Books, 1952), 161.

[23]Wilde, *Great Comedians,* 246. [24]Jolson, *Mistah,* 51.

CHAPTER 6

[1]Letter from Groucho Marx to Pete Martin, December 21, 1960, in *The Groucho Letters* (New York: Simon and Schuster, 1967), 176; Marx,

Harpo, 25.

[2]Churchill, *White Way*, 198; Allen, *Much Ado*, 237; Donald Day (ed.), *The Autobiography of Will Rogers* (Boston: Houghton Mifflin Company, 1949), 34; Fanton, "Tape," 4; Douglas Gilbert, *Lost Chords* (Garden City: Doubleday, Doran and Company, Inc., 1942), 304-5.

[3]Marx, *Groucho*, 72; Allen, *Much Ado*, 236.

[4]Lahr, *Lion*, 27.

[5]Rubin, "Handwritten," 8-9; Lahr, *Lion*, 28; Allen, *Much Ado*, 72.

[6]Allen, *Much Ado*, 61-62. [7]Shayne, "Vine Street," 9.

[8]Norman Katkov, *The Fabulous Fanny: The Story of Fanny Brice* (New York: Alfred A. Knopf, 1953), 3, 5, 11-12, 36; Marjorie Farnsworth, *The Ziegfeld Follies* (New York: G. P. Putnam's Sons, 1956), 47. There is a disagreement about Fanny Brice's age, Katkov placing it at fourteen, Farnsworth at thirteen.

[9]*Dramatic Mirror*, December 19, 1903, 50, 52.

[10]Cantor, *My Life*, 21. [11]Farnsworth, *Follies*, 69.

[12]Green, *Show Biz*, 55.

[13]West, *Autobiography*, 8, 10, 13; Interview with Mae West.

[14]*Variety*, February 3, 1906, 6; Allen, *Much Ado*, 63.

[15]Lahr, *Lion*, 19.

[16]Pearl Bailey, *The Raw Pearl* (New York: Harcourt, Brace and World, Inc., 1968), 15-16.

[17]Joey Adams, *On the Road For Uncle Sam* (New York: Bernard Geis Associates, 1963), 289.

[18]Jimmy Savo, *I Bow to the Stones* (New York: Howard Frisch, 1963), 78-80, 103.

[19]Molly Picon, as told to E. Clifford Rosenberg, *So Laugh A Little* (New York: Julian Messner, Inc., 1962), 22, 24; Sammy Davis, Jr., and Jane and Burt Boyar, *Yes I Can: The Story of Sammy Davis, Jr.* (New York: Pocket Books, 1966), 12.

[20]Langston Hughes and Milton Meltzer, *Black Magic: A Pictorial History of the Negro in American Entertainment* (Englewood Cliffs: Prentice-Hall, Inc., 1967), 172; Gene Fowler, *Schnozzola: The Story of Jimmy Durante* (Garden City: Permabooks, 1953), 64.

CHAPTER 7

[1]Gilbert, *Vaudeville*, 20, 23; Milbourne Christopher, *Houdini* (New York: Thomas Y. Crowell Company, 1969), 19; Beryl Williams and Samuel Epstein, *The Great Houdini* (New York: Julian Messner, Inc., 1954), 33.

[2]William Cahn, *Good Night, Mrs. Calabash* (New York: Duell, Sloan and Pearce, 1963), 28-9.

[3]Marian Spitzer, "The Lay of the Last Minstrels," *Saturday Evening Post*, CXCVII (March 7, 1925), 123; Carl Wittke, *Tambo and Bones: A History of the American Minstrel Stage* (Durham: Duke University Press,

1930), 127-8.

[4]Lewis, "Interview," 1-2; "Ted Lewis, 80, Suspects 'Parade's Passed Me By'," Minneapolis *Tribune*, December 13, 1970, Section E, 7; Jolson, *Mistah*, 83.

[5]Rubin, "Handwritten," 4-5. [6]*Ibid.*, 10; Rubin, "Interview," 1.

[7]Ethel Barrymore, *Memories: An Autobiography* (New York: Harper and Brothers, 1955), 177-8. Hugh Leamy, "You Ought to Go on the Stage: An Interview with Edward F. Albee," *Collier's*, LXXVII (May 1, 1926), 10, wrote, "Vaudeville audiences are exacting, more so perhaps than any others."

[8]Elbert Hubbard, *In the Spotlight* (East Aurora, New York: The Roycrofters, 1917), 12, 14, 73.

[9]Murray, "Interview," 15.

[10]Transcription of tape-recorded interview with Amy Norworth, 14; Cantor, *My Life*, 201-2.

[11]Lillian Roth, written in collaboration with Mike Connolly and Gerold Frank, *I'll Cry Tomorrow* (New York: Frederick Fell, Inc., Publishers, 1954), 91.

[12]Jolson, *Mistah*, 162-3.

[13]Letter from Harry Houdini to Robert G. Shaw, April 19, 1918, Harvard University Theatre Collection.

[14]Allen, *Much Ado*, 244. [15]*Clipper*, May 13, 1905, 298.

[16]Marks, *They All Sang*, 15; Jessel, *Autobiography*, 24.

[17]Green, *Show Biz*, 82; Allen, *Much Ado*, 246.

[18]Wilde, *Great Comedians*, 137, 271.

[19]*Ibid.*, 39-40; Hazzard, "Fellows," 62.

[20]*Variety*, November 14, 1928, 31; Laurie, *Vaudeville*, 231.

[21]Burton, *Memoriam*, 62; Rubin, "Handwritten," 6; Joey Adams, with Henry Tobias, *The Borscht Belt* (New York: Avon Books, 1967), 56.

[22]Allen, *Much Ado*, 234; Norworth, "Interview," 12.

[23]Taylor, *Fields*, 44-5; Brown, *Laughter*, 195.

[24]Rubin, "Interview," 20; Allen, *Much Ado*, 248.

[25]Donald McGregor, "The Supreme Court of the Two a Day," *Collier's*, LXXV (June 20, 1925), 38.

[26]Steve Allen, *The Funny Men* (New York: Simon and Schuster, 1956), 28; West, *Autobiography*, 44-5; Wilde, *Great Comedians*, 42.

[27]Rubin, "Interview," 19; Green, *Show Biz*, 170-1, 535-6.

[28]Cantor, *Remember*, 20.

[29]Lahr, *Lion*, 67; Blue, "Interview," 10.

[30]*Variety*, December 23, 1905, 6. [31]Allen, *Much Ado*, 129.

[32]*Variety*, December 30, 1905, 12.

[33]Octavus Roy Cohen, "Vaudeville," *Collier's*, LXXIX (February 12, 1927), 24.

[34]Murray, "Interview," 6; Norworth, "Interview," 13.

[35]Murray, "Interview," 14; Rubin, "Handwritten," 2.

[36]Allen, *Much Ado*, 207. [37]Spitzer, *Palace*, 14.

[38]Green, *Show Biz*, 117, 175-6.

[39]Green, *Show Biz,* 175; *Variety*, November 14, 1928, 39.

[40]West, "Interview"; *Variety*, May 23, 1913, 16.

[41]*Dramatic Mirror,* October 6, 1915, 18.

[42]Allen, *Much Ado,* 245; Norworth, "Interview," 13.

[43]Earl Wilson, "Even In Death Zany Olsen & Johnson Keep Their Vaude Billing," *Variety*, January 4, 1967, 198.

[44]Rubin, "Interview," 4.

[45]Allen, *Much Ado,* 256; Fanton, "Tape," 3.

[46]Norworth, "Interview," 6; Sobel, *History*, 125.

[47]Fanton, "Tape," 3.

[48]Goldwyn, "Interview," 4.

[49]Spitzer, "People," 64.

[50]Allen, *Much Ado,* 215.

[51]Lahr, *Lion,* 7; Sobel, *History,* 55; Joe Brooks, "Never Whistle in Dressing Room," Bangor *Daily News*, July 7, 1967, 12; Allen, *Much Ado,* 248, 261; John McCabe, *Mr. Laurel and Mr. Hardy* (Garden City: Doubleday and Company, Inc., 1961), 47.

[52]Rubin, "Interview," 16; Sobel, *Heartbeat,* 142.

[53]Allen, *Much Ado,* 248; William L. Gresham, *Houdini: The Man Who Walked Through Walls* (New York: Henry Holt and Co., 1959), 81.

[54]Gilbert, *Lost Chords,* 339-40; Hazel Meyer, *The Gold in Tin Pan Alley* (New York: J. B. Lippincott Company, 1958), 157, 159; Marks, *They All Sang*, 134; David Ewen, *The Life and Death of Tin Pan Alley* (New York: Funk and Wagnalls Company, Inc., 1964), 133.

[55]*Dramatic Mirror,* November 10, 1900, 16, 18.

[56]*Variety*, January 20, 1906, 20.

[57]*Ibid.,* April 7, 1906, 4.

[58]Gilbert, *Lost Chords,* 341.

[59]Gilbert, *Lost Chords,* 341-2; Meyer, *Tin Pan Alley*, 158, 160; Ewen, *Tin Pan Alley,* 134-5.

[60]Issac Goldberg, *Tin Pan Alley* (New York: The John Day Company, 1930), 204, 207; Transcription of tape-recorded interview with Ferne Aìbee Burton, 21.

[61]Bickford, *Bulls,* 92.

[62]*Dramatic Mirror,* December 29, 1900, 18; Green, *Show Biz,* 33; Gilbert, *Vaudeville,* 235-6; Rubin, "Interview," 5-6.

[63]Waters, *Sparrow,* 75; Goldwyn, "Interview," 9.

[64]Separate letters from Harry Houdini to Dr. Waitt, April 4, 1900 and March 2, 1908, Harvard University Theatre Collection.

[65]Rubin, "Handwritten," 7-8; Rubin, "Interview," 2; Churchill, *White Way*, 208; Jolson, *Mistah,* 167; Brown, *Laughter,* 110; Carrillo, *California,* 185; Donald Day, *Will Rogers: A Biography* (New York: David McKay Co., Inc., 1962), 59.

[66]Marx, *Harpo,* 114. Harpo did not describe how all four fit into the compact upper berth, but the fact that they did glaringly points out how uncomfortable the day coaches must have been.

[67]Rubin, "Interview," 2; Carrillo, *California,* 185.

[68]Burton, "Interview," 10; Norworth, "Interview," 1-2.

[69]Goldwyn, "Interview," 8; Murray, "Interview," 14.

[70]Murray, "Interview," 13. [71]*Ibid.*

[72]Rubin, "Interview," 17.

[73]Lahr, *Lion,* 83; Johnston, "Marx Brothers," 51.

[74]John Byram, " 'Duck Vaudeville': It's for the Birds!" *Variety,* January 4, 1967, 203.

[75]Gypsy Rose Lee, *Gypsy* (New York: Dell Publishing Company, Inc., 1959), 131; Burton, "Interview," 2-3; Mary L. Coakley, *Mister Music Maker, Lawrence Welk* (Garden City: Doubleday & Company, Inc., 1958), 73; Arthur Marx, *Life With Groucho* (New York: Simon and Schuster, 1954), 42.

[76]Burton, "Interview," 13.

[77]Laurie, *Vaudeville,* 277; Cantor, *Remember*, 9; Rubin, "Interview," 7-8.

[78]Waters, *Sparrow,* 77; Davis, *Yes I Can*, 11; Adams, *Curtain,* 38.

[79]Burton, "Interview," 2, 4; Zolotow, *Show People,* 257.

[80]Gordon, *Gordon,* 64. [81]*Ibid.*

[82]Marx, *Harpo,* 115. [83]Marx, *Groucho,* 72.

[84]Marx, *Groucho,* 72; Sophie Tucker, with Dorothy Giles, *Some Of These Days: The Autobiography of Sophie Tucker* (Garden City: Doubleday, Doran and Company, Inc., 1945), 59.

[85]Eddie Shayne, *Down Front on the Aisle* (Denver: Parkway Publishing Company, 1929), 36; Gordon, *Gordon,* 66; Laurie, *Vaudeville,* 3.

[86]Tucker, *Autobiography,* 58-9. [87]Brown, *Laughter,* 77.

[88]Murray, "Interview," 15.

[89]*Ibid.* Murray's films, home-movie type shots of filmdom and its personalities, have been shown on television and in movie houses all over the world. He also developed a technique involving animals and simulated talk. His films are also shown as part of the attraction at San Simeon, the Hearst estate in California.

[90]Lewis, "Interview," 7. [91]Keaton, *Slapstick,* 15-16.

[92]McCabe, *Laurel,* 102-3; "The Death Trail" was specifically the Ackerman and Harris circuit in the Northwest.

[93]Charles Chaplin, *My Autobiography* (New York: Simon and Schuster, 1964), 135; Laurie, *Vaudeville,* 247.

[94]Rubin, "Interview," 11; Lahr, *Lion,* 69; Violet Dale, as told to Clarissa Adams, *Nothing Can Remain Hidden* (New York: New York Public Library, [n.d.]), 80; Jolson, *Mistah,* 171-2; R. DiMeglio, "Letter."

[95]Brown, *Laughter,* 119; Lahr, *Lion,* 7; Nick Grinde, "Where's Vaudeville At?" *Saturday Evening Post,* CCII (January 11, 1930), 44.

[96]Taylor, *Pianist,* 94; Zolotow, *Show People,* 164; Brown, *Laughter,* 176.

[97]Marx, *Groucho,* 106; Blue, "Interview," 11; Allen, *Much Ado,* 220; Rubin, "Interview," 7; Oscar Levant, *The Memoirs of an Amnesiac* (New York: Bantam Books, 1966), 105.

[98]Marx, *Groucho,* 101-2.

[99]West, *Autobiography,* 28; Goldwyn, "Interview," 3; Laurie, *Vaude-*

ville, 149.

[100]Granlund, *Blondes*, 162; Waters, *Sparrow*, 77-81.

[101]Laurie, *Vaudeville*, 149; Rubin, "Interview," 7; John B. Kennedy, "We've Forgotten How to Fight," *Collier's*, LXXXIII (May 11, 1929), 39; Murray, "Interview," 7-8.

[102]Goldwyn, "Interview," 5; Murray, "Interview," 10.

[103]Marx, *Life*, 32-3; Steve Allen, *Mark It and Strike It: An Autobiography* (New York: Holt, Rinehart and Winston, 1960), 4-5, 7-8.

[104]Fanton, "Tape," 1. [105]*Ibid.*, 5; Murray, "Interview," 1.

[106]Murray, "Interview," 10; Lee, *Gypsy*, 48-9; Havoc, *Early*, 180; Davis, *Yes I Can*, 17; Burton, "Interview," 1.

[107]Astaire, *Steps*, 29-30; Brown, *Laughter*, 58; Keaton, *Slapstick*, 24-26.

[108]Keaton, *Slapstick*, 31-3. That the young Keaton suffered physical abuse in the roughhouse of the family act deserves attention, of course.

[109]Blue, "Interview," 8. [110]Allen, *Much Ado*, 241-3.

[111]Fanton, "Tape," 2; Allen, *Much Ado*, 243.

[112]Roth, *Tomorrow*, 30-33. [113]Davis, *Yes I Can*, 12, 15.

[114]Lee, *Gypsy*, 24; Laurie, *Vaudeville*, 143.

[115]Miriam Young, *Mother Wore Tights* (New York: Whittlesey House, McGraw-Hill Book Company, Inc., 1944), 142, 171.

[116]*Ibid.*, 140, 171.

[117]Rubin, "Interview," 6; Cantor, *My Life*, 26, 28.

[118]Cantor, *My Life*, 28. [119]Gresham, *Houdini*, 49.

[120]Davis, *Yes I Can*, 19-20.

[121]Rubin, "Interview," 6; Jolson, *Mistah*, 110; Homer Croy, *Our Will Rogers* (New York: Duell, Sloan and Pearce, 1953), 117-18.

[122]Ken Murray, *Life on a Pogo Stick: Autobiography of a Comedian* (Philadelphia: The John C. Winston Company, 1960), 58; Rubin, "Interview," 6.

[123]Charles Beaumont, *Remember? Remember?* (New York: The Macmillan Company, 1963), 209; David Robinson, *Buster Keaton* (Bloomington: Indiana University Press, 1969), 11, 14; Keaton, *Slapstick*, 14, 27, 43-47.

[124]DiMeglio, "Letter."

[125]Willows, "Nickel," 96, 98; Katherine Merrill, "The Elective System and the Vaudeville," *New England Magazine*, XXXVI (June, 1907), 498-9; Marshall D. Beuick, "The Vaudeville Philosopher," *Drama*, XVI (December, 1925), 92.

[126]Merrill, "Elective System," 499.

[127]William T. Foster, *Vaudeville and Motion Picture Shows: A Study of Theaters in Portland, Oregon* (Portland: Reed College, 1914), 14; *Variety*, August 20, 1915, 3.

[128]Foster, *Study*, 37, 49. It is interesting to note that eight years after the Reed report, an article condemned vaudeville in similar terms: "Even more notably than the moving picture, vaudeville has refused to be uplifted and to reform itself." G. S., "Vaudeville," *Dial*, LXXIII (August 1922), 238.

[129]Foster, *Study*, 34.

[130]Beuick, "Philosopher," 92. Some obvious currency can be recognized, evidence that strong stereotypes indeed were developed via the vaudeville stage. It is also interesting to note that Max Beerbohm criticized virtually the same thing as it applied to English music-halls. His list of "ever-recurring themes" included mothers-in-law, hen-pecked husbands, old maids, fatness, baldness, stuttering, and sea-sickness. Max Beerbohm, "The Laughter of the Public," *Living Age*, CCXXXIII (April 5, 1902), 56.

[131]Rubin, "Interview," 22; Waters, *Sparrow*, 92.

[132]Lauder, *You and Me*, 213.

[133]McCabe, *Laurel*, 35. It is interesting to know that Laurel, interviewed in his later years by John McCabe, felt the United States, as it had become by the late fifties, was "cruelly civilized [and] atom-dominated."

[134]Speech by Sophie Tucker, San Francisco, May, 1959, New York Public Library, Lincoln Center branch; Goldwyn, "Interview," 2.

[135]Marx, *Groucho*, 71.

[136]Allen, *Much Ado*, 239; Havoc, "Old Vaudevillians," 114.

[137]Allen, *Much Ado*, 237-9; Spitzer, "People," 15; McLean, "Pilgrims," 73; Fanton, "Tape," 3.

CHAPTER 8

[1]Laurie, *Vaudeville*, 6, 202-3; Hughes, *Black Magic*, 282; Davis, *Yes I Can*, 35-6.

[2]*Variety*, December 20, 1912, 34. [3]Barrymore, *Memories*, 178.

[4]Hughes, *Black Magic*, 58; Ethel Waters, too, recounted that it particularly disturbed her when hotels were unable to find room for her "in towns where I'd been presented by the mayor with keys to the city." Waters, *Sparrow*, 244; Ann Charters, *Nobody: The Story of Bert Williams* (New York: The Macmillan Company, 1970), 12, 34. Churchill, *White Way*, 205, incorrectly stated of Williams, "As a vaudeville headliner, he stayed in the best hotels in each town, but he was forced to ride to his floor in the freight elevator." Though Williams indeed rode many freight elevators, the best hotels were often unavailable to him.

[5]Laurie, *Vaudeville*, 494. [6]Waters, *Sparrow*, 89-91.

[7]*Ibid.*, 151-3. White customers paid more than double the regular ticket price at black theaters. When whites attended shows scheduled for black customers only, the whites sat in the balcony. Clarence Muse and David Arlen, *Way Down South* (Hollywood: David Graham Fischer, Publisher, 1932), 49-50, 63.

[8]Waters, *Sparrow*, 153, 155-61. [9]*Ibid.*, 72.

[10]Muse, *South*, 128. [11]Davis, *Yes I Can*, 34.

[12]Rubin, "Interview," 5, 11.

[13]Mabel Rowland (ed.), *Bert Williams, Son of Laughter* (New York: The English Crafters, 1923), 97.

[14]Isaacs, *Negro,* 35; Gilbert Osofsky, *Harlem: The Making of a Ghetto* (New York: Harper & Row, Publishers, 1966), 38, 40.

[15]Laurie, *Vaudeville,* 81, 206. A recent Ph.D. study of vaudeville's racial comedy maintained that the racial comics were burlesquers who performed with "a sense of fun or playfulness, not of punitive ridicule." Paul A. Distler, "The Rise and Fall of the Racial Comics in American Vaudeville" (unpublished Doctor's dissertation, Tulane University, 1963), 95.

[16]Fred Allen, certainly not a prejudiced individual, casually wrote to a book dealer he did business with that his attention had been called to a blackface act whose case was pitiful. The blackface actor had been sitting for three weeks, in makeup, waiting for a booking. "He's afraid to wash for if he catches a job he hasn't enough dough to buy enough cork to blacken up again," concluded Allen. Letter from Fred Allen to Frank Rosengren, July 2, 1932, in Joe McCarthy (ed.), *Fred Allen's Letters* (New York: Pocket Books, 1966), 110.

[17]Fanton, "Tape," 3-4. [18]*Ibid.*, 4.

[19]Charters, *Nobody,* 6, 11; Isaacs, *Negro,* 42; Cantor, *Remember,* 49-50.

[20]Rowland, *Williams,* 16; Isaacs, *Negro,* 41.

[21]*Dramatic Mirror,* August 25, 1900, 19.

[22]Waters, *Sparrow,* 72-3. [23]Waters, *Sparrow,* 220.

[24]Waters, *Sparrow,* 75-6, 148-9, 164. [25]Richman, *Life,* 73.

[26]*Ibid.*, 118; *Dramatic Mirror,* January 7, 1905, 16; Green, *Show Biz,* 57.

[27]Billie Holiday, with William Dufty, *Lady Sings the Blues* (Garden City: Doubleday and Company, Inc., 1956), 47-8.

[28]Spitzer, *Palace,* 58; Carrillo, *California,* 198; Charters, *Nobody,* 50; Ewen, *Tin Pan Alley,* 86; Laurie, *Vaudeville,* 201. Laurie contended that Hogan was pressured to stop singing his famous song, but that Hogan "kept on using it until he died." Laurie strongly implied that Hogan never felt the shame and regret that Ewen and Charters, on the other hand, mentioned in their works. Ethel Waters said of the term, "coon shouter," that it was "an expression whose passing from the common language none of us laments." Waters, *Sparrow,* 129.

[29]Tucker, *Autobiography,* 35.

[30]Waters, *Sparrow,* 176; Keaton, *Slapstick,* 78.

CHAPTER 9

[1]Taubman, *Theatre,* 129; Bickford, *Bulls,* 133; Spitzer, *Palace,* 72; Rudy Vallee, with Gil McKean, *My Time is Your Time* (New York: Ivan Obolensky, Inc., 1962), 77; Saul Carson, "Theatre: Vaudeville," *New Republic,* CXX (June 13, 1949), 19; Laurence Lader, "The Palace Theater: Broadway's Shrine," *Coronet,* XXXII (July, 1952), 51; Sobel, *History,* 90; Donald Wayne, "The Palace," *Holiday,* VII (March, 1950), 65; Allen, *Much Ado*, 208; Burton, *Memoriam,* 70. Fred Allen also referred to the Palace as

"the towering symbol of vaudeville," his book appearing in 1956. Donald Wayne, in a 1950 article, termed it "the towering arch symbol of vaudeville." Wayne, *Ibid.*, 63. Wayne, Allen, and Sobel, the last published in 1961. all supplied the description, "diploma of merit."

[2]Green, *Show Biz,* 162, 353; Brooks Atkinson, *Broadway* (New York: The Macmillan Company, 1970), 118; Allen, *Much Ado,* 346; Tucker, *Autobiography,* 131. Max Gordon, writing more than a dozen years after Green and Laurie, also termed the Palace "the White House of vaudeville." Gordon, *Gordon,* 77.

[3]Spitzer, *Palace,* 57; Wilde, *Great Comedians,* 44; Murray, *Pogo,* 59; Zolotow, *Show People,* 162.

[4]Wilde, *Great Comedians,* 145-6; Cantor, *My Life,* 204; Laurie, *Vaudeville,* 183.

[5]Tucker, *Autobiography,* 151; Bernard Sobel, *A Pictorial History of Burlesque* (New York: G. P. Putnam's Sons, 1956), 37; Barrymore, *Memories,* 177; Spitzer, *Palace,* 26, 38; Spitzer, "Morals," 37.

[6]Murray, *Pogo,* 59; Spitzer, *Palace,* 75; Bickford, *Bulls,* 133; Vallee, *My Time,* 77; Sobel, *History,* 90.

[7]Spitzer, *Palace,* 75, 90. [8]Murray, "Interview," 6-7.

[9]Spitzer, *Palace,* x, 110; Rudy Vallee, *Vagabond Dreams Come True* (New York: Grosset & Dunlap Publishers, 1930), 126-7.

[10]Gordon, *Gordon,* 77-8; Green, *Show Biz,* 31; Spitzer, *Palace,* 36, 137-8; Adams, *Curtain,* 31; Ethel Merman, as told to Pete Martin, *Who Could Ask For Anything More* (Garden City: Doubleday & Company, Inc., 1955), 66; Sobel, *Heartbeat,* 237.

[11]Spitzer, *Palace,* 91; Rubin, "Interview," 4; Adams, *Borscht,* 57; Adams, *Curtain,* 107. The Somerset Coffee House subsequently became Gus and Andy's.

[12]Spitzer, *Palace,* 64-6; Gordon, *Gordon,* 92; Tucker, *Autobiography,* 151.

[13]Gilbert, *Vaudeville,* 213-14; Spitzer, *Palace,* 70; Gordon, *Gordon,* 92-3.

[14]Spitzer, *Palace,* 76-7; Leamy, "Stage," 10. Laurie, *Vaudeville,* 489, put Wednesday as the day for morning tryouts.

[15]Spitzer, *Palace,* 95, 97; Laurie, *Vaudeville,* 484; Lader, "Palace," 53. Spitzer, Laurie, and Lader disagreed on the source of the painting idea. Spitzer and Laurie gave credit to Darling while Lader credited Albee.

[16]Green, *Show Biz,* 43; Keaton, *Slapstick,* 68-9; Day, *Rogers Autobiography,* 31; Jessel, *Autobiography,* 17; George Blumenthal, as told to Arthur H. Merkin, *My Sixty Years in Show Business: A Chronicle of the American Theater, 1874-1934* (New York: Frederick C. Osberg, Publishers, 1936), 112.

[17]Sobel, *History,* 79; Gresham, *Houdini,* 177; Blumenthal, *Ibid.*; Vincent Sheean, *Oscar Hammerstein I: The Life and Exploits of an Impresario* (New York: Simon and Schuster, 1956), 110-11, 114.

[18]Burton, *Memoriam,* 66-8; Sheean, *Oscar I,* 112.

[19]Burton, *Memoriam,* 39, 68; Sheean, *Oscar I,* 116; Laurie, *Vaudeville,* 273; Day, *Rogers Autobiography,* 32. In Sheean's book he ascribed Sober Sue's inability to laugh to "the simple reason that her face muscles were paralyzed." Will Rogers, on the other hand, claimed that when she divulged her secret of being deaf and short-sighted, she laughed while telling about it. Rogers added that it was "too late to do us any good. She was one afflicted person after this that I could never seem to sympathise with."

[20]Laurie, *Vaudeville,* 333; Christopher, *Houdini,* 22; Grau, *Observation,* 2; Parker Morell, *Lillian Russell* (New York: Random House, 1940), 4; Gilbert, *Rhyme,* 36; Sobel, *Burlesque,* 30-1.

[21]Gresham, *Houdini,* 32; Marks, *They All Sang,* 32; Gilbert, *Rhyme,* 25; David Ewen, *The Story of George Gershwin* (New York: Henry Holt and Company, 1943), 38.

[22]Ewen, *Tin Pan Alley,* 21; Carrillo, *California,* 186; *Dramatic Mirror,* November 10, 1900, 18.

[23]Keith's Jefferson must have been one of the worst vaudeville houses in the nation. Fred Allen described it as follows: The Jefferson . . . had a mongrel audience: the theater was going to the dogs. . . . Alcoholics of all sizes and in varying conditions . . . used the Jefferson as a haven from the elements and a slumber sanctuary. At some performances the Jefferson took on the appearance of a flophouse that had put in vaudeville. At one supper show, during my monologue I heard a sort of "clunk!" noise that was repeated at regular intervals. . . . On the aisle, in the third row, sat a simian-faced specimen. Between his feet he was holding a wooden bucket; on the seat next to him he had a bag filled with oysters. As I was struggling through my monologue, this combination bivalve addict and theater patron was shucking his oysters and dropping the shells into the bucket. Allen, *Much Ado,* 253.

[24]Allen, *Much Ado,* 135, 203; Ewen, *Tin Pan Alley,* 21; Ewen, *Gershwin,* 59-60. Gershwin did not flee vaude altogether, however, for he later served as an accompanist for both Louise Dresser and Nora Bayes.

[25]Rubin, "Interview," 4; Green, *Show Biz,* 28; Gresham, *Houdini,* 126; Tucker, *Autobiography,* 116, 118; Jessel, *Autobiography,* 42; Gilbert, *Rhyme,* 40-1; Gilbert, *Vaudeville,* 216. It is interesting to note that Sophie Tucker placed the Colonial at 61st and Broadway, Jessel at 62nd and Broadway, Gresham at 63rd, Rubin at 65th or 66th, and Gilbert at 66th.

[26]*Dramatic Mirror,* June 14, 1902, 16; December 9, 1905, 18; *Variety,* December 23, 1905, 9.

[27]Waters, *Sparrow,* 167; Allen, *Much Ado,* 206; Murray, *Pogo,* 55; Ewen, *Tin Pan Alley,* 261.

[28]Cantor, *My Life,* 205-7.

[29]Julius Cahn, *Julius Cahn's Official Theatrical Guide* (New York: Empire Theatre Building, 1909), 75; Goldwyn, "Interview," 9; Marks, *They All Sang,* 129-30; Atkinson, *Broadway,* 119; Spitzer, "Morals," 35. Cahn's *Guide* was indispensable to the vaudevillian, 840 pages of railroad and hotel information, plus data on theater dimensions, city newspapers and their dramatic editors, traveling companies and their managers, and maps of key loca-

tions.

[30]Granlund, *Blondes,* 41-2. [31]*Ibid.,* 42-3; Murray, *Pogo,* 55.

[32]Laurie, *Vaudeville,* 500. [33]Bickford, *Bulls,* 89-91.

[34]Allen, *Much Ado,* 136.

[35]Cantor, *My Life,* 97; Vallee, *Vagabond,* 124; *Variety,* December 12, 1928, 39.

[36]Adams, *Gags,* 26; Green, *Show Biz,* 263; Murray, "Interview," 25.

[37]Young, *Tights,* 122; Vallee, *Vagabond,* 130; Vallee, *My Time,* 79.

[38]Tucker, *Autobiography,* 139-40; Gilbert, *Rhyme,* 221-2.

[39]Gilbert, *Rhyme,* 47. [40]Marx, *Harpo,* 146.

[41]*Dramatic Mirror,* January 6, 1900, 18; Sheean, *Oscar I,* 114-15; West, *Autobiography,* 31.

[42]Dayton Stoddart, *Lord Broadway: Variety's Sime* (New York: Wilfred Funk, Inc., 1941), 89; *Variety,* January 27, 1906, 2.

[43]*Dramatic Mirror,* January 27, 1900, 18; March 31, 1900, 18; Green, *Show Biz,* 168.

[44]A. G. Macdonell, *A Visit to America* (New York: The Macmillan Company, 1935), 46; Chesterton, *America,* 33.

[45]"If Troupers Make Good They'll Go Back to the Sticks," *Newsweek,* V (June 29, 1935), 23; Marks, *They All Sang,* 221; Fowler, *Schnozzola,* 51; Churchill, *White Way,* 13; George Jessel, *Elegy in Manhattan* (New York: Holt, Rinehart and Winston, 1961), 56.

[46]Gilbert, *Rhyme,* 40; Johnston, "Marx Brothers," 50.

[47]Rubin, "Interview," 13; Spitzer, *Palace,* 79-80; West, *Autobiography,* 40.

[48]Jolson, *Mistah,* 73-4. [49]McClintic, *Me and Kit,* 88.

[50]Shayne, *Down Front,* 37; Keaton, *Slapstick,* 43.

[51]Allen, *Much Ado,* 120-7.

[52]Carrillo, *California,* 197; Brown, *Laughter,* 114, 116; Chaplin, *Autobiography,* 120; McCabe, *Laurel,* 33-4. The Yandis Court was owned for a time by vaude comic, Lou Holtz. Laurie, *Vaudeville,* 280.

[53]McClintic, *Me and Kit,* 90; Francis J. Brady, *Recollections of the Theatre of Fifty and More Years Ago* (No publication data), 14; Allen, *Much Ado,* 127-8.

[54]Rubin, "Interview," 2; Gilbert, *Rhyme,* 15; Jolson, *Mistah,* 87.

[55]Marx, *Harpo,* 60; Harry Golden, "Tales of a Truly Wayward Inn, N. Y.'s Hotel Markwell In the Depression," *Variety,* January 4, 1967, 4, 56; Lahr, *Lion,* 79; Fanton, "Tape," 1.

[56]Allen, *Much Ado,* 216; Carrillo, *California,* 189; Letter from Fred Allen to Mark Leddy, December 10, 1931, in McCarthy, *Letters,* 57.

[57]Allen, *Much Ado,* 240.

[58]*Variety,* January 9, 1929, 1.

[59]Stoddart, *Lord Broadway,* 140; Granlund, *Blondes,* 31; Laurie, *Vaudeville,* 279.

[60]Astaire, *Steps,* 33; Levant, *Memoirs,* 146.

[61]Gilbert, *Rhyme,* 38.

[62]Letter from Nick Lucas to the writer, September 3, 1970; Holtz, "Tape," 2; R. DiMeglio, "Letter."

[63]Jolson, *Mistah,* 86,

[64]Dale, *Hidden,* 81; McClintic, *Me and Kit,* 78, 81.

[65]Allen, *Much Ado,* 124-5.

[66]Lahr, *Lion,* 31-2; Brady, *Recollections,* 13-14.

[67]Jessel, *Elegy,* 9; Adams, *Curtain,* 142; Laurie, *Vaudeville,* 279; Gordon, *Gordon,* 96; *Variety,* January 2, 1929, 29; Waters, *Sparrow,* 245.

[68]Marks, *They All Sang,* 294-311, has what the author called "an exhaustive index of addresses and circumstances under which good fellows gathered," a list of hotels, boardinghouses, restaurants, bars, and dives that, although not "exhaustive," is nevertheless the most complete list available for reference. Laurie, *Vaudeville,* 176-86, in a chapter titled "Three Meals a Day—and a Bluff," described many boardinghouses, hotels, and restaurants, both in and out of New York City.

CHAPTER 10

[1]Allen, *Much Ado,* 185, 191; Robert J. Conkey, *One-To-Fill of 1922* (Chicago: Published by Bob Conkey, 1922), 3; Robert Grau, *The Business Man in the Amusement World* (New York: Broadway Publishing Company, 1909), 323.

[2]Conkey, *One-To-Fill*, 13, 15, 17, 19; Allen, *Much Ado,* 186.

[3]Allen, *Ibid.,* 191; Cahn, *Laugh Makers,* 52-3; Albert Britt, *Turn of the Century* (Barre, Massachusetts: Barre Publishers, 1966), 15; Eddie Foy and Alvin F. Harlow, *Clowning Through Life* (New York: E. P. Dutton & Company, 1928), 273.

[4]Foy, *Clowning,* 274-81. Foy's account was either distorted because of his involvement in the pressure-packed situation, or else other witnesses and the usual summaries were wrong. For example, Eddie Cantor, *Remember,* 38, followed the general story, that Foy was onstage when the fire started. William Brady reported that he had been summoned into the Iroquois by its manager, Harry Powers, to see Eddie Foy perform. Foy was onstage. He watched Foy for awhile, then left the theater. Brady claimed he was less than a hundred feet from the Iroquois when a man tore past him, shouting about the fire. William A. Brady, *Showman* (New York: E. P. Dutton & Company, Inc., 1937), 252-3.

[5]Cantor, *Ibid.*

[6]Jack Benny quoted on the "Joey Bishop Show," October 10, 1969; Hubbard, *Spotlight,* 14.

[7]Astaire, *Steps,* 51-3.

[8]Tucker, *Autobiography,* 72, 90, 98.

[9]Marx, *Harpo,* 137; Waters, *Sparrow,* 165-6.

[10]Transcription of tape-recorded interview with Mary Dentinger, 2; Sobel, *Burlesque,* 62.

[11]Carrillo, *California*, 176-8. [12]*Ibid.*, 178-9.

[13]Carrillo, *California*, 180-4.

[14]Laurie, *Vaudeville*, 244; Astaire, *Steps*, 56.

[15]Hallie Flanagan, *Arena* (New York: Duell, Sloan and Pearce, 1940), 134; Hoagy Carmichael, with Stephen Longstreet, *Sometimes I Wonder* (New York: Farrar, Straus and Giroux, 1965), 179; Waters, *Sparrow*, 204-5.

[16]Oscar Levant, *The Unimportance of Being Oscar* (New York: G. P. Putnam's Sons, 1968), 51.

[17]Green, *Show Biz*, 112-13.

[18]Rubin, "Interview," 7; Chaplin, *Autobiography*, 126-7.

[19]*Dramatic Mirror*, May 19, 1900, 18; "Social Welfare in Vaudeville," *Survey*, XXIII (February 26, 1910), 794.

[20]Allen, *Much Ado*, 191-2; Lee, *Gypsy*, 8; Laurie, *Vaudeville*, 283.

[21]*Clipper*, September 29, 1906, 843; Chaplin, *Autobiography*, 127.

[22]Shayne, *Down Front*, 39.

[23]Morell, *Russell*, 34; Carrillo, *California*, 166-7.

[24]Allen, *Much Ado*, 144; Laurie, *Vaudeville*, 14-15; Johnson, *Along*, 206.

[25]From a speech by Sophie Tucker in San Francisco, May, 1959, at New York Public Library, Lincoln Center branch; Tucker, *Autobiography*, 103, 207.

[26]Chaplin, *Autobiography*, 129; Jolson, *Mistah*, 99.

[27]Edmond M. Gagey, *The San Francisco Stage: A History* (New York: Columbia University Press, 1950), 199, 210.

[28]Eugene C. Elliott, *A History of Variety-Vaudeville in Seattle: From the Beginning to 1914* (Seattle: University of Washington Press, 1944), 49-50; Laurie, *Vaudeville*, 27; Will M. Cressy, *Continuous Vaudeville* (Boston: Richard G. Badger, 1914), 14.

[29]Carrillo, *California*, 174-6. [30]Brown, *Laughter*, 62-4.

[31]Fowler, *Schnozzola*, 65; Allen, *Much Ado*, 184; Jolson, *Mistah*, 94-5.

[32]Brown, *Laughter*, 64-6.

[33]Taylor, *Fields*, 78. Taylor gave credit for the explanation about Bushnell's importance to John Chapman.

[34]Green, *Show Biz*, 52. [35]Richman, *Life*, 137-8.

[36]*Ibid.*, 135; Jolson, *Mistah*, 94.

[37]Astaire, *Steps*, 48; Chaplin, *Autobiography*, 129; Brown, *Laughter*, 249.

[38]Johnson, *Along*, 204-5.

[39]Rubin, "Interview," 4-5, 11; Lahr, *Lion*, 79.

[40]Fowler, *Schnozzola*, 134; Elliott, *Seattle*, 57; *Dramatic Mirror*, June 2, 1900, 12.

[41]*Variety*, December 23, 1905, 11; Allen, *Funny*, 57.

[42]Blue, "Interview," 4; Norworth, "Interview," 9; Astaire, *Steps*, 39.

[43]Shayne, "Vine Street," 9; Granlund, *Blondes*, 40.

[44]Cantor, *My Life*, 203.

[45]As quoted in Foster, *Study*, 34-5.

[46]Allen, *Much Ado,* 80-1, 85-6; Marx, *Harpo,* 103-4; Kyle Crichton, *The Marx Brothers* (Garden City: Doubleday & Company, Inc., 1950), 71-2. Crichton's version had the tobacco juice coming from the gallery, a minor error.

[47]Gilbert, *Vaudeville,* 245.

[48]William A. Dillon, *Life Doubles in Brass* (Ithaca, New York: The House of Nollid, 1944), 99; McLean, *Ritual,* 94; McLean, "Pilgrims," 2-3; Gilbert, *Rhyme,* 68.

[49]Gilbert, *Vaudeville,* 244; Allen, *Much Ado,* 113; Cressy, *Vaude,* 16.

[50]Allen, *Much Ado,* 113-14; *Variety,* November 5, 1915, 2; Royle, "Theatre," 488.

[51]Allen, *Much Ado,* 87-8; Laurie, *Vaudeville,* 283.

[52]Allen, *Much Ado,* 87, 90; *Clipper,* September 29, 1906, 843. Allen stated that the William Tell "Hotel" charged five dollars a week. The *Clipper*'s advertisement stated "About $6 week."

[53]Allen, *Much Ado,* 87, 90; Picon, *Laugh,* 9.

[54]Laurie, *Vaudeville,* 282; Adams, "Frisco," 54.

[55]Chaplin, *Autobiography,* 129.

[56]Astaire, *Steps,* 25; Rubin, "Interview," 19; *Variety,* December 20, 1912, 34.

[57]DeLeon, "Wow Finish," 44; Gilbert, *Rhyme,* 65; Cahn, *Laugh Makers,* 48; Edward Jablonski and Lawrence D. Stewart, *The Gershwin Years* (Garden City: Doubleday & Company, Inc., 1958), 52; Joseph Finnigan, "Guess Who's Coming to Dinner," *TV Guide,* XVI (May 25, 1968), 8; Letter from Estelle Major Smith to the writer, October 13, 1970.

[58]Cantor, *My Life,* 110; Adams, *Gags,* 82-3; Cahn, *Laugh Makers,* 50.

[59]Gilbert, *Vaudeville,* 241-2; Taubman, *Theatre,* 128-9.

[60]Murray, *Pogo,* 21-2.

[61]Dale, *Hidden,* 208.

[62]Taylor, *Fields,* 129-30; Gordon, *Gordon,* 64-5.

[63]Macdonell, *Visit,* 77; Adams, *Curtain,* 61.

[64]Keaton, *Slapstick,* 43; Laurie, *Vaudeville,* 281; Dale, *Hidden,* 219.

[65]Bob Thomas, *The Life and Times of Harry Cohn* (New York: G. P. Putnam's Sons, 1967), 11-12.

[66]Dale, *Hidden,* 211-12.

[67]Marx, *Harpo,* 150.

[68]Jimmy Durante settled a court case in Pittsburgh for several thousand dollars. He was coming down the aisle when he acted as if a member of the audience were a long lost girlfriend. What was intended as typical horseplay was later interpreted as "an unlawful, illegal assault." It was in Pittsburgh, too, that a blackface comedian was ordered by a supermoral manager to eliminate the line, "Catfish don't have kittens." Zolotow, *Show People,* 107; Spitzer, "Morals," 38.

[69]Gordon, *Gordon,* 88; Tucker, *Autobiography,* 148-9.

[70]Eddie Leonard, *What a Life I'm Telling You* (New York: Published by Eddie Leonard, 1934), 71, 148; *Dramatic Mirror*, January 6, 1900, 20; Elsie Janis, *So Far, So Good: An Autobiography of Elsie Janis* (New York: E. P. Dutton & Company, Inc., 1932), 22; Murray, "Interview," 9; Rubin,

"Interview," 5.

[71]Rubin, "Interview," 5.

[72]Fowler, *Schnozzola,* 143-4; Cahn, *Calabash,* 72.

[73]Murray, "Interview," 8; Young, *Tights,* 122, 124.

[74]Laurie, *Vaudeville,* 15.

[75]Wilde, *Great Comedians,* 272. Hope added that, since the days of vaude, because of radio and television, *all* audiences have become the same. "They're just as fast in Texas or in Oklahoma or anywhere you go because they see all the shows, they hear all the jokes. You're working to the same audience all the time."

[76]Murray, "Interview," 18; Burton, "Interview," 12.

[77]Marx, *Groucho,* 157.

[78]McClintic, *Kit and Me,* 10-11; Savo, *Stones,* 108; Tucker, *Autobiography,* 102.

[79]Elliott, *Seattle,* 44; Brown, *Laughter,* 55-6.

[80]Elliott, *Seattle,* 52.

[81]Elliott, *Seattle,* 59; Ellis Lucia, *Klondike Kate* (New York: Hastings House Publishers, 1962), 202.

[82]Laurie, *Vaudeville,* 267; Spitzer, *Palace,* 101-2; Jessel, *Elegy,* 53; Jessel, *Autobiography,* 21-2.

[83]Muse, *South,* 94.

[84]Shayne, *Down Front,* 37; Ewen, *Tin Pan Alley,* 81-2; Havoc, *Early,* 252; Lee, *Gypsy,* 58-9, 63.

[85]Dillon, *Brass,* 104-5; Bing Crosby, as told to Pete Martin, *Call Me Lucky* (New York: Simon and Schuster, 1953), 47-8.

CHAPTER 11

[1]Spitzer, "Business," 19. [2]DeLeon, "Wow Finish," 16.

[3]Rubin, "Interview," 16; Allen, *Much Ado,* 245; Tucker, *Autobiography,* 39, 147.

[4]Spitzer, *Palace,* 63; Jan Kindler, "Elysian Fields," *Playboy,* XVI (March, 1969), 118; Taylor, *Fields,* 69-70.

[5]Dale, *Hidden,* 236; Adams, *Gags,* 47.

[6]Marx, *Groucho,* 71; Havoc, *Early,* 176.

[7]Art Cohn, *The Joker is Wild: The Story of Joe E. Lewis* (New York: Random House, 1955), 50-1.

[8]Astaire, *Steps,* 47.

[9]Tucker, *Autobiography,* 39; *Vaudeville Year Book, 1913* (Chicago: Vaudeville Year Book, 1913), 47, 49, 55, 57, 59, 61; Goldwyn, "Interview," 10; Hughes, *Black Magic,* 67; Muse, *South,* 15; Rubin, "Handwritten," 3; Rubin, "Interview," 9-10.

[10]Bickford, *Bulls,* 64; Wilde, *Great Comedians,* 372; Keenan Wynn, as told to James Brough, *Ed Wynn's Son* (Garden City: Doubleday & Company, Inc., 1959), 26. Ed Wynn described the piano site as "a whorehouse,

practically," while his son, Keenan, called it "a recently opened speak-easy."

[11]Burton, "Interview," 10; Flanagan, *Arena,* 273; Green, *Show Biz,* 85.

[12]Jessel, *Autobiography,* 27; Allen, *Much Ado,* 108-109, 112.

[13]Allen, *Much Ado,* 113.

[14]Keaton, *Slapstick,* 21; Gilbert, *Rhyme,* 60.

[15]Astaire, *Steps,* 45; Allen, *Much Ado,* 235.

[16]West, *Autobiography,* 41-43.

[17]Astaire, *Steps,* 44; *Dramatic Mirror,* August 3, 1901, 16; Rubin, "Interview," 7.

[18]W. Charles Barber, "A Great Show Town: Golden Age of Elmira's Theaters, Movies," *Chemung Historical Journal,* VII (June, 1962), 975, 977. The Mozart Theatre was renamed the Strand.

[19]Interview with Nancy Welford Morris.

[20]Murray, *Pogo,* 61.

[21]*Dramatic Mirror,* January 3, 1903, 18.

[22]Adams, *Borscht,* 79-80, 84, 154-155; Adams, *Gags,* 54; Cantor, *Remember,* 59.

[23]Jessel, *Autobiography,* 20; Cantor, *Remember,* 58.

[24]Marx, *Groucho,* 64-65.

[25]*Dramatic Mirror,* March 25, 1905, 21; Blumenthal, *Chronicle,* 181; *Variety,* February 10, 1906, 2; March 24, 1906, 2; July 14, 1906, 2. Douglas Gilbert, *Vaudeville,* 220, refers to Mozart as Fred Mozart.

[26]Gilbert, *Vaudeville,* 220; Grau, *Observation,* 19-20; Richard Gehman, "Pool, My Dad, and Show Biz," *Variety,* January 4, 1967, 41; Allen, *Much Ado,* 252.

[27]Murray, "Interview," 14-15.

[28]Cantor, *My Life,* 22; Crichton, *Marx Brothers,* 75-76.

[29]He was such a superior talent that, despite the stigma of a walkout, he later played the Palace. Burton, "Interview," 7-8; Laurie, *Vaudeville,* 175; Spitzer, *Palace,* 103.

[30]Wilde, *Great Comedians,* 194-195.

[31]Blue, "Interview," 4. [32]Allen, *Much Ado,* 186-187.

[33]Marx, *Groucho,* 115-116. [34]Marx, *Ibid.,* 90-91; Marx, *Harpo,* 98.

[35]Chaplin, *Autobiography,* 124.

[36]Laurie, *Vaudeville,* 407-409; Richard B. Gehman, "Daddy of the Small Time," *Collier's,* CXXVI (May 23, 1950), 30.

[37]Marx, *Groucho,* 72-73; Gehman, *Ibid.,* 72.

[38]Lewis, "Interview," 1. [39]Allen, *Much Ado,* 251.

[40]*Ibid.,* 189-190.

[41]From the South Bend *Daily News,* as quoted in *Vaude Year Book,* 17.

[42]*Dramatic Mirror,* October 5, 1901, 18.

[43]The vaude grapevine had it that Root deliberately provoked arguments in order to have the final word with his fists. Wolfie Gilbert was booked to play what he called a "shredded" week, three days in Burlington, three in Ottumwa, then back to Burlington for the Sunday shows. He was so bad in Burlington that the Ottumwa manager made him the opening act.

Furious, he telephoned Root in Burlington, made an appeal, and Root ordered him changed to fourth spot. This greatly pleased Gilbert but antagonized the Ottumwa manager, who so berated Gilbert that the vaudevillian punched him to the floor. When Gilbert returned to Burlington, Root told him he was not only going to deduct ten dollars for punching his theater manager, but that he was going to work Gilbert over. Gilbert ran to his hotel room, explained his plight to Alex Hanlon and Sam Kramer, two burly acrobats, and with them for protection, he got his ten dollars back. Gilbert, *Rhyme*, 54-58.

[44]Allen, *Much Ado*, 187-188; Marx, *Harpo*, 142-143.

[45]Allen, *Much Ado*, 225; Letter from Fred Allen to Sammy Tishman, February 3, 1921, in McCarthy, *Letters*, 46.

[46]*Clipper*, July 17, 1915, 4. The towns in Iowa were Atlantic, Clarinda, Creston, and Red Oak. In Nebraska, Falls City, Nebraska City, and Plattsmouth.

[47]Astaire, *Steps*, 10; Dale, *Hidden*, 231; Allen, *Much Ado*, 188; Letter from Fred Allen to Sammy Tishman, December 25, 1920, in McCarthy, *Letters*, 45.

[48]Cantor, *I See It*, 200-201; Dale, *Hidden*, 234; Marx, *Harpo*, 119-120.

[49]*Dramatic Mirror*, November 24, 1900, 20.

[50]Norworth, "Interview," 10-11.

[51]Laurie, *Vaudeville*, 284; Marx, *Harpo*, 100.

[52]Marx, *Harpo*, 99.

[53]Marx, *Harpo*, 106.

[54]*Ibid.*, 99; Dale, *Hidden*, 259.

[55]Laurie, *Vaudeville*, 243; Richman, *Life*, 74.

[56]Ruth Hunter, *Come Back on Tuesday* (New York: Charles Scribner's Sons, 1945), 6, 10; Morris, "Interview."

[57]McClintic, *Me and Kit*, 38.

[58]Norman Bel Geddes, *Miracle in the Evening: An Autobiography*, edited by William Kelley (Garden City: Doubleday & Company, Inc., 1960), 99.

[59]Morris, "Interview"; Astaire, *Steps*, 25.

[60]Fanton, "Tape," 7.

[61]Chaplin, *Autobiography*, 128.

[62]Richman, *Life*, 80.

[63]*Ibid.*, 81-82; Chaplin, *Autobiography*, 128; Marx, *Harpo*, 132.

[64]Sandra Dallas, *No More Than Five in a Bed: Colorado Hotels in the Old Days* (Norman: University of Oklahoma Press, 1967), 48-49.

[65]Keaton figured that in 1901 their family act cleared $120 a week. Room and board for the three was usually twenty-six dollars, traveling expenses about thirty dollars, and his father's beer and other luxuries about fifty dollars. Keaton, *Slapstick*, 24.

[66]Rubin, "Interview," 7, 16-17.

[67]Marx, *Life*, 20-21; Johnston, "Marx Brothers," 49.

[68]Lee, *Gypsy*, 157-158.

[69]Brown, *Laughter*, 55.

[70]*Variety*, December 20, 1912, 52; Gilbert, *Rhyme*, 44-45.

[71]Hunter, *Tuesday*, 13.

[72]Bickford, *Bulls*, 92-93.

[73]*Ibid.*, 94-96.

[74]Lewis, "Interview," 2-3.

[75]Richman, *Life,* 74-75.

[76]Taylor, *Running Pianist,* 92; Allen, *Much Ado,* 199; Goldwyn, "Interview," 3.

[77]Gilbert, *Rhyme,* 29; Cohn, *Joker,* 52-53.

BIOGRAPHY

Vaudeville was a natural subject for John E. DiMeglio, whose father was a child vaudevillian, singing and dancing in an act with the author's aunt, and whose grandfather, "Prof. John DiMeglio," tried to teach the author some tricks from his days as a vaude magician. The father, Richard A. DiMeglio, used his powers of persuasion to discourage the author from trying his lot in the world of show business, remembering the disappointments of the old days, and wishing his son to pursue a career that would offer more security. Thus, instead of leaving Bethlehem, Pennsylvania, for an undergraduate program in theater arts at Ithaca College, as the author had hoped, the father's advice prevailed and young John found himself instead as a teaching degree candidate in nearby Kutztown State College. One good thing came out of that—John met his bride-to-be, Alice, and they married soon after their senior year. They have six handsome children, five boys and one girl.

From Kutztown, DiMeglio took a teaching job at Liberty High School in his hometown of Bethlehem, stayed there for nine years, and then entered the graduate program at the University of Maine. Majoring in American history, DiMeglio received the M.A. and Ph.D., in the meantime teaching another year in Bethlehem and accepting a position at Mankato State College in southern Minnesota. Presently, the author is Chairman of the History Department at Mankato, with special interests in popular culture, oral history, organized crime, and the preparation of teachers. DiMeglio has had articles in the *Journal of Popular Culture, The History Teacher, Social Studies,* and *Variety,* and his name is included in the 1972 edition of *Outstanding Educators of America.*

BIBLIOGRAPHY

A. BOOKS

Adams, Joey. *The Curtain Never Falls.* New York: Frederick Fell, Inc., 1949.

__________. *From Gags to Riches.* New York: Frederick Fell, Inc., 1946.

__________. *On the Road For Uncle Sam.* New York: Bernard Geis Associates, 1963.

__________, with Henry Tobias. *The Borscht Belt.* New York: Avon Books, 1967.

Allen, Fred. *Much Ado About Me.* Boston: Little, Brown and Company, 1956.

Allen, Steve. *The Funny Men.* New York: Simon and Schuster, 1956.

__________. *Mark It and Strike It: An Autobiography.* New York: Holt, Rinehart and Winston, 1960.

Astaire, Fred. *Steps in Time.* New York: Harper & Brothers, Publishers, 1959.

Atkinson, Brooks. *Broadway.* New York: The Macmillan Company, 1970.

Bailey, Pearl. *The Raw Pearl.* New York: Harcourt, Brace & World, Inc., 1968.

Barrymore, Ethel. *Memories: An Autobiography.* New York: Harper & Brothers, 1955.

Beaumont, Charles. *Remember? Remember?* New York: The Macmillan Company, 1963.

Bel Geddes, Norman. *Miracle in the Evening: An Autobiography,* ed. William Kelley. Garden City: Doubleday & Company, Inc., 1960.

Bernheim, Alfred L., assisted by Sara Harding. *The Business of the Theatre: An Economic History of the American Theater, 1750-1932.* New York: Benjamin Blom, 1964.

Bickford, Charles. *Bulls, Balls, Bicycles & Actors.* New York: Paul S. Eriksson, Inc., 1965.

Bier, Jesse. *The Rise and Fall of American Humor.* New York: Holt, Rinehart and Winston, 1968.

Blumenthal, George, as told to Arthur H. Merkin. *My Sixty Years in Show Business: A Chronicle of the American Theater, 1874-1934.* New York: Frederick C. Osberg, Publisher, 1936.

Brady, Francis J. *Recollections of the Theatre of Fifty and More Years Ago.*

No publication data.

Brady, William A. *Showman.* New York: E. P. Dutton & Co., Inc., 1937.

Brazier, Marion H. *Stage and Screen.* Boston: M. H. Brazier, Publisher, 1920.

Britt, Albert. *Turn of the Century.* Barre, Massachusetts: Barre Publishers, 1966.

Brown, Joe E., as told to Ralph Hancock. *Laughter is a Wonderful Thing.* New York: A. S. Barnes and Company, 1956.

Burton, Jack. *In Memoriam–Oldtime Show Biz.* New York: Vantage Press, 1965.

Caffin, Caroline. *Vaudeville.* New York: Mitchell Kennerley, 1914.

Cahn, Julius. *Julius Cahn's Official Theatrical Guide.* New York: Empire Theatre Building, 1909.

Cahn, William. *Good Night, Mrs. Calabash: The Secret of Jimmy Durante.* New York: Duell, Sloan and Pearce, 1963.

__________. *The Laugh Makers: A Pictorial History of American Comedians.* New York: Bramhall House, 1957.

Cantor, Eddie. *As I Remember Them.* New York: Duell, Sloan and Pearce, 1963.

__________, with Jane Kesner Ardmore. *Take My Life.* Garden City: Doubleday & Company, Inc., 1957.

__________. *The Way I See It,* ed. Phyllis Rosenteur. Englewood Cliffs: Prentice-Hall, Inc., 1959.

Carmichael, Hoagy, with Stephen Longstreet. *Sometimes I Wonder: The Story of Hoagy Carmichael.* New York: Farrar, Straus and Giroux, 1965.

Carrillo, Leo. *The California I Love.* Englewood Cliffs: Prentice-Hall, 1961.

Chaplin, Charles. *My Autobiography.* New York: Simon and Schuster, 1964.

Chaplin, Charles, Jr., with N. and M. Rau. *My Father, Charlie Chaplin.* New York: Popular Library, 1961.

Charters, Ann. *Nobody: The Story of Bert Williams.* New York: The Macmillan Company, 1970.

Chesterton, G. K. *What I Saw in America.* New York: Da Capo Press, 1968.

Christopher, Milbourne. *Houdini: The Untold Story.* New York: Thomas Y. Crowell Company, 1969.

Churchill, Allen. *The Great White Way.* New York: E. P. Cutton & Co., Inc., 1962.

Coakley, Mary Lewis. *Mister Music Maker, Lawrence Welk.* Garden City: Doubleday & Company, Inc., 1958.

Cohn, Art. *The Joker is Wild: The Story of Joe E. Lewis.* New York: Random House, 1955.

Conkey, Robert J. *One-To-Fill of 1922.* Chicago: Published by Bob Conkey, 1922.

Cressy, Will M. *Continuous Vaudeville.* Boston: Richard G. Badger, 1914.

Crichton, Kyle. *The Marx Brothers.* Garden City: Doubleday & Company, Inc., 1950.

Crosby, Bing, as told to Pete Martin. *Call Me Lucky.* New York: Simon and Schuster, 1953.

Croy, Homer. *Our Will Rogers.* New York: Duell, Sloan and Pearce, 1953.

Dale, Violet, as told to Clarissa Adams. *Nothing Can Remain Hidden.* New York: New York Public Library, [n.d.].

Dallas, Sandra. *No More Than Five in a Bed: Colorado Hotels in the Old Days.* Norman: University of Oklahoma Press, 1967.

Davis, Sammy, Jr., and Jane and Burt Boyar. *Yes I Can: The Story of Sammy Davis, Jr.* New York: Pocket Books, 1966.

Day, Donald (ed.). *The Autobiography of Will Rogers.* Boston: Houghton Mifflin Company, 1949.

__________. *Will Rogers: A Biography.* New York: David McKay Company, Inc., 1962.

Dillon, William A. *Life Doubles in Brass.* Ithaca, New York: The House of Nollid, 1944.

Elliott, Eugene C. *A History of Variety-Vaudeville in Seattle: From the Beginning to 1914.* Seattle: University of Washington Press, 1944.

Everson, William K. *The Art of W. C. Fields.* Indianapolis: The Bobbs-Merrill Company, Inc., 1967.

Ewen, David. *The Life and Death of Tin Pan Alley.* New York: Funk and Wagnalls Company, Inc., 1964.

__________. *The Story of America's Musical Theater.* New York: Chilton Company's Book Division, 1961.

__________. *The Story of George Gershwin.* New York: Henry Holt and Company, 1943.

Farnsworth, Marjorie. *The Ziegfeld Follies.* New York: G. P. Putnam's Sons, 1956.

Flanagan, Hallie. *Arena.* New York: Duell, Sloan and Pearce, 1940.

Ford, Corey. *The Time of Laughter.* Boston: Little, Brown and Company, 1967.

Foster, William T. *Vaudeville and Motion Picture Shows: A Study of*

Theaters in Portland, Oregon. Portland: Reed College, 1914.

Fowler, Gene. *Schnozzola: The Story of Jimmy Durante.* Garden City: Permabooks, 1953.

Foy, Eddie, and Alvin F. Harlow. *Clowning Through Life.* New York: E. P. Dutton & Company, 1928.

Gagey, Edmond M. *The San Francisco Stage: A History.* New York: Columbia University Press, 1950.

Gibson, Walter B., and Morris N. Young. *Houdini's Fabulous Magic.* New York: Chilton Book Company, 1968.

Gilbert, Douglas. *American Vaudeville: Its Life and Times.* New York: Whittlesey House, McGraw-Hill Book Company, Inc., 1940.

__________. *Lost Chords: The Diverting Story of American Popular Songs.* Garden City: Doubleday, Doran and Co., Inc., 1942.

Gilbert, L. Wolfe. *Without Rhyme or Reason.* New York: Vantage Press, 1956.

Goldberg, Isaac. *Tin Pan Alley.* New York: The John Day Company, 1930.

Gordon, Max, with Lewis Funke. *Max Gordon Presents.* New York: Bernard Geis Associates, 1963.

Granlund, Nils Thor, with Sid Feder and Ralph Hancock. *Blondes, Brunettes, and Bullets.* New York: David McKay Company, Inc., 1957.

Grau, Robert. *The Business Man in the Amusement World.* New York: Broadway Publishing Company, 1910.

__________. *Forty Years Observation of Music and the Drama.* New York: Broadway Publishing Company, 1909.

Green, Abel, and Joe Laurie, Jr. *Show Biz: From Vaude to Video.* Garden City: Permabooks, 1953.

Gresham, William L. *Houdini: The Man Who Walked Through Walls.* New York: Henry Holt and Company, 1959.

Havoc, June. *Early Havoc.* New York: Simon and Schuster, 1959.

Hecht, Ben. *A Child of the Century.* New York: Simon and Schuster, 1954.

Holiday, Billie, with William Dufty. *Lady Sings the Blues.* Garden City: Doubleday & Company, Inc., 1956.

Hopper, Hedda, and James Brough. *The Whole Truth and Nothing But.* New York: Pyramid Books, 1963.

Hubbard, Elbert. *In the Spotlight: Personal Experiences of Elbert Hubbard on the American Stage.* East Aurora, N.Y.: The Roycrofters, 1917.

Huff, Theodore. *Charlie Chaplin.* New York: Henry Schuman, 1951.

Hughes, Langston, and Milton Meltzer. *Black Magic: A Pictorial History of the Negro in American Entertainment.* Englewood Cliffs: Prentice-Hall, Inc., 1967.

Hunter, Ruth. *Come Back on Tuesday.* New York: Charles Scribner's Sons, 1945.

Isaacs, Edith J. R. *The Negro in the American Theatre.* New York: Theatre Arts, Inc., 1947.

Jablonski, Edward, and Lawrence D. Stewart. *The Gershwin Years.* Garden City: Doubleday & Company, Inc., 1958.

Janis Elsie. *So Far, So Good: An Autobiography of Elsie Janis.* New York: E. P. Dutton & Company, Inc., 1932.

Jessel, George. *Elegy In Manhattan.* New York: Holt, Rinehart and Winston, 1961.

__________. *So Help Me: The Autobiography of George Jessel.* New York: Random House, 1943.

__________. *This Way, Miss.* New York: Henry Holt and Company, 1955.

Johnson, James Weldon. *Along This Way: The Autobiography of James Weldon Johnson.* New York: The Viking Press, 1968.

__________. *Black Manhattan.* New York: Arno Press and The New York *Times,* 1968.

Jolson, Harry, as told to Alban Emley. *Mistah Jolson.* Hollywood: House-Warven, Publishers, 1951.

Katkov, Norman. *The Fabulous Fanny: The Story of Fanny Brice.* New York: Alfred A. Knopf, 1953.

Keaton, Buster, with Charles Samuels. *My Wonderful World of Slapstick.* Garden City: Doubleday & Company, Inc., 1960.

Knight, Arthur. *The Liveliest Art: A Panoramic History of the Movies.* New York: The Macmillan Company, 1957.

Lahr, John. *Notes On A Cowardly Lion: The Biography of Bert Lahr.* New York: Alfred A. Knopf, 1969.

Lauder, Sir Harry. *Between You and Me.* New York: The James A. McCann Company, 1919.

Laurie, Joe, Jr. *Vaudeville: From the Honky-Tonks to the Palace.* New York: Henry Holt and Company, 1953.

Lee, Gypsy Rose. *Gypsy.* New York: Dell Publishing Co., Inc., 1959.

Leonard, Eddie. *What a Life I'm Telling You.* New York: Published by Eddie Leonard, 1934.

Levant, Oscar. *The Memoirs of an Amnesiac.* New York: Bantam Books, 1966.

Levant, Oscar. *The Unimportance of Being Oscar.* New York: G. P. Putnam's Sons, 1968.

Lucia, Ellis. *Klondike Kate: The Life and Legend of Kitty Rockwell.* New York: Hastings House Publishers, 1962.

Macdonell, A. G. *A Visit to America.* New York: The Macmillan Company, 1935.

McCabe, John. *Mr. Laurel and Mr. Hardy.* Garden City: Doubleday & Company, Inc., 1961.

McClintic, Guthrie. *Me and Kit.* Boston: Little, Brown and Company, 1955.

McLean, Albert F., Jr. *American Vaudeville as Ritual.* Lexington: University of Kentucky Press, 1965.

McNally, William. *Mack's Vaudeville Guide.* New York: Published by Wm. McNally, 1920.

Marks, Edward B., as told to Abbott J. Liebling. *They All Sang: From Tony Pastor to Rudy Vallee.* New York: The Viking Press, 1935.

Marston, William H., and John H. Feller. *F. F. Proctor: Vaudeville Pioneer.* New York: Richard R. Smith, 1943.

Martin, Pete. *Pete Martin Calls On. . . .* New York: Simon and Schuster, 1962.

Marx, Arthur. *Life With Groucho.* New York: Simon and Schuster, 1954.

Marx, Groucho. *Groucho and Me.* New York: Dell Publishing Co., Inc., 1959.

Marx, Harpo, with Rowland Barber. *Harpo Speaks!* New York: Published by Bernard Geis Associates, Distributed by Random House, 1961.

Mayer, Arthur. *Merely Colossal: The Story of the Movies from the Long Chase to the Chaisè Longue* [sic]. New York: Simon and Schuster, 1953.

Merman, Ethel, as told to Pete Martin. *Who Could Ask for Anything More.* Garden City: Doubleday & Company, Inc., 1955.

Meyer, Hazel. *The Gold in Tin Pan Alley.* New York: J. B. Lippincott Company, 1958.

Morehouse, Ward. *George M. Cohan: Prince of the American Theater.* New York: J. B. Lippincott Company, 1943.

Morell, Parker. *Lillian Russell: The Era of Plush.* New York: Random House, 1940.

Morris, Lloyd. *Incredible New York.* New York: Random House, 1951.

Murray, Ken. *Life on a Pogo Stick: Autobiography of a Comedian.* Philadelphia: The John C. Winston Company, 1960.

Muse, Clarence, and David Arlen. *Way Down South.* Hollywood: David Graham Fischer, Publisher, 1932.

Nathan, George Jean. *Encyclopaedia of the Theatre.* New York: Alfred A. Knopf, 1940.

Newquist, Roy. *Showcase.* New York: William Morrow & Co., Inc., 1966.

O'Brien, P. J. *Will Rogers: Ambassador of Good Will, Prince of Wit and Wisdom.* Philadelphia: The John C. Winston Company, 1935.

Osofsky, Gilbert. *Harlem: The Making of a Ghetto.* New York: Harper & Row, Publishers, 1966.

Page, Brett. *Writing for Vaudeville.* Springfield, Massachusetts: The Home Correspondence School, 1915.

Patton, Cornelius H., and Walter T. Field. *Eight O'Clock Chapel: A Study of New England College Life in the Eighties.* Boston: Houghton Mifflin Company, 1927.

Picon, Molly, as told to Eth Clifford Rosenberg. *So Laugh A Little.* New York: Julian Messner, Inc., 1962.

Richman, Harry, with Richard Gehman. *A Hell Of A Life.* New York: Duell, Sloan and Pearce, 1966.

Robinson, David. *Buster Keaton.* Bloomington: Indiana University Press, 1969.

Roth, Lillian, written in collaboration with Mike Connolly and Gerold Frank. *I'll Cry Tomorrow.* New York: Frederick Fell, Inc., Publishers, 1954.

Rourke, Constance. *American Humor: A Study of the National Character.* Garden City: Doubleday Anchor Books, 1953.

Rowland, Mabel (ed.). *Bert Williams, Son of Laughter.* New York: The English Crafters, 1923.

Savo, Jimmy. *I Bow to the Stones.* New York: Howard Frisch, 1963.

Schlesinger, Arthur M. *The Rise of the City: 1878-1898.* New York: The Macmillan Company, 1933.

Schoener, Allon (ed.). *Portal to America: The Lower East Side 1870-1925.* New York: Holt, Rinehart and Winston, 1967.

Seldes, Gilbert. *The 7 Lively Arts.* New York: Sagamore Press Inc., 1957.

Shayne, Eddie. *Down Front on the Aisle.* Denver: Parkway Publishing Company, 1929.

Sheean, Vincent. *Oscar Hammerstein I: The Life and Exploits of an Impresario.* New York: Simon and Schuster, 1956.

Sobel, Bernard. *Broadway Heartbeat: Memoirs of a Press Agent.* New York: Hermitage House, 1953.

Sobel, Bernard. *A Pictorial History of Burlesque*. New York: G. P. Putnam's sons, 1956.

__________. *A Pictorial History of Vaudeville*. New York: The Citadel Press, 1961.

Spitzer, Marian. *The Palace*. New York: Atheneum, 1969.

Stagg, Jerry. *The Brothers Shubert*. New York: Random House, 1968.

Stoddart, Dayton. *Lord Broadway: Variety's Sime*. New York: Wilfred Funk, Inc., 1941.

Stuart, Lyle. *The Secret Life of Walter Winchell*. Boar's Head Books, 1953.

Taubman, Howard. *The Making of the American Theatre*. New York: Coward McCann, Inc., 1965.

Taylor, Robert Lewis. *The Running Pianist*. Garden City: Doubleday & Company, Inc., 1950.

__________. *W. C. Fields: His Follies & Fortunes*. New York: Bantam Books, 1951.

Thomas, Bob. *The Life and Times of Harry Cohn*. New York: G. P. Putnam's Sons, 1967.

Treadwell, Bill. *50 Years of American Comedy*. New York: Exposition Press, 1951.

Tucker, Sophie, with Dorothy Giles. *Some of These Days: The Atuobiography of Sophie Tucker*. Garden City: Doubleday, Doran and Company, Inc., 1945.

Vallee, Rudy. *Vagabond Dreams Come True*. New York: Grosset & Dunlap Publishers, 1930.

__________, with Gil McKean. *My Time Is Your Time: The Story of Rudy Vallee*. New York: Ivan Obolensky, Inc., 1962.

Vaudeville Year Book, 1913: Published as a Compendium of General Information for the Vaudeville and Tabloid Field in the West and South. Chicago: Vaudeville Year Book, 1913.

Waters, Ethel, with Charles Samuels. *His Eye Is On the Sparrow: An Autobiography*. London: W. H. Allen Limited, 1958.

West, Mae. *Goodness Had Nothing to Do With It: The Autobiography of Mae West*. Englewood Cliffs: Prentice-Hall, Inc., 1959.

Wilde, Larry. *The Great Comedians Talk About Comedy*. New York: The Citadel Press, 1968.

Williams, Beryl, and Samuel Epstein. *The Great Houdini: Magician Extraordinary*. New York: Julian Messner, Inc., 1954.

Wittke, Carl. *Tambo and Bones: A History of the American Minstrel Stage*. Durham: Duke University Press, 1930.

Wynn, Keenan, as told to James Brough. *Ed Wynn's Son.* Garden City: Doubleday & Company, Inc., 1959.

Young, Miriam. *Mother Wore Tights.* New York: Whittlesey House, McGraw-Hill Book Company, Inc., 1944.

Zolotow, Maurice. *No People Like Show People.* New York: Bantam Books, 1952.

B. NEWSPAPERS

New York *Clipper,* 1900-1918.

New York *Dramatic Mirror,* 1900-1922.

Variety, 1905-1937.

C. ARTICLES

Adams, Franklin P. "Olympic Days," *Saturday Evening Post,* CCI (June 22, 1929), 18+.

Adams, Joey. "Happiness was a Thing Called F-F-Frisco," *Coronet,* VI (April, 1968), 50-54.

"The Apotheosis of Vaudeville," *Current Literature,* XXXIII (November, 1902), 523.

Bakshy, Alexander. "Vaudeville Must Be Saved," *Nation,* CXXIX (July 24, 1929), 98-100.

__________. "Vaudeville's Prestige," *Nation,* CXXIX (September 4, 1929), 258.

Barber, W. Charles. "A Great Show Town: Golden Age of Elmira's Theaters, Movies," *Chemung Historical Journal,* VII (June, 1962), 975-82.

Bayes, Nora. "Holding My Audience," *Theatre,* XXVI (September, 1917), 128.

Beerbohm, Max. "The Laughter of the Public," *Living Age,* CCXXXIII (April 5, 1902), 52-7.

Beuick, Marshall D. "The Vaudeville Philosopher," *Drama,* XVI (December, 1925), 92-3+.

Brooks, Joe. "Never Whistle in Dressing Room," Bangor *Daily News,* July 7, 1967, 12.

"Browsing for Vaudeville Talent," *Theatre,* XX (December, 1914), 281-2+.

Byram, John. " 'Duck Vaudeville': It's For The Birds!" *Variety,* January 4, 1967, 203.

"California's Gold Mine," *Time,* XLV (February 12, 1945), 44+.

Canfield, Mary C. "The Great American Art," *New Republic,* XXXII (November 22, 1922), 334-5.

Carson, Saul. "Theatre: Vaudeville," *New Republic,* CXX (June 13, 1949), 19-20.

Cohen, Octavus Roy. "Vaudeville," *Collier's,* LXXIX (February 12, 1927), 24.

Collins, Sewell. "Breaking Into Vaudeville," *Collier's,* XLII (March 20, 1909), 20+.

Copley, Frank B. "The Story of a Great Vaudeville Manager," *American Magazine,* XCIV (December, 1922), 46-7+.

Crane, Warren E. "Alexander Pantages," *System,* XXXVII (March, 1920), 501-3.

"The Decay of Vaudeville," *American Magazine,* LXIX (April, 1910), 840-48.

DeLeon, Walter. "The Wow Finish," *Saturday Evening Post,* CXCVII (February 14, 1925), 16+.

DiMeglio, John E. "New York vs. Rural America . . . Who Ruled Vaudeville?" *Mankato State College Today,* II (Fall, 1970), 8-9.

__________. "Old Vaudevillians Fade When Invited to 'Tape' Their Memoirs for a Ph.D." *Variety,* January 7, 1970, 153.

Disher, M. Willson. "The Music-Hall," *Quarterly Review,* CCLII (April, 1929), 259-71.

Distler, Paul A. "Exit the Racial Comics," *Educational Theatre Journal,* XVIII (October, 1966), 247-54.

Douglas, W. A. S. "The Passing of Vaudeville," *American Mercury,* XII (October, 1927), 188-94.

"Editor's Easy Chair," *Harper's Monthly Magazine,* CVI (April, 1903), 811-15.

"Enter the Italian on the Vaudeville Stage," *Survey,* XXIV (May 7, 1910), 198-9.

Ferguson, Otis. "Daughters and Others," *New Republic,* XCVII (January 18, 1939), 315.

Finnigan, Joseph. "Guess Who's Coming to Dinner," *TV Guide,* XVI (May 25, 1968), 6-8.

"From Honky-Tonk to Palace," *Life,* XXXV (December 7, 1953), 38.

Gehman, Richard B. "Daddy of the Small Time," *Collier's,* CXXVI (May 23, 1950), 30-1+.

__________. "Pool, My Dad, and Show Biz," *Variety,* January 4, 1967, 41.

"The Golden Age of Vaudeville," *Current Literature,* XLII (June, 1907), 669.

Golden, Harry. "Tales of a Truly Wayward Inn, N. Y.'s Hotel Markwell In the Depression," *Variety,* January 4, 1967, 4, 56.

Grau, Robert. "The Amazing Prosperity of the Vaudeville Entertainers," *Overland,* LVII (June, 1911), 608-9.

__________. "B. F. Keith," *American Magazine,* LXXVII (May, 1914), 86-8.

Green, Abel. "Chas. Evans Hughes 'Saves' Albee," *Variety,* January 4, 1967, 196.

Green, Helen. "The Vaudevillians," *Collier's,* XLIV (October 23, 1909), 20+.

Grinde, Nick. "Where's Vaudeville At?" *Saturday Evening Post,* CCII (January 11, 1930), 44-6.

Hartley, Marsden. "Vaudeville," *Dial,* LXVIII (March, 1920), 335-42.

Havoc, June. "Old Vaudevillians, Where Are You Now?" *Horizon,* I (July, 1959), 112-20.

Hazzard, John E., and Robert G. Anderson. "Fellows of Infinite Jest," *Saturday Evening Post,* CCII (November 16, 1929), 60-69.

Hoffman, Arthur S. "Who Writes the Jokes?" *Bookman,* XXVI (October, 1907), 171-81.

"If Troupers Make Good They'll Go Back to the Sticks," *Newsweek,* V (June 29, 1935), 23.

Johnston, Alva. "The Marx Brothers," *Woman's Home Companion,* LXIII (September, 1936), 12-13+.

__________. "Those Mad Marx Brothers," *Reader's Digest,* XXIX (October, 1936), 49-52.

Kennedy, John B. "We've Forgotten How to Fight," *Collier's,* LXXXIII (May 11, 1929), 39-42.

Kindler, Jan. "Elysian Fields," *Playboy,* XVI (March, 1969), 116-18, 187-99.

"A King of the Vaudeville Stage," *Current Literature,* XLVI (January, 1909), 84-6.

Lader, Lawrence. "The Palace Theater: Broadway's Shrine," *Coronet,* XXXII (July, 1952), 51-4.

Laurie, Joe, Jr. "The Early Days of Vaudeville," *American Mercury,* LXII (February, 1946), 232-6.

__________. "Vaudeville," *Theatre Arts,* XXXII (August, 1948), 54-5.

__________. "Vaudeville Dead? It's Never Been," New York *Times Magazine,* October 14, 1951, 25+.

Leamy, Hugh. "You Ought to Go on the Stage: An Interview with Edward F. Albee," *Collier's,* LXXVII (May 1, 1926), 10+.

McGregor, Donald. "The Supreme Court of the Two a Day," *Collier's,* LXXV (June 20, 1925), 38.

McLean, Albert F., Jr. "Genesis of Vaudeville: Two Letters from B. F. Keith," *Theatre Survey,* I (1960), 82-95.

Merrill, Katherine. "The Elective System and the Vaudeville," *New England Magazine,* XXXVI (June, 1907), 498-9.

Nathan, George Jean. "A Matter of Life and Death," *Newsweek,* XIII (April 17, 1939), 27.

"1942 Handbook of MPAA Recalls the Then No-No's," *Variety,* March 25, 1970, 1, 61.

Nye, Russel B. "Notes on a Rationale for Popular Culture," pamphlet published by the Popular Culture Association, 1970, 1-12.

Odenwald-Unger, J. "The Fine Arts as a Dynamic Factor in Society," *American Journal of Sociology,* XII (March, 1907), 656-74.

Prill, Arthur. "The 'Small Time' King," *Theatre,* XIX (March, 1914), 139-40+.

"Psychology of the American Vaudeville Show From the Manager's Point of View," *Current Opinion,* LX (April, 1916), 257-8.

Reed, Edward. "Vaudeville Again," *Theatre Arts Monthly,* XVII (October, 1933), 802-6.

Revell, Nellie. "Speed Mania Afflicts Vaudeville," *Theatre,* XXVI (October, 1917), 216.

__________. "Vaudeville Demands Cheerful Patriotism," *Theatre,* XXVI (December, 1917), 364.

__________. "Vaudeville Doing Its Best," *Theatre,* XXVI (August, 1917), 90.

__________. "Yellow Peril Threatens Vaudeville," *Theatre,* XXV (May, 1917), 290+.

Royle, Edwin M. "The Vaudeville Theatre," *Scribner's Magazine,* XXVI (October, 1899), 485-95.

S., G. "Vaudeville," *Dial,* LXXIII (August, 1922), 237-8.

Shayne, Bob. "Vaudeville is Dead and Living on Vine Street," A.C.T. Program for performance of "Hair," Geary Theater, San Francisco, August, 1969, 7-10.

Sherlock, Charles R. "Where Vaudeville Holds the Boards," *Cosmopolitan,* XXXII (February, 1902), 411-20.

"Social Welfare as Vaudeville," *Survey,* XXIII (February 26, 1910), 794-5.

Spitzer, Marian. "The Business of Vaudeville," *Saturday Evening Post,* CXCVI (May 24, 1924), 18-19+.

Spitzer, Marian. "The Lay of the Last Minstrels," *Saturday Evening Post,* CXCVII (March 7, 1925), 12-13+.

__________. "Morals in the Two-A-Day," *American Mercury,* III (September, 1924), 35-9.

__________. "The People of Vaudeville," *Saturday Evening Post,* CXCVII (July 12, 1924), 15+.

"Springtime in the 40s," *Newsweek,* XXXIII (May 30, 1949), 76-7.

"Ted Lewis, 80, Suspects 'Parade's Passed Me By,' " Minneapolis *Tribune,* December 13, 1970, Section E, 7.

"The Trend in Vaudeville," *Independent,* LIII (May 9, 1901), 1092-3.

Wayne, Donald. "The Palace," *Holiday,* VII (March, 1950), 62-3+.

Willows, Maurice. "The Nickel Theatre," *Annals of the American Academy of Political and Social Science,* XXXVIII (July, 1911), 95-9.

Wilson, Earl. "Even In Death Zany Olsen & Johnson Keep Their Vaude Billing," *Variety,* January 4, 1967, 198.

Woolf, S. J. "Gus Edwards' Academy," New York *Times Magazine,* March 23, 1941, 12+.

"A Word for Vaudeville," *Literary Digest,* LII (April 22, 1916), 1151.

D. UNPUBLISHED WORKS

Distler, Paul A. "The Rise and Fall of the Racial Comics in American Vaudeville." Unpublished Doctor's dissertation, Tulane University, 1963.

McLean, Albert Forbes, Jr. "Pilgrims and Palaces: The Meaning of American Vaudeville." Unpublished Doctor's dissertation, Harvard University, 1960.

E. INTERVIEWS, LETTERS, SPEECHES, NARRATIVES

Allen, Fred. Letter to Bernard Sobel. April 16, [n.d.]. New York Public Library, Lincoln Center branch.

Blue, Ben. Tape-recorded interview. Summer, 1969. Tape in possession of the writer.

Burton, [Mrs.] Ferne Albee. Tape-recorded interview. Winter, 1968-9. Tape in possession of the writer.

Dentinger, [Mrs.] Mary. Tape-recorded interview. Summer, 1969. Tape in possession of the writer.

DiMeglio, Richard A. Personal correspondence with the writer, n.d.

Fanton, Al. Tape-recording sent to the writer. Spring, 1970.

Goldwyn, [Mrs.] Mitzi. Tape-recorded interview. Fall, 1969. Tape in possession of the writer.

The Groucho Letters: Letters From and To Groucho Marx. New York: Simon and Schuster, 1967.

Holtz, Lou. Tape-recording sent to the writer. Spring, 1971.

Houdini, Harry. Letters to Dr. Waitt. April 4, 1900, November 20, 1906, March 2, 1908. Harvard University Theatre Collection.

Lewis, Ted. Tape-recorded interview. Summer, 1970. Tape in possession of the writer.

Lucas, Nick. Personal correspondence with the writer. September 3, 1970.

McCarthy, Joe (ed.). *Fred Allen's Letters.* New York: Pocket Books, 1966.

Morris, Nancy Welford. Personal interview. Summer, 1969.

Murray, Ken. Tape-recorded interview. Summer, 1969. Tape in possession of the writer.

Norworth, [Mrs.] Amy. Tape-recorded interview. Summer, 1969. Tape in possession of the writer.

"Playboy Interview: Mae West," *Playboy,* XVIII (January, 1971), 73-82.

Rubin, Benny. Personal correspondence with the writer. Spring, 1969.

__________. Tape-recorded interview. Summer, 1969. Tape in possession of the writer.

Smith, [Mrs.] Estelle Major. Personal correspondence with the writer. October 13, 1970.

Stark, Samuel. Personal interview. Summer, 1969.

"Testimonial Dinner to Sophie Tucker," March 4, 1947. New York: Printed by Horne & Shell, Inc. New York Public Library, Lincoln Center branch.

Tucker, Sophie. Transcriptions of four speeches. 1954 Golden Jubilee Dinner, May, 1959 in San Francisco, undated in Philadelphia, and undated in honor of George Jessel. New York Public Library, Lincoln Center branch.

West, Mae. Personal interview. Summer, 1969.

Williams, Harry. Letter to Charles Dillingham. May 7, 1919. New York Public Library, Lincoln Center branch.

F. OTHERS

Benny, Jack. Quoted on the "Joey Bishop Show." October 10, 1969.

In Vaudeville. Official Organ Oakland Orpheum. Scattered issues. California Historical Society Theatre Collection.

Modern Stars—Lillian Russell. Associated Press obituary of Lillian Russell Moore. June 6, 1922. Harvard University Theatre Collection.

INDEX

A

Aborn Circuit of Polite Vaudeville Houses, 179
Academy Hotel, New York City, 136
Academy of Music, New York City, 127
Ackerman and Harris Circuit, 187
Actors' Fund, 27, 56
Adams, Franklin P., 5, 40
Adams, Joey, 4, 68, 123, 131, 162, 173, 178
Albee, Edward F., 15, 19-20, 22-25, 33, 47-48, 50-51, 86, 123-124, 129, 144, 163
Albee (E. F.) Theatre, Brooklyn, 131
Albee Sisters, 33, 86-87, 90-91, 180
Alexander's Ragtime Band (film), 161
Alhambra Theatre, New York City, 86, 116
Ali, Hadji, 31
"All Coons Look Alike to Me," 117
Allardt Circuit, 174
Allen, Fred, 15-16, 51, 63-65, 75, 77, 79-80, 82-84, 91-92, 100, 107, 119, 135, 137, 139, 141-142, 147-148, 154, 156, 158, 161-162, 172, 175-176, 181, 184-185, 193
Allen, Gracie, 159-160, 165
Allen, Steve, 97-98
Ameche, Don, 160
American Music Hall, Chicago, 144
American Music Hall, New York City, 129, 155
American Roof, New York City, 129
Ancient Order of Hibernians, 44
"Angle Worm Wiggle," 146
Animal Crackers (film), 161
Anna Christie (film), 161
Anson, Cap, 125
Anti-Defamation League of B'nai Brith, 44
Apollo Theatre, New York City, 68-69, 116-117
Arcade Theatre, Easton, Pa., 180
Armstrong, Louis, 110
Artists and Models (film), 160
Associated Rabbis of America, 44
Astaire, Adele, 99, 143-144, 154, 159, 176
Astaire, Fred, 22, 35, 57, 99, 138, 143-144, 154, 159, 161, 173-174, 176, 185, 189
Auditorium Theatre, Quebec, Canada, 194
Automat Restaurants, New York City, 139
Avon Comedy Four, 85

B

Back to Hicksville (act), 30
Bailey, Pearl, 68
Baker, Belle, 60, 85, 133-134
Bakshy, Alexander, 13, 15
Balducci, Carolyn, 8
Baltimore, Maryland, 163-164, 170
Barrymore, Ethel, 34, 36, 44, 73
Barrymore, Lionel, 110
Bartholdi Inn, New York City, 137-138
Basselin, Olivier, 19
Bayes, Nora, 33, 40, 47, 88
Baylos, Gene, 76
Beacon Theatre, Boston, 155
Beck, Martin, 12, 20, 25-26, 34, 36, 75
Bel Geddes, Norman, 188
Belle of the Nineties (film), 161
Bennett, Richard, 152
Benny, Jack, 3, 16, 60, 75-76, 78, 81-82, 96, 120, 122, 143, 160
Benny, (Jack) and Woods, 120
Bergen, Edgar, 16
Berle, Milton, 59, 123, 162
Bernard, Sam, 77

Bernhardt, Sarah, 44
Bernie, Ben, 161
Besser, Joe, 72
Bethlehem, Pa., 180-181, 229
Bickford, Charles, 56, 87, 120-121, 130, 175, 192-193
Big Broadcast of 1932, The (film), 159
Big Broadcast of 1937, The (film), 160
Big Gurn, 107
Bimm, Bomm, B-r-r-r (act), 30
Bishop, Joey, 76
Black, Johnny, 173, 194
Blake, Eubie, 117
Block (Jesse) and Sully (Eve), 83
Blonde Crazy (film), 160
Blondell, Joan, 160-161
Blossom, Henry, 76
Blue, Ben, 7, 40-41, 77, 79, 96, 100, 122, 154, 160, 181
Boardinghouses (theatrical), 134-136, 148, 163-164, 166, 169
Bolger, Ray, 160-161
Bond Building, New York City, 122
Bonett, Renee, 49-50
Bonner, Cleveland, 74
Born to Dance (film), 160
Borscht Belt, The, 76-77, 178
Boston, Massachusetts, 155-158, 170
Boston Theatre, Boston, 157
Bowen, Eli ("The Legless Wonder"), 148
Braatz's Dogs, 31
Brevoort Hotel, St. Louis, 169
Brice, Fanny, 65-66, 85, 160
Brice, Lew, 65
Brittons and Rita, The, 32
Broadway Melody of 1936 (film), 160
Brock, H. I., 13
Brody, Bill (pianist), 126
Brooks, Corny, 88
Brooks (Corny); Burton and, 88
Broun, Heywood, 114-115
Brown, Joe E., 16, 36, 53, 77, 93, 95-96, 99, 135, 150-153, 160, 167-168, 191-192
Browne, Ray, 8
Brown's Chop House, New York City, 139
Brown's Hotel, Loch Sheldrake, N. Y., 76
Bryan, William Jennings, 32
Bryant (Lester) Booking Exchange, Chicago, 141
Buck and Bubbles, 124
Buck's Cafeteria, Baltimore, 164
Buffalo Bill Show, 60
Buffalo, New York, 165
Burke's Juggling Dogs, 30
Burns, George, 16, 30, 59, 75, 120, 159-160, 165, 181
Burton and Brooks, 88
Burton, Ferne Albee, *see* Albee Sisters, 7, 91, 99, 175
Bushnell's (photographer), 152
Butte, Montana, 189-190
Butterfield Circuit, 174
Buttons, Red, 76

C

Cagney, James, 160
California Theatre, San Francisco, 148
Callahan, Emmett, 135
Calumet Hotel, New York City, 138
Calumet Juvenile Protective League, South Chicago, 147
Camp Street Theatre, Dallas, 166
Canada, 166-167, 192-194
Cantor, Eddie, 21, 34, 41-43, 56, 58, 66, 73-74, 78, 102, 114, 122, 128, 146, 155, 159, 178, 180, 185-186
Cantor (Eddie) and Lee (Al), 41, 143
Cantor, Marjorie, 102
Capitol Theatre, New York City, 131
Capone, Al, 146
Carnegie Hall, New York City, 138

Carrillo, Leo, 53, 88, 135, 137, 144-146, 148, 150, 160
Carroll, Earl, 123
Catlett, Walter, 161
Cawthorne, Joseph, 160
Cedar Rapids, Iowa, 184-185
Chaplin, Charles, 34, 94, 135-136, 146-149, 153, 158-159, 182-183, 189-190
Charles (Mrs.) Boardinghouse, New York City, 134-135
Chase Theatre, Washington, D C., 163
Chasing Rainbows (film), 160
Cherry Sisters, The, 125, 184
Cherry; Wishbone and, 188
Chicago, Illinois, 141-148
Chicago Anti-Stage Jew Ridicule Committee, 44
Chicago Opera House, Chicago, 144
Chicago *Tribune,* 142
Chief, The (film), 161
Churchill, Allen, 133
Chutes Theatre, San Francisco, 149
Cincinnati, Ohio, 152-153, 170
Circle Theatre, Chicago, 144
Circle Theatre, New York City, 67, 116
Circuits; Theatrical, 174, 179, 181, 187
City Theatre, New York City, 127
Clark, Bobby, 43, 95-96, 193
Clayton, Lou, 151, 165-166
Cleveland, Ohio, 164-165
Cocoanuts, The (film), 161
Coffee Dan's, San Francisco, 149
Cohan, George M., 56, 60, 133, 162
Cohen, Myron, 76
College Holiday (film), 160
College Humor (film), 159
College Humor (magazine), 75
Collins and Hart, 30
Colon Theatre, El Paso, Texas, 191
Colonial Theatre, Boston, 157
Colonial Theatre, New York City, 127
Columbia Theatre, Boston, 67
Columbia Theatre, St. Louis, 169
Concord Hotel, Kiamesha Lake, N. Y., 76
Cone Circuit, 174
Conkey, Robert, 141
Connolly, Eugene, 165
Connors, Babe, 169
Conrad, Ethel, 125
Considine, John, 154, 167-168
Continental Hotel, Los Angeles, 158
Continental Hotel, San Francisco, 151
Cook, Joe, 43
Coolidge, Calvin, 162
Corbett, James J., 125, 146
Corporal Arthur Fields and Private Flatow (act), 47
Crescent Circuit, 174
Crescent Theatre, Brooklyn, 132
Cressy, Will, 157
Crosby, Bing, 169-170
Curley, (Mayor) James, 157

D

Daisy Lunch, Boston, 158
Dale (Charles); Smith (Joe) and, 78
Dale, Violet, 31, 95, 163-164, 172-173, 185-187
Dallas, Texas, 166
Dancing Lady (film), 161
Darling, Eddie, 124
Davies, Acton, 13
Davis, Sammy, Jr., 68, 98-99, 101-103, 109, 112
Davis, Sammy, Sr., 102-103
Davis Theatre, Pittsburgh, 165
Dawes, Charles Gates, 163
Delancey Street Theatre, New York City, 130
Delaney Circuit, 174
Delmar Circuit, 174
Demarest, William, 160-161
Dempsey, Jack, 33, 37
Dentinger, Mary, 8
Diamond Tony's, Coney Island,

N. Y., 71
Dickinson's Saloon, New York City, 139
Dillingham, Charles, 120
Dillon, Bobby, 169
DiMeglio, Amelia, 61
DiMeglio, Professor John, 9, 61, 229
DiMeglio, Richard A., 9, 61, 95, 104, 229
Dinner at Eight (film), 161-162
"Dinty" Moore's Saloon, New York City, 140
Disher, M. Willson, 13-14
Doctor Bull (film), 161
Dr. Kronkheit (sketch), 78
Dolly Sisters, 37
Donahue, Jack, 73-74
Drako's Sheep and Goats (act), 30
Dramatic Mirror, 52
Dresser, Louise, 85, 161-162
Dressler, Marie, 56, 160-161
Drown, Clarence, 159
Duck Soup (film), 161
Duffy and Sweeney, 168
Durante, Jimmy, 60-61, 71, 122, 165-166

E

Eastman, Joel W., 8
Easton, Pa., 180
Ebsen, Buddy, 160
Edwards, Cliff, 160
Edwards, Gus, 37, 60, 160
Edwards (Gus) Music Publishing Co., 85
Ehric House, New York City, 135
Eighty-First Street Theatre, New York City, 130
Elmer the Great (film), 160
Eltinge, Julian, 32, 72
Empire Theatre, San Francisco, 149
Empress Theatre, Chicago, 116
Erlanger, Abe, 20, 22
Errol, Leon, 160
Etting, Ruth, 33, 37, 82, 159

F

Fairbanks, Douglas, Sr., 36
Fanton, Al, 7, 31, 64, 83, 98, 100, 108, 114
Fanton, Joe, 32-33, 59, 83
Fay, Frank, 24, 160
Faye, Joey, 76
Feiber and Shea Circuit, 179
Ferguson, Otis, 14-15
Fiddler and Shelton, 109-110
Fields and Harrington, 48
Fields (Lew); Weber (Joe) and, 59
Fields, W. C., 41, 43, 59-60, 77, 114, 159, 161, 163, 172
Fifth Avenue Theatre, New York City, 82, 127-128
Finkelstein and Rubin Circuit, 174
Fink's Mules, 37, 90
Finn and Heiman Circuit, 174
Fireman Save My Child (film), 160
Fish, Mrs. Stuyvesant, 133
Fisher, Edward J., 168
Fitzgerald Building, New York City, 139
Five Marvelous Ashtons, 151
Flatbush Theatre, Brooklyn, 132
Flippen, Jay C., 154
Flying Down to Rio (film), 161
Follow the Leader (film), 161
Folly Theatre, Brooklyn, 131
Fontanne, Lynn, 120
Footlight Parade (film), 160
Ford, Corey, 43-44
Forrest Hotel, New York City, 136
Fort Worth, Texas, 166
Foster, Phil, 76
Four Nightingales, The. *See* The Marx Brothers, 156, 179
Four Small Brothers, 110
Fowler, Gene, 133
Fox, Della, 82
Fox, William, 131
Foy, Bryan, 142
Foy, Eddie, 56, 67, 133, 142-143, 154, 160
Frazier's (Mrs.) Dining Room, New

York City, 140
Free and Easy (film), 161
Friar's Club, New York City, 140, 153-154
Fricso, Joe, 154, 158
Fynes, J. Austin, 26, 126

G

Gaiety Theatre, New York City, 140
Gaiety Theatre, Utica, N. Y., 178
Garland, Judy, 161
Garvey, Marcus, 118
George, "The Turtle Boy," 148
Gershwin, George, 127, 162
Gerson's (Mother) Fudge Shop, New York City, 140
Gibson, Charles Dana, 120
Gilbert, L. Wolfe, 32, 131, 138, 156-157, 176, 192
Girl of the Golden West, The (film), 160
Girl of the Rio (film), 160
Gleason, Jackie, 76
Glorifying the American Girl (film), 159
Gold Diggers of Broadway (film), 160
Gold Diggers of 1935 (film), 160
Goldberg, Isaac, 86
Golden Gate Hotel, San Francisco, 151
Goldwyn, Mitzi, 8, 83, 89, 96-97, 193-194
Goode, Paul, 147
Goodman, Maurice, 86
Gordon, Max, 26, 29, 39-40, 92, 123, 140
Gotch, Frank, 125
Gotham Theatre, Brooklyn, 132
Gottlieb, George A., 35
Gottlob, Mr. & Mrs. Earle, 30
Graham, Lillian, 125
"Grand Old Flag, A," 162
Grand Theatre, Chicago, 116
Grandma's Pantry Restaurant, Jamestown, North Dakota, 188
Granlund, Nils T., 48, 96, 155
Grant Hotel, Chicago, 147
Grau, Robert, 26
Grauman, Dave, 150-151
Great McGonigle, The (film), 161
Great Northern Hippodrome, Chicago, 146
Great Northern Hotel, New York City, 138
Great Ziegfeld, The (film), 160
Greeley Theatre, New York City, 130
Green, Abel, 7, 23
Green Room (restaurant), Joplin, Missouri, 112
Green, Rosie, 101
Greenpoint Theatre, Brooklyn, 131
Grossinger's Hotel, Grossinger, N.Y., 76, 178
Gus Edwards' Song Revue (act), 60

H

Hakola, John W., 8
Haley, Jack, 21, 161
Hallelujah, I'm a Bum (film), 159
Ham and Eggs (act), 30
Hammerstein, Oscar, I, 20, 33, 124-125, 132
Hammerstein, Oscar, 2d, 29-30
Hammerstein, Willie, 11, 20, 125
Hammerstein's Victoria Theatre, New York City, 56, 124-126, 144, 201
Happy Days (film), 161
Harding, Warren G., 162
Harrigan and Hart Theatre Comique, New York City, 126, 139
Harris Circuit; Ackerman and, 187
Hartmann, Sadakichi, 32
Hathaway Theatres, 174
Haveman's Animals, 82
Havoc, June, 55-56, 98, 107, 169, 173
Hayes and Post, 32

Hayes, Cardinal Patrick Joseph, 120
Haymarket Music Hall, San Francisco, 151
Haymarket Theatre, Chicago, 144-146
Hazzard, John, 76
Healey, Ted, 137
Hecht, Ben, 14
Heiman; Finn and, 174
Hellzapoppin (revue), 14
Her Majesty Love (film), 161
"Her Name Was Mary Wood But Mary Wouldn't," 146
Herkert and Meisel, aka: H&M (theatrical luggage), 100
Herman, Al, 76
Hicks, Leonard, 147
Higgins Hotel, Boston, 158
Hill Sisters, 97
Hippodrome, New York City, 128-129
Hoboken, New Jersey, 154-155
Hodkins Lyric Vaudeville Circuit, 174
Hogan, Ernest, 34, 115, 117
Holiday, Billie, 117
Hollywood, California, 159-162
Hollywood Revue of 1929 (film), 160
Holtz, Lou, 8, 34, 138
Hoover, Herbert, 51
Hope, Bob, 75, 123, 166
Hoppe, Willie, 33, 165
Hopper, DeWolf, 75
Horse Feathers (film), 161
Houdini, 22, 33-34, 74-75, 87-88, 102-103
Howard, Sammy, 67
Howard Theatre, Boston, 155-156
Howard, Willie, 67, 123
Hubbard, Elbert, 73, 143, 152
Humphrey, H. B., 148
Hurtig and Seamon, 126

I

"I Didn't Raise My Boy to Be a Soldier," 86
"I Don't Want to Get Well," 47
"I Love My Wife but Oh, You Kid," 146
If I Had a Million (film), 161
I'm No Angel (film), 161
Imhof, Roger, 83, 161
Imhof (Roger) and Corinne, 161
Imperial Japs, The (act), 30
Interstate Circuit, 166, 174
Irish by Name but Coons by Birth (act), 113
Iroquois Theatre, Chicago, 142-143
Irwin, May, 56, 162
"It'll Be a Hot Time for the Old Boys When the Young Men Go to War," 46

J

Jackson, Eddie, 154, 165-166
Jacobs, Abe, 126
James Madison's *Budget,* 75
Jazz Singer, The (film), 159
Jeanie (midget), 90
Jefferson Hotel, New York City, 136
Jefferson, Stan. *See* Laurel, Stan.
Jefferson Theatre, New York City, 127
Jersey City, New Jersey, 154
Jessel, George, 4, 60, 122, 124, 128, 140, 175, 178
Johnson, Chic, 82
Johnson, James Weldon, 148, 153
Jolson, Al, 21, 34, 52, 57, 72, 77, 86, 122, 134, 146, 149, 159
Jolson, Harry, 24, 57, 72, 74, 88, 95, 134
Jones, Irving, 117
Jones, Will, 7

K

Kaiserhof Restaurant, New York City, 139
Kansas City, Missouri, 153-154, 170
Kaye, Danny, 76

Kazana (Egyptian snake charmer), 30
Keaton, Buster, 25-26, 94, 99-100, 103-104, 117, 124, 135, 160-161, 176, 190
Keaton, Joe, 25-26, 94, 99-100, 103, 135
Kedzie Theatre, Chicago, 144
Keeney, Frank, 65
Keeney's Theatre, Brooklyn, 65, 67, 79
Keith-Albee, 22-23, 29, 50-51, 127, 156, 183
Keith, Benjamin F., 6, 19-20, 26, 48-50, 52
Keith, B. F., Vaudeville Booking Exchange, 23, 127
Keith Circuit, 23-24, 50-51, 86, 126-127, 141, 156, 165
Keith-Orpheum Circuit, 169
Keith's Theatre, Boston, 156-157
Keith's Theatre, Washington, D. C., 162-163
Keller, Helen, 33
Keller's (Mrs.) Boardinghouse, Chicago, 148
Kellogg's Cafeteria, New York City, 123
Kelly, Father, 120
Kelly, Patsy, 21, 161
Keno and Green, 101
Kid from Spain, The (film), 159
King, Alan, 76
Kingsley, Walter J., 108
Kiss and Tell (act), 30
Klaw, Marc, 22
Klee, Mel, 76
Knickerbocker Hotel, New York City, 139
Knowles, R. G. (Dick), 52
Kohl, Charles F., 27
Kohl and Castle Circuit, 27
Kutsher's Hotel, Monticello, N. Y., 76

L

Lackaye, Wilton, 44, 161
Lafayette: The Great (mimic), 82
La Guardia, Fiorello, 51
Lahr, Bert, 4, 42-43, 59, 64-65, 67-68, 77, 79, 90, 95, 136, 139, 153-154, 161
Lancaster, Pa., 179-180
Larsen, Robert, 156-157
Lauder, Sir Harry, 5, 43, 48, 107, 163
Laurel, Stan, 84, 94, 107, 135-136, 160
Laurie, Joe, Jr., 3-4, 6, 25-26, 53, 76, 93, 97, 109, 113, 138, 148, 164, 183
Lee, Al, 41, 143
Lee, Gypsy Rose, 90, 98, 169, 191
Lefkowitz, Al, 131
Lehigh University, Bethlehem, Pa., 180
Lemmon, Jack, 16
Leonard, Eddie, 72
Leonard, Jack E., 76
"Let Me Call You Sweetheart," 93
Levy, Bert, 141
Lewis, Jerry, 76
Lewis, Joe E., 173, 194
Lewis, Ted, 3, 8, 42, 55, 72, 94, 130-131, 160, 183, 193
Life (magazine), 4
Lillian Russell (film), 160
Lillie, Beatrice, 160
Lincoln Hotel, New York City, 137
Lincoln Theatre, Baltimore, 111-112
Lindy's Restaurant, New York City, 140
"Little Egypt" (act), 52
Loew Circuit, 11, 20, 26, 129-132, 155
Loew, Marcus, 12, 23, 25, 129-130
Loew's Metropolitan Theatre, Brooklyn, 23
Loew's State Theatre, New York City, 110, 129-130
Longworth, Alice Roosevelt, 162

Los Angeles, California, 158-159
Lowery's (Mrs.) Boardinghouse, New York City, 136
Lowry Hotel, St. Paul, 166
Lucas, Nick, 8, 138, 160
Lunt, Alfred, 120
Lyric Theatre, Hoboken, N. J., 154-155

M

Madison, James, 75
Madison Theatre, New York City, 68
Mahoney, Will, 47
Majestic Theatre, Brooklyn, 69
Majestic Theatre, Chicago, 143
Majestic Theatre, Elmira, N. Y., 177
Majestic Theatre, Cedar Rapids, Iowa, 184-185
Major and Minor (act), 30, 33
Mammy (film), 159
Mankato (Minn.) *Free Press* 8
Mansfield Hall Hotel, New York City, 98, 136
Mardo, Al, 60, 65
Marion, Sid, 76
Market Street Cafe, San Francisco, 151
Marks, Edward B., 34, 46
Markus, Fally (booking), 174
Markwell Hotel, New York City, 136
Marquard, Rube, 23
Martin's (Mrs.) Theatrical Boardinghouse, New York City, 136
Marx, Arthur, 97
Marx Brothers, 15, 21-22, 24, 31, 43, 60, 90, 92, 96, 132, 156, 161, 180-183, 185-186, 191
Marx, Chico, 60, 165
Marx, Groucho, 3, 7, 14-15, 22, 25, 42, 63-64, 88, 92, 96-97, 107, 167, 173, 179-180, 186-187, 191
Marx, Harpo, 14, 22, 24-25, 30, 59, 63, 88, 132, 156, 165, 182, 186-187, 190
Marx, Samuel, 133
Mastin, Will, 102
Maurice and Walton, 47
May, Marty, 76
Maybe It's Love (film), 160
Medicine Man (film), 160
Merman, Ethel, 21
Merry Wop, The (act), 113
Metropolitan Opera House, New York City, 133
Meyerfeld, Morris, 75
Mick and the Policeman, The (act), 113
Midsummer Night's Dream, A (film), 160
Million Dollar Legs (film), 161
Min and Bill (film), 161
Miner, Henry Clay, 66
Miner's Bowery Theatre, New York City, 66
Minneapolis, Minnesota, 165-166, 170
Minneapolis *Tribune,* 7
Monkey Business (film), 161
Monogram Theatre, Chicago, 116
Montfort's (Mrs.) Boardinghouse, New York City, 135
Monticello Theatre, Jersey City, N. J., 154
Montreal, Canada, 166-167
Moonlight and Pretzels (film), 160
Moore, Victor, 161
Morgan and Stone, 21
Morris, Nancy Welford. *See* Welford, Nancy.
Morris, William, 20, 22-24, 29, 163
Mother Howard's Boardinghouse, Baltimore, 164
Mother Irish's Boardinghouse, Washington, D. C., 163
Motogirl (act), 31-32
Mozart, Edward, 179-180
Mozart Theatre, Elmira, N. Y., 177, 179
Mr. Antonio (film), 160
Murdock, John J., 24, 26-27, 86
Murphy, "Con," 157

Murray, Ken, 8, 21, 36-37, 73, 79-80, 89, 93-94, 97-98, 120, 131, 163, 165-166, 178, 180
Muse, Clarence, 161
Music Publishers Protective Association, 86
Musliner's Pigs (act), 30
Myers, Barney, 79

Mc

McCarthy, (Senator) Joseph, 23
McClintic, Guthrie, 139, 167, 188
McGurk; Sablosky and, 174
McPherson, Aimee Semple, 51

N

Nathan, George Jean, 14
National Theatre, San Francisco, 149
National Vaudeville Artists, Inc., 77-78
New England Circuit, 174
New Haven, Connecticut, 176-177
New Orleans, Louisiana, 168-169
New Palace Theatre, New York City, 116
New Sheridan Hotel, Telluride, Colorado, 190
New York Child Welfare Committee, 105
New York *Clipper* (trade paper), 26, 80, 185
New York *Dramatic Mirror*, 78, 81, 85
New York *Morning Telegraph,* 80
New York *Sun,* 26
New York Theatre, New York City, 32, 129
Newark, New Jersey, 155
Night after Night (film), 161
Night at the Opera, A (film), 161
Night in the Slums of Paris, A (act), 105
Norton, Harry, 175-176
Norworth, Mrs. Jack (Amy), 7, 79, 88, 154
Novelty Theatre, Brooklyn, 132

O

Oakland, Ben, 131
O'Connor, John J., 86
"Old George" (stage doorman), 150
Old South Theatre, Boston, 157
Olive Lunch, New York City, 139
Olsen, Ole, 82
Olympic Theatre, New York City, 68
On with the Show! (film), 160
105th Street Theatre, Cleveland, 164-165
Orpheum Circuit, 25, 75, 103, 116, 128, 141, 144, 153, 169
Orpheum Theatre, Brooklyn, 31, 52, 132
Orpheum Theatre, Denver, 189
Orpheum Theatre, Los Angeles, 159
Orpheum Theatre, Minneapolis, 165
Orpheum Theatre, New Orleans, 168
Orpheum Theatre, Oakland, California, 49
Orpheum Theatre, San Francisco, 149-150
Orpheum Theatre, South Bend, Indiana, 184
Osofsky, Gilbert, 113
"Over There," 162

P

Painted Faces (film), 160
Palace Cafeteria, New York City, 123
Palace Hotel, Chicago, 148
Palace Theatre, Boston, 155
Palace Theatre, Chicago, 143-144
Palace Theatre, Cleveland, 164
Palace Theatre, New York City, 21, 24, 26, 35-36, 43, 47, 50-51, 76, 81, 83, 93, 98, 116, 119-124, 126, 128, 131, 136-137, 140, 159, 201
Pantages, Alexander, 12, 20, 27, 167-168, 174
Pantages Theatre, Seattle, 167-168

Papinta, 82
Paradise Roof, New York City, 124
Paradise Theatre, New York City, 128
Parks, Eddie, 60
Parlor, Bedroom and Bath (film), 161
Pastor, Tony, 19, 75
Pearl, Jack, 76, 84, 136
Pearl Theatre, Philadelphia, 68
Pennington, Ann, 160
People's Theatre, Seattle, 168
Philadelphia, Pennsylvania, 154
Piccolo Midgets, The, 30
Picon, Molly, 68
Pigskin Parade (film), 161
Pittsburgh, Pennsylvania, 165
Plaza Hotel, Fallsburgh, N. Y., 175
Plaza Music Hall, New York City, 30
Poli Circuit, 174
Poli, Sylvester, 20, 177
Poli's Theatre, New Haven, 176
Poultney, George, 7
President Theatre, Chicago, 144
Proctor, F. F., 20, 26-27, 49, 127-128
Proctor's 23rd Street Theatre, New York City, 49
Proctor's 58th Street Theatre, New York City, 128
Prospect Theatre, Brooklyn, 132
Prudential Pawn Shop, New York City, 64

Q

Qualey's (Mrs.) Boardinghouse, St. Paul, 166

R

Raines Act (law), 138
Rastelli (juggler), 36
Rath Brothers, 36
Reed College, Portland, Oregon, 104-105
Reed, Edward, 41
Revell, Nellie, 40
Revere House, Chicago, 147
Rexford Hotel, Boston, 157
Rhythm Boys, The, 169-170
Richman, Harry, 50-51, 152, 188-190, 193
Rico, Puerto (comedian), 68-69
Rilling's (Dave) Boardinghouse, St. Louis, 169
Ring, Blanche, 56
Rivoli Theatre, Toledo, Ohio, 30
Roberta (film), 161
Rogers, Will, 34, 37, 64, 88, 103, 124, 137, 154, 161-162
Roman Scandals (film), 159
Rooney, Mickey, 160
Rooney, Pat, Sr., 97, 119
Roosevelt, Franklin Delano, 162
Roosevelt, Theodore, 162-163
Root (Jack) Theatres, 184
Roth, Lillian, 74, 101, 161
Roth Sisters, 36
Rourke, Constance, 43-44
Royal, John, 6
Royal Polo Team (act), 30
Royal Theatre, Baltimore, 112
Royal Theatre, Brooklyn, 67, 131-132
Royle, Edwin, 49, 157
Rubin, Benny, 8, 21-22, 36-37, 46, 51, 59, 64-65, 72-73, 76, 80, 82, 84, 87-89, 91, 94-95, 97, 102, 106, 112, 122, 127, 136, 146, 153, 159, 165, 172, 174, 177, 190-191
Rubin; Finkelstein and, 174
Russell, Annie, 49
Russell Brothers, The, 44-45
Russell, Lillian, 21, 85, 160
Ruth, Babe, 21, 37

S

Sablosky and McGurk Circuit, 174
Sailor and Yeoman, The (act), 48
St. Francis Hotel, San Francisco, 151

St. Hubert Hotel, New York City, 138
St. Louis, Missouri, 169-170
"Saint Patrick's Day Is No Day for a Man with a Face Like Mine," 117
St. Paul, Minnesota, 166, 170
St. Regis Cafe, New York City, 122, 140
Sale, Charles "Chic," 34, 153
Salt and Pepper (act), 30
Salt Lake City, Utah, 153
Sam T. Jack Theatre, Chicago, 144
San Francisco, California, 148-152, 158
Sandow, 125
Saratoga Hotel, Chicago, 147
Sardi's Restaurant, New York City, 139
Savo, Jimmy, 68, 167
Say It with Songs (film), 159
Scenic Theatre, Westbrook, Maine, 175
Schenck, Joseph M., 11, 26
Schenck (Joe); Van (Gus) and, 37, 82
Schreyer, Lowell, 8
Seattle, Washington, 167-168
Seldes, Gilbert, 13
Seville Hotel, New York City, 136
She Done Him Wrong (film), 161
Shea; Feiber and, 179
Shea, Mike, 165
Shean, Al, 63
Sheedy Time (circuit), 175
Sheldon, Gene, 161
Shelton; Fiddler and, 109-110
Shenandoah, Pennsylvania, 180
Shindler's Theatre, Chicago, 146
Show Biz (book), 56, 119
Show of Shows, The (film), 160
Shrapnel Dodgers, The (act), 46
Shubert Brothers, 20, 23-24
Shubert, J. J., 20, 22, 84
Shubert, Lee, 20, 22
Shulem's Restaurant, New York City, 140
Sidewalks of New York (film), 161
Sidman, Sam, 66, 77
Silverman, Sime, 23, 80
Singer, Leo, 30
Singer's Midgets, 30
Singing Fool, The (film), 159
Sissle, Noble, 117
Six American Dancers (act), 60
Skelton, Red, 3, 123
Slaski, Eugene, 8
Slattery, William J., 184-185
Smith, David C., 8
Smith, Estelle Major, 8, 162
Smith (Joe) and Dale (Charles), 78
Snow Brothers, The, 82
So This Is London (film), 161
Sobel, Bernard, 15, 26, 121
Sober Sue (act), 125-126
Society for the Prevention of Cruelty to Children, 99
Somerset Coffee House, New York City, 122
Somerset Hotel, New York City, 122, 136-137
Sonny Boy (film), 159
Soul of the Violin, The (recitation), 58
South (Old) Theatre, Boston, 157
Sparrows Boardinghouse, Baltimore, 164
Spitzer, Marian, 26, 34, 50, 119, 121, 123-124
Stanley Hotel, New York City, 137
Stanton, Val and Rennie, 36
Star Theatre, New York City, 130
Stark, Samuel, 7
State Fair (film), 161
Steamboat 'round the Bend (film), 161
Stettler, Myron, 8
Stop and Go (act), 30
Strauss Hotel, Cincinnati, 153
Sullivan-Considine Circuit, 167-168, 174, 192
Sully; Block and, 83
Sun, Gus, 33, 141, 174, 183

Sweeney; Duffy and, 168
Swing Time (film), 161
Swor, Bert, 72, 77, 154, 186
Swor, John, 77
Sylvester, Everett, 82

T

Taft, William Howard, 32, 107
Tamarack Hotel, Greenfield Park, N. Y., 76
Tammany Building, New York City, 126
Tanguay, Eva, 21, 34, 67, 81
Tannen, Julius, 96, 161, 166
Taubman, Howard, 15
Taylor, Dot, 154
Tejan, Fred, 34
Templeton, Fay, 56
Texas Tommy Dancers, 135
Thaw, Evelyn Nesbit, 125
Theatre Comique. *See* Harrigan and Hart Theatre Comique.
Theatre Owners Booking Association, 174
Theatrical Drugstore, New York City, 123
Theilen Circuit, 174
They Had to See Paris (film), 161
Thornton, James J., 180-181
Tillie and Gus (film), 161
Tillie's Punctured Romance (film), 161
Tobias, George, 76
Tony Pastor's Music Hall, New York City, 75, 126, 201
Top and Bottom (act), 30
Trafalgar Hotel, New York City, 136
Tucker, Sophie, 34, 60, 85, 93, 117, 119, 144, 146, 149, 165, 167, 172
Tumulty, Joseph, 162
Tunney, Gene, 33
Turklu Apartments, San Francisco, 151
Twentieth Century Club, Boston, 155
Tysner (restaurant owner), 138-139

U

Union Square Theatre, New York City, 126
Unique Theatre, San Francisco, 150-151
United Booking Offices, 46
United Irish Societies of New York, 44
United States Amusement Company, 22-23
University of Chicago, 147

V

Valencia, Doty, 150
Vallee, Rudy, 121-122, 131
Van (Gus) and Schenck (Joe), 37, 82
Vancouver, B. C., Canada, 167
Variety (trade paper), 7, 20, 23, 30-31, 45-48, 76-77, 79-81, 85-86, 109, 128, 130-133, 137, 154, 157, 159, 179
Vaudeville Managers' Protective Association, 77-78
Vesta, Nettie, 85
Victoria Theatre. *See* Hammerstein's Victoria Theatre.
Von Tilzer, Harry, 138

W

"Wait Till the Sun Shines, Nellie," 68
Wake Up and Live (film), 161
Walker, George W., 34, 36, 72, 115. *See* Williams and Walker.
Walker, James J., 51
War Brides (act), 163
Warner Brothers Studio, 160
Warwick, Robert, 36
Washington, Booker T., 114
Washington, D. C., 162-163
Washington Theatre, Washington, D. C., 162

Watermelon Trust, The (act) 113
Waters, Ethel, 21, 25, 34, 59, 87, 91, 96-97, 106, 111-112, 115-117, 128, 140, 144
Wayne, Hortense, 82
Weber (Joe) and Fields (Lew), 59, 160
Webster's (George) Circuit, 187-188
Webster Vaudeville Circuit, Chicago, 141
Weiss, George, 67
Welford, Nancy, 7, 160, 177, 188-189
Welk, Lawrence, 90
Welle's Restaurant, New York City, 140
Wells Circuit, 174
West, Mae, 7, 11, 26, 40, 50-51, 67, 78, 81, 96, 161, 176-177
Western Vaudeville Circuit, 181, 185
Western Vaudeville Managers Association, Chicago, 141-142
Whalen, Grover, 51
Wheeler, Bert, 84
White, Stanford, 125
Whiteman, Paul, 169
Whiz Bang (magazine), 75
Whoopee (film), 159
Wichman, George A., 82
Wigwam Theatre, San Francisco, 149
Wilde, Larry, 60
Willard Theatre, Chicago, 144
William Tell House, Boston, 158
Williams, Bert, 34, 67, 72, 110, 114-115
Williams (Bert) and Walker (George), 36
Williams, Percy, 20, 26-27, 52, 127, 131
Wills, Nat M., 126-127
Wilson Avenue Theatre, Chicago, 144
Wilson, Woodrow, 162
Winchell, Walter, 47, 161
Winthrop Hall, Dorchester, Mass., 175
Wishbone and Cherry, 188
"Without a Wedding Ring," 146
Wizard of Oz, The (film), 161
Wolpin's Restaurant, New York City, 140
Wonder Bar (film), 159
Woods; Benny (Jack) and, 120
Woods, George, 166
Woolworth, F. W., 179
Wynn, Ed, 43, 136, 161, 175

Y

Yale University, New Haven, 176-177
Yandis Court Boardinghouse, New York City, 135
Yes and No (act), 30
You and Me (act), 30
Young, Miriam, 101-102

Z

Zat Zams (act), 30
Ziegfeld, Florenz, 15, 73, 120, 123, 132
Ziegfeld Follies (revue), 34, 115
Zimmerman, Willie, 32